A HIGHER STANDARD

A HIGHER STANDARD

LEADERSHIP STRATEGIES
from AMERICA'S FIRST FEMALE
FOUR-STAR GENERAL

✶ ✶ ✶ ✶

GENERAL
ANN DUNWOODY (RET.)
WITH TOMAGO COLLINS

Da Capo
LIFE
LONG

A Member of the Perseus Books Group

Editorial production by Lori Hobkirk at the Book Factory

Set in 11.5-point Goudy Oldstyle STD

Cataloging-in-Publication data for this book is available from the Library of Congress.

First Da Capo Press edition 2015
ISBN: 978-0-7382-1779-6 (hardcover)
ISBN: 978-0-7382-1780-2 (ebook)

Published by Da Capo Press
A Member of the Perseus Books Group
www.dacapopress.com

Da Capo Press books are available at special discounts for bulk purchases in the U.S. by corporations, institutions, and other organizations. For more information, please contact the Special Markets Department at the Perseus Books Group, 2300 Chestnut Street, Suite 200, Philadelphia, PA, 19103, or call (800) 810-4145, ext. 5000, or e-mail special.markets@perseusbooks.com.

10 9 8 7 6 5 4 3 2 1

To my parents, who taught me anything was possible.
To the leaders who blazed trails before me.
To the leaders who never gave up on me.
To the next generation of leaders on the bench—this
book is for you.
To my husband, who made this journey possible.

CONTENTS

FOREWORD

by Sheryl Sandberg

IN THIS BOOK, Ann Dunwoody writes, "A hero is an average person who has done something extraordinary." As unusual as it is to start a foreword for a book by disagreeing with its author, I have to say that I disagree with Ann. I do not believe anyone would ever describe Ann as an average person. She has certainly done many extraordinary things. And to me, she is a true hero.

Ann and I were introduced through a mutual friend who thought we'd like each other, even though we work in starkly different cultures. At the Facebook office, we have signs on the walls that read, "Move fast and break things." Obviously, our military leaders know better than to adopt this policy themselves. Still, from our first e-mail exchange, Ann and I felt connected. She once described it so beautifully, saying, "We are kindred spirits in very different worlds."

In 2014, Ann accepted my invitation to speak at Facebook's North America Women's Leadership Day. That afternoon, I watched her inspire fifteen hundred women, offering both practical advice and encouragement. She told us to put our passion before our fear. She spoke of how things were changing. In 1995, she had attended a high-level military meeting where "there was not one woman sitting at the table. The only women in that room were delivering coffee." Twenty years later, she urged the women of Facebook to look around. "Look at this room, look at your-selves," she said. "I am just so proud of you, I am getting goose bumps just thinking about it."

I get those same goose bumps thinking about what Ann has achieved. And I'm so glad she wrote this book so that more women—and men—can be inspired by her wisdom and her story.

When Ann became the first female four-star general in the United States military. Her father put it this way: "I have followed her career for thirty-three years. Every assignment she has ever had, she's done in an outstanding manner. So it really doesn't sur-prise me she was the first woman selected for four stars." In turn, Ann credits her father with teaching her never to accept defeat and shares how her family's history of service paved her path. Her great-grandfather, grandfather, father, and brother all graduated from West Point. She herself might have attended the military academy except for one hitch: they didn't admit women at the time. Rather than giving up, Ann found a way. She knew she wanted to serve, and she never lost sight of that goal.

Once Ann joined the Army, she pushed to be the best soldier she could be. In 2005, she became the Army's top-ranking woman when she received her third star. Three years later, she made United States history by becoming our first-ever female four-star general. While Ann credits the Army with shattering the "brass ceiling," it was her uniform that was pinned with that fourth star.

I concluded my book *Lean In* with my hope that "in the future, there will be no female leaders. There will just be leaders." I did not know Ann when I wrote that, but she is exactly who I had in mind. What distinguishes Ann is not that she's a woman, but that she is a spectacular and inspiring leader.

Deano Roberts was an Army captain who served under Ann when she led the Joint Logistics Command in Uzbekistan. Back then, Deano was an aviation liaison officer. Today, Deano is one of my colleagues at Facebook who works in data center logistics. I asked him to describe what made General Dunwoody unique. He acknowledged that being a woman made her different, but that it was her talent as a logistician that made her stand out.

"In the military it is said that you can often fool your boss, you can sometimes fool your peers, but you can never fool your soldiers," Deano explained. "General Dunwoody commanded the trust and service of her soldiers, not as a function of her rank or position, but rather as a function of her mastery of her profession [logistics] and her willingness to always place the needs of the soldier first."

Deano remembers one night in Karshi-Khanabad, Uzbekistan, when he was working in a makeshift US outpost in a Soviet-era air base—a far cry from Silicon Valley. The conditions were miserable. Rats and rain both streamed in. There was no hot water. The soldiers were stressed and fatigued and still hard at work one night at 2 a.m. when "an energetic and vibrant General Dunwoody" walked into the tactical operations center, still in uniform, and sat down with the soldiers. "In the most concerned and legitimate way, she asked if there was anything she could do for me," Deano said. They spoke at length, and her words and demeanor were both motivating and inspiring. "She had an emotional empathy that wasn't part of her training. It was just part of her character," Deano concluded.

I could not love this story more. Study after study sadly reveals that too often, in the workplace, if a woman is competent, she does not seem nice enough. And if a woman seems really nice, she is considered more nice than competent. Ann proved that competence and compassion are not mutually exclusive. Deano praised his commander for being "the smartest person in the room when it came to what was happening on the ground." He also recalled the way she patted him on the shoulder, which he found both "calming and reassuring."

There is a popular saying in feminism that "you got to see it to be it," but that wasn't true of Ann. In all her years serving, she never reported to a woman. Out of necessity, Ann leaned on family members and male mentors for support. As she points out, the men she reported to "either believed in me or didn't." She is grateful to the ones who did, especially Sergeant First Class Wendell Bowen, who vowed to make her the best platoon leader in the Army. His confidence in her fed her desire to rise to his challenge. He also encouraged her to be true to herself, something that is important in every profession.

As we all do, Ann stood on the shoulders of the many women who cleared a path before her. Women first became a formal part of the US military more than a century ago with the creation of the Army Nurse Corps. During World War I, thirty-five thousand women served their country as nurses, interpreters, and clerks. In 1942, President Roosevelt authorized the creation of women's auxiliaries/reserves for the Army, Navy, and Coast Guard, and during World War II, about 350,000 women served. While most of these women worked in health care, administration, and communications, a growing number began serving in technical and command roles. Still, at the war's conclusion, these trained and seasoned personnel were not encouraged to remain in the military but were urged to return to civilian life and domestic responsibilities.

In 1948, the Women's Armed Services Integration Act enabled women to serve as regular members of the US Armed Forces. This was a step forward but not a leap. Other legislation prevented women from serving in direct combat roles and prohibited women from serving in a rank higher than lieutenant colonel. It also limited the number of women allowed in the military to 2 percent of the armed forces. President Ford signed a law that allowed women to enroll in military academies in 1975. That same year, fresh out of State University of New York College at Cortland, Ann joined the Women's Army Corps, the women's branch of the United States Army.

Over the thirty-seven years that Ann served in the US Army, many policies evolved. Revisions were made to the laws governing the role of women in the military, with each round opening up more positions to women. In 1994, a new policy was implemented that allowed for a less restrictive rule about ground combat and opened up 80 percent of all military positions to women. By 2012, when Ann retired from the military, women made up almost 15 percent of the active duty force and 16 percent of the active duty officers.

The hope is that with growing numbers comes growing strength and support. Two years ago, I visited an Air Force base in Minneapolis and met a group of courageous women who formed a Lean In Circle because, as they explained, being a woman in the military can be an "isolating experience." They described how they are still subtly—and not so subtly—undermined, even as they stand side by side with men wearing the same uniform. After discovering how helpful their Circle was on their base, they expanded online to reach other women in the military. As one of them told us, "Now no one has to feel like the only woman in her unit." And as many of them noted, the example of great female military leaders such as Ann has motivated them, demonstrating the real possibility that they too can serve their country at the highest levels and with the greatest impact.

My admiration for Ann is boundless—not just because of what she achieved but how she achieved it. Ann's story is the story of a true soldier. She ends every talk with this: "In the end we're all just soldiers, but that's the highest thing you could claim to be." Her story—and this book—will inspire anyone who wants to serve and lead.

INTRODUCTION

First to Four: A Collective Smile

———

November 14, 2008

THE PENTAGON

As I scanned the large auditorium, an insurgent thought infiltrated my mind: *Okay, Ann, don't screw this up.* The audience was filled with military dignitaries, war heroes, mentors, colleagues, family, friends, and other curious onlookers. Television cameras rolled, and there stood Old Glory and the Army flag: it was quite a remarkable scene, all for the purpose of promoting a woman, the first woman in history, to receive a fourth star. Questions swirled in my head: Am I sweating? Will I forget to thank anyone? Will I sound like Charlie Brown's teacher?

Relax, Ann. You can do this. You have deployed with thousands of paratroopers into combat zones. You bleed olive-drab green. You have given your entire professional life to the service of your country.

I had spoken to soldiers and audiences literally tens of thousands of times—so much so that I got tired of hearing myself talk.

1

And I'm sure my husband got tired of listening. So there was no need for stage fright.

But this was different. Months earlier I was petrified, as I started preparing for the speech of my life.

On June 23, 2008, President George W. Bush nominated me to become the first female four-star general in US military history. I didn't initially understand all the fuss, much less the magnitude of President Bush's decision. I was proud of my accomplishment, but I was just as proud for being a Dunwoody, a soldier, and an American, as I was for being a woman.

The nomination made headlines around the world.

"First Woman Ann Dunwoody Makes Four-Star US General," the *Australian*
    "Army Gets First Female Four-Star General," *NBC News*
    "Ann Dunwoody Becomes First Female 4-Star General," the *Kansas City Star*
    "Military Milestone," Scholastic
    "Four Stars—Finally," *U.S. Army Reserve* magazine
    "An American Original," *Columns*, SUNY Cortland Alumni News, Spring 2009
    "Four-Star and First," the *Fayetteville Observer*
    "Dunwoody Becomes First Female Four-Star General," the *Seattle Times*

US Senator Hillary Clinton, representative of my native New York, said, "Today another glass ceiling has been shattered in our nation with the nomination of a woman to the rank of [four-star] General for the first time in the history of America's armed forces."

As the first woman to four-star general, I was determined to lead and create even greater opportunities for deserving men and women throughout the military. First, however, I had to get through the confirmation process and prepare for my speech.

I was excited, emotional, proud, and nervous, as my official four-star ceremony approached. It was impossible, however, to not occasionally flash back to one of the most embarrassing moments of my life. I couldn't shake the time that, as a young 1st lieutenant in 1977, at Fort Sill, Oklahoma, I had my first speaking role in front of a large audience. After that experience I wasn't sure whether I would ever stand in front of a microphone again.

I had just been selected to be the battalion adjutant, which meant I was the chief paper pusher for the battalion. One of my duties was to read the orders and citations for promotion and award ceremonies. So the first time I had the opportunity to excel as an adjutant was at an award ceremony. The battalion commander was going to present the Meritorious Service Medal to an outgoing company commander.

The audience was seated in the 250-seat auditorium, and the commander, his aide, the awardee, and I were on stage. After the normal introductions and comments, the battalion commander nodded at me—my cue to begin.

"Attention to orders," I said into the microphone, trying to avoid a squeaky, high-pitched voice and make a good impression with my best Barry White baritone imitation. Immediately everyone sprang to their feet and snapped to attention. So far, so good. But then I froze.

With everyone staring at me, the only thing I could feel from the audience was pity, and the only thing I could hear was my heart pounding. I swallowed hard and tried to look down at the citation I was supposed to read.

My hands trembled, then I held on to both sides of the podium with a death grip. I was shaking so badly that I was unable to talk. I was horrified. I'd never had anything like this happen before. The battalion commander kept looking over at me and making some not-so-subtle gestures to tell me to get on with the reading.

> To all . . . ummmm . . . who shall see . . . uhhh . . . these pres-
> ents, greeting. This . . . this uh this . . . is to . . . ssss-sss . . . certify
> that da-da the president of the United States . . . of Amer-
> ica . . . America . . . ah-ah . . . authorized by act . . . uhh . . . of
> Congress . . . umm on 2 July 1978, has awarded the . . . the . . .
> Mary . . . Meritorious Service Medal . . . to . . . Captain James C.
> Hall . . . uhh . . . Untied States Army . . . uhhh Headquarters. . . .
> 100th Supply and Service Battalion . . .

I felt my battalion commander staring at me. Everyone in front of me looked at me as if I didn't know how to read. I struggled on:

> For exceptionally . . . mer, mer . . . meritorious service while ser . . .
> serving as Commander . . . uhhh . . . 225th Main . . . maintenance
> Company, 100th Supply and Service Ba . . . battalion at Fort Sill
> Oklahoma . . . fr . . . ummm . . . from 2 June 1976 to . . . to 25 May
> 1978. Cap . . . Captain Hall was personally re . . . responsible for
> the excep . . . exceptional main . . . maintenance readiness of the
> Corps Artillery at Fort Sill. His proactive . . . uhhh . . . approach
> and streamline . . . streamlining of maintenance oper . . . oper-
> ations . . . in-in . . . enhanced readiness rates to an all time . . .
> ummm . . . high of 93 percent. Captain Hall's disting . . . distin-
> guished performance of duty is in keeping with the highest tra . . .
> traditions of the . . . U . . . United States Army. Giv . . . given
> under my hand in the City of . . . ummm . . . Washington this 2nd
> day of July 1978. Signed Joe Sch . . . Schmidt, Commander, Field
> Artillery, Head . . . Headquarters, Fort Sill, Okla . . . homa.

Somehow I stuttered and stammered my way through the seem-ingly eternal three minutes. Afterward I felt humiliated. I made the long walk to my battalion commander's office, certain that my short-lived tenure as his adjutant was over. I knocked on his door, and he invited me in. "Sir, I am so sorry!" I said. "I don't know what happened to me."

He replied, "Ann, don't worry about it." Then he smiled and asked whether it had been my first time speaking in front of a large audience. I said that it was. "Next time you'll do better," he said. Next time! You can imagine my relief.

He could have handled that so much differently. He could have further shattered my confidence with ridicule. He could have fired me. Instead, he made that experience a growth opportunity. And while I was grateful that I still had a job as his adjutant, I learned some other valuable lessons that day. One of those lessons was to be better prepared! Another, just as important, is that nobody is perfect. When leaders help subordinates overcome weaknesses or mistakes, they help the subordinate, they help the organization, and they help themselves become better leaders.

I could have run away from the experience. I could have quit. I could have delegated those responsibilities to my assistant. Or I could just suck it up, realizing that I needed to work harder and improve.

In this instance I watched my commander underwrite an error. I can assure you that I never walked into a situation like that again without being prepared. But the nerves still exist. To this day, deep down inside, I worry that stage fright will sabotage me again. And, as a lifelong skill, I have worked on developing the skill of giving people chances to improve their performance after a failure.

THIRTY YEARS LATER not even that tongue-tied disaster could have prepared me for this speech in front of this audience. Weeks of media training. Years of delivering speeches. Decades of leading and counseling soldiers. Not even my childhood as a military brat or adulthood as a soldier. This day seemed unthinkable and improbable for a pig-tailed tomboy who grew up dreaming of becoming a coach and teacher. This opportunity was impossible back in 1974, when I joined an Army that had a separate Women's Army Corps and embraced separate training for men and for women. What a transformation my Army had undergone, and to think that I played some small role in that wonderful change.

When the All-Volunteer Force construct became a reality in 1973, the opportunities for women in the military were greatly expanded. Women were now being recruited, and the number of WACs in the Women's Army Corps (WAC) grew from roughly 12,000 in 1972 to nearly 53,000 by 1978. The Reserve Officer Training Corps (ROTC) was beginning to open up for women, and in 1976 the first women were accepted into the military academies. More women were being given the opportunity to serve alongside men in integrated units. Finally, in 1978, having outlived its usefulness, the WAC was disbanded.

The military was no longer just a man's world. My appointment was another affirmation that the Army was evolving from generations of snubbing women for jobs based solely on gender. Standards for entry into the Army became the same for women as for men, and more job specialties were transitioning to gender-integrated training.

On that day in November 2008 General George Casey, Army Chief of Staff, officially promoted me, Lieutenant General Ann Dunwoody, to four-star general. I became the first woman in US history to achieve the highest active military rank.

The ceremony was so well attended that US Defense Secretary Robert Gates joked that everyone except the fire marshal had been invited. The largest auditorium in the Pentagon held a standing-room-only crowd filled with male and female soldiers of all races and backgrounds. The Army had come a long way and truly represented the "Army of One" slogan used years ago.

Secretary Gates's opening words were gratifying:

General Dunwoody ascends to this post with thirty-three years
of service as a soldier and leader of the highest caliber. She is recognized as one of the best military logisticians of her generation.

General Casey followed Gates with a heartwarming speech discussing my accomplishments while paying tribute to our family's
five-generation history in the military and to our current patri-
arch, my father, Hal.

He recounted my dad's thirty-one years of selfless service and
sacrifice. My dad nearly lost his leg and his life fighting in three
wars. He was severely wounded in Germany during World War II,
only to recover and lead a battalion into combat during the Korean
War. He was wounded again and awarded the Distinguished Service Cross to go along with his two Purple Hearts. He also fought
in Vietnam. I always knew my dad was a hero, but now General
Casey was telling everyone what a star he was.

General Casey said he had never seen such a "collective smile"
at a military ceremony. As he continued his introduction, emotions and memories came flooding back, especially when I looked
at my frail father beaming in his wheelchair. Next to my dad were
my four siblings, each accomplished in their own right in business
or in the military. But two people were missing. My mother, Betty,
who had died of a massive stroke just a few years earlier, would
have been the proudest parent on the planet. She kept our family
together as Dad fought in Germany, Korea, and Vietnam and as
we moved from military base to military base around the world.
She created a home filled with love, God, and accountability. One
sister was also absent that day. Kay, the oldest, I never really knew.
She was a special-needs child and never stood a chance. Merci-
fully, she died at age ten, with no memory that she had ever lived.

My best friend from my youth, Elaine, was there. Growing up, she was my greatest partner in mischief—Girl Scouts, sports, cheerleading, silly crushes on silly boys, fishing for crab on the Chesapeake Bay. We were inseparable in middle school before another inevitable move to yet another military base—this time in Belgium—separated us for forty years until a chance encounter brought us back together. If only we'd had e-mail, Facebook, and GChat in the 1960s.

Elaine became a schoolteacher and taught for twenty-nine years in Arlington, Virginia. She had taught two children of a colleague of mine, Robert Wilkie, who worked in the Pentagon. Elaine recalls being home, making dinner and watching the news. She heard the reporter say General Ann Dunwoody will become the first four-star female Army general. She reached out to Mr. Wilkie's wife, Julie, via e-mail, hoping they could provide contact information.

My parents and Elaine's mother had exchanged Christmas cards over the years, so we kept tabs on each other, but we had no personal contact, and I had no idea she was teaching third grade less than twenty minutes from the Pentagon until Robert called and asked whether he could pass along my phone number and e-mail. He did, and we got together for lunch a few weeks later and are as close today as when we first became friends in fifth grade.

Sitting a few inches to my left was my soul mate and a military professional of his own renown: my husband, Craig Brotchie. A lifelong Air Force special operator, he has been more influential during my career than anyone. We had been together for more than twenty years and survived countless months apart during various deployments and assignments around the world.

Our constant inside joke was, "Behind every successful woman stands an astonished man." But Craig is my rock. No one has been more supportive of my career. He is strong and sensitive, caring and courageous. Even as I struck out in my first attempt at marriage, I hit a five-hundred-foot grand slam when I met Craig. He has been there almost every step of my advancement in the Army. Without him this book wouldn't be possible. He is my copilot and coauthor in life. No one knows me better. He knows what makes me tick and what ticks me off. When I introduce him I always refer to him as Mr. Wonderful, and he is. Having Mr. Wonderful a few feet from the podium was all the support I needed.

Craig and I practiced my speech dozens of times leading up to my milestone promotion—while enjoying our normal early morning run, hitting balls on the driving range, in the car on the way to the grocery store. Craig believed in me and said I'd nail the speech. When General Casey introduced me, I was ready to give thanks and get to work.

General Casey and Craig placed my four stars on my right and left shoulders. My normally sure-handed husband fumbled the snap a bit, as it took him a couple of tries to get the shoulder board properly snapped in place. Then Craig and I shared the most public smooch ever witnessed at a military promotion ceremony.

With butterflies and a sense of pride, I was determined not to screw up this historic moment. Just as they had done when we initially entered the auditorium, the audience gave me a wonderful ovation. I wish I could describe the incredible feelings of gratitude, humility, and love that consumed me as I walked to the podium. The extended applause gave me a chance to compose myself, and I took a final drink of water before delivering the most memorable speech of my life.

I couldn't help but shake my head when I was introduced as "General Ann Dunwoody." Did I really hear those words? There was no way to thank everyone who had helped me along the way, but I had to try. Had I been accepting an Academy Award, the music to shoo me off the stage would have started playing.

At the heart of my speech was my father. My role model. A leader who instilled integrity, courage, and a sense of values in my siblings and me. My stubborn father shouldn't have even been in attendance. Not only had he been wounded in multiple wars, but he had also survived cancer four times. He had life-threatening surgery weeks earlier. But he made it clear to me and the doctors that there was no way in hell he was going to miss his daughter's promotion. He gathered every bit of strength in his broken-down, ninety-year-old body and was there, front and center.

My voice quivered as I looked at my dad, but I pressed on. That's what good soldiers do. That's what my dad did during decades of service to his country. So much of my success was a result of what I had learned from him as a father, a patriot, and a soldier. He was the proudest person in the room. He was also probably the most shocked. Dad never pushed me to join the military. He simply pushed me to always give my best in everything—academics, sports, even board games.

It took years for everything he instilled in me to really sink in, as I progressed through the military ranks. But to say I had an inherent advantage over so many fellow war fighters, male and female, would be the biggest understatement. My dad still jokes that the only reason he earned his second Purple Heart was because he was a slow learner. That type of self-deprecation and humor, even when reflecting on the most harrowing moments of war, is a gift that I would truly appreciate later in life. My dad was my first four-star teacher. He was my General George Washington.

While Dad instilled military values, my mom handled the family values. My parents mastered two of the toughest jobs on the planet: soldiering and parenting. I know Mom was smiling from her heavenly home during my promotion ceremony, not just because she was proud of me but because it created another opportunity for a Dunwoody family reunion, the first time we had all gathered since her funeral a few years earlier.

My mother spent the last eight months of her life bedridden, fighting death and trying to recover from a stroke. It was the medical system, not a lack of determination, that let her down. But she was brave-hearted until her final breath. The most difficult period in my life was watching the Lord take her home months after a stroke permanently paralyzed the left side of her body. Believe what you will, but I believe she is in heaven.

She was eighty-two. She fought valiantly to recover but died on May 1, 2006, just three days shy of my parents' sixtieth wedding anniversary. I was stationed at Fort Lee, Virginia, on August 29, 2005, when I was notified about the stroke. I flew to see her and my dad immediately. My father was devastated, and we were all in shock. Mom was six years younger than Dad. She still played tennis at least three times a week and was fiercely competitive. She even painted the garage the night before her stroke. In later years she was always the healthy one, taking care of our legally blind and ailing father. No one ever thought Mom would be the first to go. Her faith and spirit kept us believing that she would recover. For eight long months the family, scattered all over the country, flew in to see her.

I flew down at least every two weeks, Richmond through Atlanta and on to Sarasota, and it was still another forty-five-minute drive to Englewood. Dad, approaching ninety and not very mobile, visited her every day. My sister Sue and her husband, Jim, bought a house right around the corner from Mom and Dad to tend to both of them. That was a tremendous sacrifice, as Sue and Jim did the heavy lifting for the family during this tough time. From the moment she was admitted into the hospital, Mom never once complained or said a negative word. She was always so polite and said "thank you" to anyone who did the slightest thing to assist her. It was painful to watch her body deteriorate. But her beautiful face never changed. Her blue eyes sparkled, and her smile was radiant and genuine as ever.

Our family and friends shared so many memories and laughs over those grueling months. Mom had such a distinct laugh, and fortunately (or unfortunately) all three of her daughters inherited her infectious laugh. It was a loud, happy cackle times four. When we were all together laughing, people would stare. All my life I had put my dad, the war hero from the Greatest Generation, on a pedestal. As my mom lay dying, I realized in a much more finite way what Dad knew all along: my mom was the real hero of the family. A lady of great faith, she never gave up on any of us. Although Lord knows we all gave her reason to do so at one time or another.

I remember Mom telling us during one of my last visits that the accomplishment she was most proud of was that she taught herself and her children to swim, because she was afraid of the water when she was young. She made sure that each of her kids had no such fears. In fact, she raised five dolphins. To this day we all still love lakes and oceans. None of us knew the courage it took for her to overcome her fears as she taught us to strive for better.

She raised six demanding kids while my dad was away serving our country. She taught us the importance of self-confidence and perseverance. She always told us that "nothing could rain on our parade." Her words helped me forge ahead in my military career the few times I was slighted or passed over for an assignment based on my gender rather than my qualifications. Looking back on it, I couldn't have asked for a better instructor in my early leadership training.

Sitting in the audience were my brother Buck, another West Point grad and successful businessman who put his career on hold to care for my father; my sister Sue, who became the third helicopter pilot in Army history; my sister Jackie, a mother of two beautiful daughters; and my brother Bill, who was a land surveyor turned construction supervisor.

Leadership begins in the home, but that's hardly where it ends. My first platoon leader in 1976 was Sergeant First Class Wendell Bowen. He was the best noncommissioned officer (NCO) in the company and the reason I stayed in the Army.

If he's the reason I stayed, my husband, Craig, is the reason I became the first woman to get four stars thirty-two years later.

EARLY IN MY career I married my high school sweetheart, another West Point man. I was ready to follow him around the world while he served our nation. Even though we loved each other, we grew apart. The Vietnam War divided the United States and, in many ways, our marriage. My first husband began to question a lot of things about life, liberty, and love. When we married, I thought the plan was to raise a big family; I'd do my best impersonation of my maternal role model—my mother. It was clear that my husband was not prepared to enlist in that type of idyllic matrimony, and understandably so. We both had changed so much from our puppy love days. We ultimately divorced.

During my speech I fought back tears a few times. Who wouldn't? After all, we had finally made it. We, the hundreds of thousands of women who had fought sexism and stereotypes just to serve their country long before my four-star promotion. We, the mothers and wives who had fought to keep their families together while praying that their sons and husbands came home alive. We, the Dunwoody clan, who had fought in every military conflict since the Spanish-American War. We, the male and female fighters who had heeded a higher calling and higher standard to protect and defend the United States of America. We, the hundreds of thousands of women who had fought tradition, sexism, and stereotypes just to serve our country.

My promotion was our victory.

As I concluded my speech I reflected on a remarkable career made possible by so many. I had thought I was born to coach athletes, but instead my real team consisted of thousands of soldiers in nearly 145 countries. My new job as leader of the Army Materiel Command would include nearly sixty-nine thousand civilians and soldiers working together to supply our troops with almost everything needed to get the job done. My team could fill almost any football stadium in the United States.

During his Pro Football Hall of Fame induction speech earlier that year, Washington Redskins wide receiver Art Monk said something that will forever resonate with me: from the first day he put on a football uniform, he knew that playing the game was all he ever wanted to do. Even though I thought I was coming to the Army for two years, I realized that I had known from the day I first donned my uniform that soldiering was all I ever wanted to do.

I felt a sense of relief as I wrapped up my speech, and I was eager to pay a final tribute to the man sitting in the front row. I delivered a bouquet of yellow roses and an "Army Strong" hat to my father and gave him a warm Dunwoody hug. More hugs, kisses, and flowers followed for my siblings, nieces, and in-laws in attendance.

After a few minutes I hopped back on stage, ready to start my assignment as the Army's newest four-star general. Ready to continue striving toward a higher standard.

one

★ ★ ★ ★

WALK THE WALK

"LIVE TO A HIGHER STANDARD"

SUMMER 1997, FORT DRUM, NEW YORK

ARMY HELICOPTERS CIRCLED above the wooded area. Search dogs combed the ground. Military and civilian police were trying to find the lost battalion commander. We knew we would locate our missing comrade, but the question was whether he would be alive or dead. Had he killed himself after his transgressions? If he hadn't, would he be a danger to his own battalion that was trying to rescue him? Days earlier he knew he had been caught in lies and lapses of judgment. His immoral choices would undoubtedly end an Army career that had been fast-tracked for early promotion and greater leadership posts. But right now I was more concerned about saving his life.

The fear of losing his family and military career weighed him down. The guilt of violating multiple oaths, vows, and creeds crushed his spirit. He snapped, deserting his command and country after being caught betraying his wife and his uniform. He left behind his military ID and an address book with the names of female soldiers and civilians we suspected he had affairs with—but no clues as to his whereabouts. His address book had the names of women, adorned with stars, presumably indicating the ladies he had slept with. He had breached the Army's code of ethics on numerous fronts, including affairs with civilians and possibly subordinates.

An anonymous letter was the first clue that reached my office. I was the brigade commander, and it was my job to get to the bottom of the sordid allegations. It didn't say much—more innuendo than specifics. We investigated and found nothing that could be substantiated. I also talked to the battalion commander himself, and he denied everything. But days later a second letter appeared, and it was much more specific—names, places, and dates. At first it was incomprehensible that there could be merit to the charges. The accused was a rising star. Unfortunately the evidence was damning. The shame and guilt were too much when we confronted him. He ran from his demons.

The massive search lasted for hours. We feared the worst. The military demands conduct from soldiers that no other industry expects of its employees. Often it's one strike and you're out. Get caught cheating on a test or on your spouse, and your career could be over. In most businesses, affairs and white lies are common and rarely lead to dismissal. In the military such actions are verboten for soldiers who swear to uphold a higher standard the moment they enlist. The standards are so high and the guilt can be so great that, in a disgraced soldier's mind, suicide sometime seems only the way out. A year earlier Admiral Jeremy Boorda, Chief of Naval Operations, committed suicide after being accused of wearing an undeserved combat "V" device, used to honor combat heroism, on one of his medals. He was humiliated and couldn't bear bringing disgrace to the Navy or his family. Unfortunately he thought suicide was the only honorable path open to him.

I worried that our missing battalion commander might be in a similar mental state. We decided to put every available person in the battalion online to join the search. About five hundred soldiers, many of whom reported directly to the missing leader, searched both sides of the Black River, a scenic river with good fishing that runs along the southern boundary of the main post area of Fort Drum. About 4 p.m. I received a call from one of the NCOs in the battalion: we found him.

One of his direct reports discovered him curled up in the fetal position along the river bank. He was incoherent and a broken man—not from myriad tours of duty in a war zone but because he had failed to live up to the higher standard mandated of all war fighters when they enlist or are commissioned in the US Army. He violated the very ethos that makes the Army strong: honor, integrity, and loyalty. He could have been found guilty of sexual misconduct in a court of law or adultery in the eyes of God.

The officer was smart, charming, and loved his country. Many of his soldiers looked up to him. But I think he would be the first to admit that he let success and power go to his head. In his mind he let down not only his family and the service but also his soldiers.

I wasn't going to give up on him. Yes, his military career was over, a once-promising future derailed. The rest of his life, however, wasn't over. Similar mistakes have been overlooked, ignored, or covered up, from Wall Street to the White House. But he wasn't a businessman or a politician; he was a soldier, and he had dishonored the Code. Soldiers commit to a different set of rules—actually a different set of values that represent a higher standard of personal conduct.

After speaking with the battalion commander in the local hospital, I promised to get him the help for his recovery. He received psychiatric evaluation and was admitted to Walter Reed

Army Medical Center in Bethesda, Maryland. The easy thing would be to desert him. Getting him whole was important. He gave his adult life to the military and deserved to transition to civilian life with some compassion and grace. Most businesses would eventually fire an employee for such transgressions, leaving them with a severance or unemployment check. Few companies would care about the employee's mental well-being or the root cause of the behavior. The Army could have easily discharged him and wiped its hands clean of him. That would ignore the principles that I signed up for forty years ago when I joined the family business: the US Army.

I knew what I was getting into. I grew up idolizing my father. He was a third-generation West Point man and a war hero. His word was law. My siblings and I were expected to be on our best behavior. Our actions could have negative consequences on our father's career if we did anything to discredit the family name.

My father still reminds me of the time he blistered my behind for cheating in Sister Inez's second-grade class in Arlington County, or when, as a three-year-old, I summoned my inner Picasso and vandalized our freshly painted white walls with crayons at our house in Fort Leavenworth, Kansas, as we were preparing to move to a new base. The constant threat of a switch to the fanny was real and had our full attention. My father held himself and his family to a higher standard. At West Point, if a cadet knew that a classmate was lying, cheating, or stealing, he had to report it or risk being expelled. These principles and expectations were instilled in me almost from birth. This was a huge advantage throughout my career.

When I enlisted in the Army Reserves in 1974 it was a turbulent time for the military and the country. The Vietnam War was "officially" ending, and with it came relentless backlash and scrutiny for the Armed Forces. Despite the protests and outrage by millions, my admiration for the Army did not waver. Although I admit that I saw it through rose-colored corneas, the Army I loved affected almost everything I valued and stood for: family, discipline, respect, and teamwork.

The end of the Vietnam War came as doors were opening for women in ways unthinkable a decade earlier—equal rights, equal pay, Title IX. New opportunities were being presented to women in the workplace, classrooms, sports fields, and battlefields. I knew I wouldn't be a lifer, but becoming a soldier was an opportunity I couldn't turn down. My great-grandfather, grandfather, and father were proud veterans of the US Army. Now their baby girl was following in their decorated footsteps, even if just for a few years and even if my father wasn't completely supportive or understanding of women in the military.

When I received my fourth star, I became the leader of the largest logistics organization in the military, the US Army Materiel Command (AMC). I was responsible for leading a $60 billion enterprise with more than sixty-nine thousand employees operating in fifty states and 145 countries. If a soldier shoots it, drives it, flies it, wears it, or eats it, AMC provides it. Think Walmart. Think Amazon. Think Department of Defense.

Months into my promotion Oprah's O magazine named me on their first-ever "power list" of women, and I was asked to participate in a *Fortune* "most powerful women" summit. In 2012 I was recognized by the United Service Organizations (USO) as their "Woman of the Year." That type of recognition was embarrassing at times and led to good-natured ribbing from friends, family, and colleagues. I never set out for headlines or stars; I just wanted to be the best soldier and leader I could be. I can't tell you how many people have asked me, "Why you?" and "How did you break that brass ceiling?" People wanted to know how I took on a sexist institution that was dead set against allowing women access to its ranks and battlefields. After all, the Army had been around for more than two hundred years before I became the first female four-star general. Though I am proud to be the first, clearly there have been many dedicated and deserving women war fighters.

The truth is that many male mentors fought for me throughout my career. Although it's important to acknowledge that not everyone was gracious and accommodating, I was able to advance through the ranks on my own merits and credentials with the willingness of male supervisors to judge me based on those merits and credentials rather than my gender. No one gets to the top of their profession without the support of many, but the real story of my success and the lessons I learned along the way are far more interesting and informative than a story about moving up in a male-dominated profession. It's more about leadership than about gender. In my entire thirty-eight-year career I never reported to a woman. I worked for male leaders who either believed in me or didn't.

I remember when I first reported to the 82nd Airborne Division in 1988. I had to go to the firing range with my unit to qualify on a 9mm pistol. Although I had qualified on an M-16 rifle and a .45 caliber pistol in the past, I had never handled or fired a 9mm before, and quite frankly there wasn't anyone there eager to show me how. Well, I "bolo'd." Translation: the fourth-generation Army brat flunked. I scored fifteen out of forty, the highest failing grade— so close to being barely mediocre. Back then some of the logistics NCOs enjoyed it when officers didn't qualify. Imagine how much they loved knowing that the first female field grade officer in the division couldn't shoot straight. They undoubtedly had some good laughs over that one. I'm sure several members of my family would have joined in with the NCOs. My father, my sister Sue, and my brother Buck were all not only expert shooters but also members of the National Rifle Association (NRA).

I told my Air Force Special Operations husband about my disaster, but he wouldn't let me wallow in self-pity. "Well, we've got to fix that," he said. "My guys will show you how to fire Expert on

9mm, and they won't let you leave until you do." That's one of the things that makes Craig so special: he didn't want me to simply pass; he wanted me to kick ass. In his mind, just qualifying wasn't enough, nor was qualifying as Marksman or Sharpshooter. So he set up a training session for me with his NCO weapons experts.

Master Sergeant Harry Walker and Technical Sergeant John Roller were professionals, airmen trained to shoot for a living. I can't say the same about my logistics NCOs, who were responsible for the firing range in my unit. They did not shoot routinely. Craig's NCOs were impressed that a field grade officer had asked for their help, and they gladly agreed to teach me. They had 9mm pistols, ammunition, and headphones for hearing protection ready the next morning. The special operators have multiple firing ranges and configurations—indoor shoot houses, outdoor static training ranges, and ranges with a variety of target options. They took me out to the basic 9mm range with static targets. They focused on technique—how to stand, how to hold the weapon, how to breathe, and how to align the sight. They told me to line up the two white dots on the front and rear sights to look like a snowman. I knew none of this. A day earlier I had just gone out, pointed at the target, fired, and failed.

No wonder I had bolo'd. But Walker and Roller were patient and serious. "Breathe easy. Inhale, hold your breath, fire, exhale. Repeat. Steady, steady. Nice shot. Raise your sight a little." As I hit more targets, they continued to reinforce the good performance with comments like "Great shot! That's it! Keep it up." I practiced their techniques for about thirty minutes on stationary paper targets with giant bull's eyes. I started gaining confidence as I hit targets. We went to another nearby range that had pop-up targets, more in line with the Army's, for about thirty minutes, and I couldn't believe the difference. I felt as if I had all day to aim, fire, and shoot at each target. The targets looked like gray human silhouettes—waist up. They were made out of metal and would pop up and down on signal from the NCO. Watching the targets go "down" was exhilarating. This wasn't hard. It's like golf or tennis: there's a technique to the swing, and you will succeed if you take the time to master that technique.

I couldn't wait for my do-over. The special operators made me feel like a character from a John Wayne movie, whereas the preparation and training in my own unit was pedestrian and embarrassing. We were taught all the safety requirements: loading, clearing, breaking down, and cleaning a gun. Safety, of course, was paramount. The actual training on how to fire the weapon, however, was practically read verbatim from a manual. My logistics trainers lacked personal knowledge and experience.

When I returned a few days later for my mulligan, I could sense their cynicism: *Here she comes again. I hope she can get seventeen this time.* But I proved them wrong and Craig right. I qualified Expert, hitting thirty-eight out of forty targets after barely hitting a third of that number just days earlier. My stunned NCOs high-fived me. They were happy for me—and perplexed. "How did you do that?" they asked. I told them I had received training from the special operators NCOs. Craig's men did what mine should have done: they coached me. My NCOs learned a lesson that day. They were embarrassed, knowing that they had failed by not being expert trainers. Their days of laughing about officers who bolo'd were over. They realized that success on the range was based in part on their ability to train. You train people so they don't flail or fail— you train them to succeed.

As I rose through the ranks, I always visited ranges to make sure soldiers were receiving proper training before going for qualification. Some of the trainers didn't really know how to fire the weapon. It was easier to laugh about no-gos than to learn how to train them. We fixed that—I made sure people understood that if you were prepared, then you would not fail.

MY FATHER TAUGHT me to not accept defeat. Like most World War II vets and men of his generation, however, he would never be mistaken for a feminist. It was not easy for him to wrap his mind around the idea of a woman being anywhere near a combat zone. When I was deploying to Saudi Arabia with the 82nd Airborne Division in support of Desert Shield/Desert Storm, I thought my mom would be the one worried to death, but it was actually my dad. "Stay in touch when you can," he asked me. I told him not to fret; the Army had prepared me well, and this is what I was trained to do. My father provided me with lifelong insight into the dangers of war. But it was tough for him, probably because he knew the ugly side of war and couldn't imagine his little Annie going off to fight with the mighty 82nd Airborne.

He kept asking me questions and making small talk while constantly chewing on his fingernails—he was a notorious nail-biter. How long are you going to be gone? Where are you staying? When will you call?

I don't think my father was scared, but he was anxious. The idea that I couldn't check in regularly, as I always did, was disconcerting. Our communication now was going to be through letters and the occasional phone call. I told him I would touch base with him as often as I could and that as long as Craig was stateside I would have him check in as well.

Dad's concern was touching, but he had prepared me for the challenges and demands of war. He gave me advice that I have used in almost every aspect of service and personal life:

- If you don't think you're the best at what you do, no one else will.
- If winning isn't everything, why bother playing? (Now, I never took this to mean, "Win at all costs." I took it to mean, "Be a fighter and don't give up on the things you believe in.")

- The higher up the flagpole you ascend, the more your ass is exposed. (Translation: "The higher your rank, the more visibility you and your actions receive.")

Dad's tenets and those I've adopted throughout my career have ultimately led me to write this book. But writing a book never crossed my mind as I spent decades training troops to protect our freedom. I'm a war fighter, not a writer. My promotion to general changed my outlook, however. I received hundreds of media requests from mainstream, right-wing, left-wing, and feminist outlets. Journalists and well-wishers repeatedly asked me when I was going to share my story. At first I would politely change the subject or deflect the question. My rise through the ranks was a result of a life spent learning, listening, and, ultimately, leading. The Army was never about me or the accomplishments achieved on my watch. (One of my great friends and mentors told me that he never reads memoirs or books on any subject written by the people he served with because he thinks the books are part chest beating, part revisionist history, and part fiction.) This book is not an autobiography. It will share some personal experiences—life lessons gleaned through failures, do-overs, and successes—in hopes that others can learn, grow, and, most important, help develop the next generation of leaders.

This is not a manual about how to become a general, nor will I reveal a secret recipe for becoming a great leader. There are scores of books on leadership. Some people think that great leaders are born, whereas others think that leadership can be taught. Whatever you believe about the nature of leadership, true leaders never stop learning, refining, growing, and adapting—and that's the primary focus of this book.

It's no coincidence that I chose A *Higher Standard* as the book's title. Those words became the foundation of my leadership philosophy and a central part of how I tried to live my life. I didn't invent it, and I certainly wasn't born with it. It became instilled in me through sixty-plus years of relationships with my husband, family, friends, coaches, and soldiers.

I discovered that the military not only encourages soldiers to meet their standards but also rewards those who exceed them. This sounds practical and reasonable, but how many organizations really encourage people to ruin the curve? Usually it means that you will have to work harder and do more. Unions are notorious for crushing "go-getters" or "overachievers." Just do your job; don't try to set the world on fire. In the military, overachievers are usually respected for raising the bar. Those who run faster, do more push-ups, or fire Expert are recognized with well-earned qualification badges, patches, or decorations. No one ever frowns upon the fastest runner or the most accurate shooter—they want them on their team. This is a dangerous profession, and you want the best of the best on your side, on and off the battlefield.

Meeting the standard is the expectation, but those who strive to exceed the standard send a signal about their character and their competence. To be honest, as a woman, I felt that there was more expected of me in order to gain acceptance and respect in this man's Army. Although the oath we take and the Uniform Code of Military Justice hold our troops to a higher standard than our civilian counterparts, our ethos and our creeds tug at the human dimension of being the best.

Although it has been intuitively obvious to many of us, it wasn't until recently that many people, inside or outside the military, really understood that everyone in the Army is first and foremost a rifleman. History is full of great soldiers who died heroically for their nation. We know that war brings with it the grim reality that we will lose great soldiers and friends. What we cannot afford is to lose great soldiers because we failed to equip them with the best tools or train them to standard so they can protect themselves and carry out their mission. We cannot accept anything less.

WHENEVER PEOPLE ASK whether I always knew that I'd become a four-star general, my answer is always the same: not in my wildest dreams! My Army experience was intended to be a brief, two-year detour on the road to the fitness profession. Even at a young age, I was never satisfied with just getting by. I am my daddy's girl. I was always goal oriented and competitive. I wanted to give a little more and to be the best, or at least do my best. That was the case during my first command, when I led two hundred soldiers. It was the case during my two-star assignment, when I supported the largest deployment and redeployment of US forces since World War II in support of Operation Iraqi Freedom (OIF) and Operation Enduring Freedom (OEF). And it was the case during my final four-star position, in which I was responsible for leading tens of thousands of soldiers and civilians.

Becoming the first anything, whether it be a female general, an Asian rabbi, or an openly gay NFL player, comes with pressure, challenges, and, above all, responsibility. I always think of myself as a soldier first and foremost, not a female soldier. But to think that my gender wouldn't lead to greater scrutiny and opportunity would be naïve. The successes and failures under my command could raise or shatter those supposed brass ceilings for future generations of female soldiers. I am an unabashedly proud US Army veteran. I love the United States and all of its military branches, even my husband's Air Force. Like all institutions, however, the Army is imperfect. The problems that have plagued the military are present in every sector and profession of society: corporate America, universities, religious sects, and the sports world.

Throughout my career I was faced with decisions that could affect the lives of thousands of soldiers and civilians from all walks of life. During my last assignment as commander of AMC, I felt as if someone was directing my life with a remote control that changed channels every two minutes: one moment I was making decisions on how to provide support to a land-locked Afghanistan while the

Pakistan ground lines of communication were shut down, and the next minute I had to figure out how to best support and synchronize the removal of equipment in Iraq or respond to contingency operations in Japan or Haiti, all of this while trying to move my headquarters from Fort Belvoir, Virginia, to Redstone Arsenal in Alabama. Not long after I settled into Redstone, devastating tornadoes shook the state. It really is true: if you want adventure, join the Army.

The lessons I absorbed in the military are applicable to servicemen, senior citizens, CEOs, students, and parents. Whether you've risen through the ranks to company president or were just cut from your JV basketball team, there are strategies to help you deal with success or setbacks and to achieve your goals.

When I spoke to executives and employees at Coca-Cola, I was surprised by how much our two organizations had in common—in size, scope, global presence, and budget. I remember telling them that the biggest difference between our distribution processes is that they aren't getting shot at or blown up while trying to deliver their products.

After managing nearly sixty-nine thousand employees, one thing is clear to me: there is a higher standard that provides the foundation upon which every effective leadership journey is built. It's the difference between the leaders who excel and the leaders who fail. It's their thought process, attention to detail, and execution that enables them to inspire and motivate their workforce to create and sustain high-performing, successful organizations.

Whether it's the military, a Fortune 500 company, or a mom-and-pop store that's been in business for fifty years, not everyone in the organization needs to be what's known as a Level 5 leader as defined by Jim Collins in his number-one best-seller *Good to Great*—the kind of leadership required to achieve greatness. But to experience sustained success, you need some Level 5 leaders to inspire and motivate those around them.

In the Army "meeting the standard" is the base requirement. It is the very definition of an average performance. Imagine if you had an entire organization filled with average employees. You're going to have an average organization. If you're lucky.

In school a C student drifts along without necessarily fully comprehending the material. The student likely won't care about improving without someone providing motivation and inspiration. Often these "average" students go on to enlist in the military, looking for a better life. Once in the military, it's all about meeting the standards. On the rifle range a soldier has to hit the target sixty-five out of a hundred rounds to meet the standard. The sad reality is that a 65 percent shooter is a C student who is unlikely to be an MVP on the battlefield. We spend a lot of leadership time at the lower levels training and retraining soldiers so that all of our troops can meet the standards. For what? A whole unit of C students? That is hardly something to brag about unless we start to redefine average.

About seven years ago a squad of soldiers was on combat patrol in the Korangal Valley, one of the most dangerous regions of Afghanistan. Most of these soldiers were barely out of high school and not old enough to legally drink. They had been on patrol for six straight days. When you think of Afghanistan, think third-world war-torn country, barren and underdeveloped. These soldiers were scaling mountains at a grueling and lung-zapping eight thousand feet. They had been sleeping in ditches every night. They were cold. They were tired. But their mission was almost complete.

The squad was on its way back to base camp, some on foot and others in a heavily armored Humvee. Machine gunfire erupted from the ridge off to their left, and rocket-propelled grenades rained down on them. Bullets landed all around them. The squad was being ambushed from a stone's throw away. The first two soldiers in the squad were hit instantly. A couple of seconds later the squad leader was hit. They were about to be overrun by the enemy. But that's not how this story ends. The squad survived because of the heroic efforts of an "average" teenager from Iowa named Salvatore "Sal" Augustine Giunta. A kid who had gone to the Army recruiter in hopes of getting a free T-shirt was now front and center and living the worst day of his life.

When Specialist Giunta saw that his squad leader was wounded, he ran directly into oncoming fire to render first aid. The relentless enemy fire was so intense that Giunta was hit twice. One round was deflected by his body armor and another by the assault rifle he was carrying. Undeterred and defiant, he quickly pulled his squad leader to safety. But Giunta wasn't finished. He knew there were two other comrades still out there. So he led the rest of the squad—running, firing their rifles, and throwing grenades at the enemy. They charged ahead and found the first of the two wounded soldiers. They quickly assisted him and gave him medical aid. There was one more soldier out there: Specialist Joshua Brennan. He was one of Giunta's closest friends, and the squad wasn't going to leave him behind.

With bullets still flying all around him, Giunta spotted his friend being dragged away by two Afghan insurgents. He immediately charged the insurgents, shooting and killing one while wounding the other. Giunta grabbed his Army brother by the vest and pulled him to the closest point that could pass for cover. For thirty minutes Specialist Giunta stayed by Specialist Brennan's side. He treated his wounds until the medical evacuation helicopter arrived and the Apache helicopters were able to clear the ridge of enemy fire. Tragically Specialist Brennan died as a result of his wounds on October 26, 2007.

In spite of Specialist Giunta's courage, he sincerely downplayed his heroism. When people asked him to describe himself as a soldier, he said, "I'm average. . . . If I'm a hero, then every man that stands around me, every woman in the military, everyone who goes into the unknown, is a hero. So if you think I'm a hero—as long as you include everyone with me."

I had the privilege of meeting Sal Giunta at his Medal of Honor ceremony in November 2010. He is the first living service member to receive our nation's highest honor since the Vietnam War. Recently Sal told his own story in *Living with Honor: A Memoir*.

Giunta is without question an American hero. Yet he took absolutely no credit for saving the lives of several soldiers; he only gave thanks to those who fought alongside him. People might wonder where does the Army find soldiers like that? Well, the Army doesn't recruit superheroes. He was just like many other high school seniors in search of their next adventure.

One thing is clear, though: no matter what he does or where he goes, Sal will always serve as an example of what it means to redefine average. In the military we should strive for average to be extraordinary. As a military brat who evolved into a lifelong soldier, I was decades into my career when I truly understood the magic of "average." A kid from the cornfields of Iowa set the standard. He led under the deadliest circumstances.

The key is to teach the soldiers to be better. Yes, they should meet the standards, but that's simply a starting point. Good soldiers know the importance of rising above and beyond. Success has no ceiling. Our striving to improve as an individual, a team, a unit, and an organization should never end. The great leaders eliminate, separate, isolate, or retire those who are not willing to improve. In sports we cut or trade those who aren't improving.

The US military is the most scrutinized organization in the world. Pick up a newspaper or turn on a television, and chances are you will see a story involving the military. The stories range from money to morality to morale. Are soldiers paid enough? Should taxpayers continue to fund wars? Should we withdraw troops? Are veterans being mistreated? Are female soldiers prey to a sexist system? Are we violating human rights for prisoners of war?

Despite the constant coverage, the military remains one of the most respected institutions in our country. While trust in pluto-

crats, politicians, and priests is at an all-time low, respect for soldiers is high, regardless of metric or poll.

Our nation has come a long way from spitting in the faces of
heroes coming home from Vietnam. At sporting events soldiers
are regularly honored for their valor. Patriotic or pacifist, Americans have grown to respect our servicemen and their sacrifices.

I felt a personal responsibility to prepare our American sons
and daughters for war. Like their families and friends, I wanted
them to be proud of what they did and to be the best at what they
did. As I became part of this great institution, it was the pride
of wearing the uniform and the sense of belonging to a community that became my true calling and creed. Early on it was the
Quartermaster Corps, then the Rigger community, and then my
beloved Airborne unit.

Each group had a creed that made you feel larger than life, part
of something greater than self. These doctrines were a source of
pride and kinship. They made me want to be the best I could be
and to never be the one to let the team down.

As I rose in rank, each creed gained new meaning.

For years I carried around a copy of the Quartermaster Creed,
Airborne Creed, and Rigger Pledge. I kept these cards because
I was proud of the Quartermaster, the Airborne, and the Rigger
ethos.

Quartermaster Creed
I can shape the course of combat, change the outcome of
battle.

This has resonated with me for almost thirty years.

The Rigger Pledge
I will be sure always . . . I will remember that the other man's
life is as dear to him as mine is to me.

This one gives me chills as I think of American heroes such as Sal Giunta.

The Airborne Creed

I am an airborne trooper . . . a paratrooper. In battle I fear no foe's ability nor underestimate his prowess, power, and guile. I am a trooper of the sky! I am my nation's best! In peace and war I never fail. Anywhere, anytime, in anything.

This one takes me back to the moment when I first parachuted from a plane and truly understood one of the main reasons why God put me on Earth. I attended a Catholic mass at Fort Benning, Georgia, the day before we started jump week training. The place was packed. When I shook hands with the priest, I commented on how well attended the service was. He smiled and told me it's always that way before a jump week.

These creeds are more than just catchy phrases; they represent a way of life for every serviceman and woman regardless of branch.

In 2005 General Peter Schoomaker, Chief of Staff of the US Army, delivered a new warrior ethos: the Soldier's Creed. To this day, even though I am a retired four-star general, this creed takes precedence for me over every creed I hold dear except the Apostles' Creed:

I am an American soldier.
I am a warrior and a member of the team.
I serve the people of the United States and live the Army values.
I will always place mission first.
I will never accept defeat.
I will never quit.
I will never leave a fallen comrade.
I am disciplined, physically and mentally tough.
Trained and proficient in my warrior tasks and drills.

I always maintain my arms, my equipment, and myself.

I am an expert, and I am a professional.

I stand ready to deploy, engage, and destroy the enemies of the
United States of America in close combat.

I am a guardian of freedom and the American way of life.

I am an American soldier.

This is the creed of the American soldier. It's not a creed just for Rangers, Infantry, or other combat arms or for members of an exclusive club. It's the creed that most accurately reflects our profession, our mission, our commitment, and our warrior ethos.

The Quartermaster Creed unifies quartermasters. The Rigger Creed unites riggers. And the Airborne Creed bonds paratroopers. General Schoomaker introduced a creed that connects all soldiers.

I will always proudly wear my Quartermaster Regimental Crest, Rigger Wings, and Airborne Wings. I am equally proud of my dog tags as I am of my four stars.

two

WENDELL WOULD BE PROUD

"Never Walk by a Mistake"

THE FIRST DAY OF a new job is always tough. Will you fit in? Are you dressed properly? Will you be ostracized? When I reported to duty at Fort Sill, Oklahoma, in June 1976, I stood out. I was anything but the average soldier. I was five-feet-five inches with my boots on. I weighed 118 pounds after a good meal. Women had been serving in a coed Army for seven months at this point. But it didn't take long for me to realize I belonged. Within minutes of meeting my first platoon sergeant my life changed. He didn't see a petite blonde woman all dressed up, trying to play Army; he saw a soldier in the making.

"Lieutenant Dunwoody, I'm going to make you the best platoon leader in the United States Army," said Sergeant First Class Wendell Bowen.

"Was he talking to me?" I thought. I had half-expected him to say, "Kid, do you really know what you're signing up for?"

Instead, he immediately taught me the power of belief. I barely knew the man, yet he saw something in me instantly that made me want to prove him right.

As I have previously mentioned, when I joined the Army I had no long-term military ambitions. Becoming a one-star or four-star general never entered my mind. I had hoped to add my own small footnote to our family tradition. But I knew that the Army was just going to be a brief detour on my way to becoming a coach and physical education teacher—two years and done.

Until I met Sergeant First Class Wendell Bowen.

He was a Vietnam veteran with a classic five-foot-ten, 175-pound build straight off the Army assembly line. Married and in his thirties, the NCO walked with a strange gait, toes pointed out, sort of like a penguin. Like so many soldiers back then—officers, noncommissioned officers, and junior enlisted troops—he was a two-pack-a-day smoker.

When I first met Sergeant Bowen as a 2nd lieutenant, it was at a time when the Army was reeling from severe budget cuts. In the years to come the Army of this era would be referred to as hollow and broken. The Vietnam War was just ending, and there wasn't an urgency to build a trained and ready force. The military was a microcosm of society at large. The Vietnam era was a period of experimentation and demonstration. Many kids enlisted in those days because judges gave them two options—jail or the military. Drug and alcohol abuse was rampant. Racial tensions were high as a so-called integrated military and most of the country struggled to deal with the realities of civil rights legislation.

To ease the burden on soldiers who had been sent back for additional tours, the Army began allowing young adults who hadn't even graduated high school to enlist. A new generation of soldiers had trouble saying a full sentence without lacing it with profanity.

Sergeant Bowen, in contrast, represented all that was good about our Army. He had a strong work ethic and never complained about working ungodly hours and most weekends. He had a disarming smile and a great laugh to complement his thick Tennessee twang. He carried himself with dignity and was very detailed about his appearance. He wore his hair parted on the left, combed back with a slick Vitalis look. The only thing with a greater sheen than his hair was his spotless, spit-shined military boots.

As a first-time platoon leader, I could not have asked for a better mentor than Sergeant Bowen. We instantly clicked. So when he told me that he was going to make me the best platoon leader in the entire Army, it resonated. Sergeant Bowen wasn't prone to military bravado. His challenge pushed me to reward his confidence. However, I had a lot to learn. So much so that he brought me back to earth a few days later when he quipped, "You are going to make me work at this aren't you, Lieutenant?"

It didn't take long to settle into the daily routine of being a platoon leader. The Army has a very structured work schedule. Up at 0530 hours for physical training, shower, clean up, and breakfast. Report to work at 0800. Inspect the barracks, review the troops in formation, and then head to the maintenance shed to begin mission operations. Sergeant Bowen not only told me what was expected every day, but he also made sure I memorized Army policy governing how to wear the uniform, how to conduct an inspection, and how to run a repair parts shop. Straight from Army Regulation 670-1, Paragraph 3-1, "Soldiers will present a professional image at all times and will continue to set the example in military presence, both on and off duty. Pride in appearance includes Soldier physical fitness and adherence to weight standards."

Every day we supervised soldiers, ordering, issuing, and restocking repair parts for vehicles and equipment of our customers, the Corps Artillery, and Artillery School. Lunchtime was signaled by the arrival of the "Roach Coach" in the maintenance yard; it was at noon sharp. The Roach Coach was a meals-on-wheels kind of operation. Soldiers grabbed a quick snack, maybe a hot dog, Fritos, and a Coke from the truck, while others caught the bus back to the mess hall. Lunch for me usually included playing Double Pinochle with Sergeant Bowen, the company commander, and a few other

NCOs and officers. Sergeant Bowen wasn't required to invite me to the table, but it was another sign of his inclusive leadership style. I loved playing cards and won my fair share of games. It was another bonding activity that made me feel very much a part of the team.

On Wednesday afternoons we had beer call at the maintenance shops. Sergeant Bowen encouraged me to stay and drink a few Pearl beers while getting to know the other officers. Pearl may have been brewed in San Antonio, Texas, but it was an Oklahoma favorite. It would have been easy to just head for home after being up for twelve to fourteen hours, but Sergeant Bowen was teaching me about the Army culture of the day. Beer calls provided a time to relax, tell war stories, solve problems, and build trust. The Vietnam vets would talk about the war, especially after a couple of beers. We talked about the good soldiers and definitely about the bad. In those days we used to say it was important to work hard and play hard. After a couple of beers, I would head home and get my uniform and boots ready for the next day: starch, press, spit shine, and start all over.

Sergeant Bowen shared wisdom on many levels that guided me through every step of my military career:

1. He never once gave me advice on being a female soldier. He vowed to make me the best platoon leader in the Army, not the best female leader. In a society that still questions whether a woman can have it all, a chain-smoking military man knew that the best way for soldiers—regardless of race or gender—to coexist was to respect one another.

   There was a cover story in the *Atlantic* in 2014 titled "The Confidence Gap" that made the rounds on political talk shows and boardrooms. The article states, "Evidence shows that women are less self-assured than men and that to succeed, confidence matters as much as competence." Thanks to people like Sergeant Bowen, I never struggled with such self-doubt. I'm certain that if every woman had a Sergeant Bowen mentoring them, they wouldn't either.

2. He showed me what right looks like. The military is deeply ritualistic, with infinite rules, regulations, and traditions. What might seem trivial to civilians could ultimately mean life or death for a war fighter and those he is trying to protect. What appears mundane to laymen—making beds correctly, polishing shoes, and marching in cadence—becomes crucial as soldiers evolve into war fighters. Jumping from planes and staying in cramped barracks or ships for hundreds of days at a time while fighting wars require discipline, teamwork, and acute attention to detail.

3. He taught me to never walk by a mistake. Far too often we let little things slide. But just turn on the news and listen as the anchors lament an auto-part defect leading to deaths and multibillion-dollar recalls or a small leak in a gas pipeline causing an explosion that endangers wildlife. Recognizing when something is wrong, big or small, and holding people accountable can save industries billions and citizens their lives. Sergeant Bowen instilled in me instantly that if you *do* walk by a mistake, then you just set a new, lower standard.

4. Be true to yourself. Even though I was joining a man's Army, Sergeant Bowen made it clear that women could be themselves as they integrated into military life. We did not have to act like a macho man to be successful. We did not have to forsake our femininity. We did not have to curse, pound a dozen Pabst Blue Ribbons, or spit tobacco to show we belonged. We just had to be professional and meet or exceed the standard.

I'm not sure whether I ever became the "best platoon leader in the United States Army," but Sergeant Bowen made it clear to me that I should never settle for less than my best. By removing gender from the discussion, I would never use it as an excuse. He taught me how to write honest evaluation reports that addressed not only a soldier's performance but also his potential. He showed me how to counsel soldiers on personal and professional issues. He instructed me about the chain of command and the importance of the relationship between the platoon leader and the platoon sergeant. Constant communication was crucial. There could be no doubt among the troops that we spoke with one voice.

Sergeant Bowen also taught me the human dimension of dealing with troubled soldiers, especially during a period of heavy drug use in the military. We were still having a problem with dope in the barracks. We could smell the residue of marijuana. This was unacceptable. It was hard to catch anyone in the act; the dudes were too smart for that. I hadn't been with Sergeant Bowen very long before he told me about health-and-welfare inspections, a tool I would use throughout my career. It's hard for private citizens to imagine someone storming through their houses or offices unannounced, looking for illegal activity. But that was the purpose of these inspections—to investigate when least expected. Bowen went over every detail of the inspection. It was a complicated and covert operation.

Sergeant Bowen was a pro here. He stressed the importance of secrecy and not discussing anything with anyone. He had seen loose lips ruin many inspections—it never occurred to me that someone could be eavesdropping. He also would plan the raids on forty-eight hours' notice. He told me, "You'll know when an inspection has been compromised because you won't find any contraband."

Sergeant Bowen, myself, the company commander, a couple of higher-ups, and two security guys with their drug-sniffing dogs were the only ones who knew about the mission. Details were passed in sealed envelopes.

The team assembled in Sergeant Bowen's office around 0330. I stood in the doorway listening to his instructions: "Sergeants Ingrid and Brown, you have the first floor, Sergeant Elliott and Sergeant Smith, you have the second. Each of you will start at opposite ends of the barracks. At exactly 0400 turn on the lights and announce the health and welfare inspection. Tell the soldiers to quickly get dressed in PT gear, open their wall lockers, and stand by their beds. Security, you will follow the NCOs as they search each room for contraband."

A few minutes later we slipped into the barracks as "Operation Clean Up" commenced.

The lights came on. "Listen up! Get into your PT gear, open up your wall lockers, and stand by your bed. This is a health and welfare inspection. Come on! Get up! Now! Hurry up! Hurry up! Move like you have a sense of purpose!"

The good soldiers snapped up, got dressed, opened their lockers, and stood by their beds. "Yes, Sergeant!" they replied. Some had grins on their faces, knowing we were going to find some bootie.

The suspect soldiers grumbled, "What the f— . . . You gotta be sh—ting me."

I was shocked by the stuff flying out of the windows—bags of marijuana, some LSD, bottles of Jim Beam, Mad Dog, and Boone's Farm wine. Of course, Sergeant Bowen had his trusted NCOs standing watch outside the barracks to take notes and gather the flying contraband.

The drug dogs sniffed every inch of the barracks. Common areas, laundry rooms, and bathrooms were good hiding places for drugs because you couldn't easily trace ownership. The security guys led the dogs to the wall lockers and the beds. All of a sudden the dog would stop at a mattress, sniffing violently and waiting for the soldiers to inspect. Sergeant Brown smiled and said, "Guess this is your unlucky day, PFC Jones." He lifted up the mattress and pulled out a plastic bag full of marijuana. A recorder followed the NCO, writing down everything seized and the names of the culprits.

We busted eleven soldiers with drugs or paraphernalia. Other platoons were not as successful because details often were leaked. Soldiers were prepared and got rid of everything before the supposed surprise search. Not so with Sergeant Bowen. He showed me how to not be duped by the dope heads. This would serve me very well five years later, when I arrived at the drug-plagued 5th Quartermaster Airborne Detachment in Germany. I now knew how to flush out bad soldiers. They weren't going to get over on me. I knew some of the NCOs were in cahoots with the soldiers. The NCOs wanted to be liked, so they enabled and protected the drug users. Finding drugs was only phase one; equally important was handing down appropriate discipline. One size didn't fit all.

Each soldier was dealt with as an individual. Private Jones had multiple previous offenses and already had seen a reduction in rank. Bowen told me, "Three strikes and you're out." We started to transition Jones out of the Army. Specialist Tommey was a new soldier in the unit and a first-time offender. We gave him two weeks' extra duty—mowing grass, painting rocks, sweeping parking lots—and a $50 fine. Sergeant Bowen sat down and counseled him about his misconduct and what he wanted to do with his life. He was off to a bad start but could straighten up and make a good soldier out of himself. He did just that. Six months later he was named Soldier of the Month.

Some soldiers, like our kids, have great potential but get sucked into bad behavior by bad soldiers. I believe most soldiers can learn from slip-ups. Although I never experimented with drugs, I made several honest mistakes in my career, got my butt chewing, made the necessary corrections, and was grateful for a second chance.

Bowen gave me my first chance at being a military leader. A seasoned vet, he could have easily bullied or hazed a rookie female platoon leader just a few years out of State University of New York at Cortland. An NCO's path to leadership starts in the trenches, not on a cushy university campus. They don't take the commissioned, college graduate route. It would be only human for NCOs to resent college kids with no real experience entering with higher status and making more money. But Sergeant Bowen, like all great NCOs, didn't care about commissions and titles. He only cared about doing right by his soldiers, his Army, and his country.

My assignment to Sergeant Bowen's platoon was a combination of luck and smart strategic planning by the company commander, Captain James Casey. When I arrived at the company, Bowen was the only sergeant without a platoon leader. Truth be told, he was so good that most people thought he really didn't need a platoon leader. But Captain Casey knew that Sergeant Bowen was the best NCO he had to train an inexperienced "butter bar" like me.

"Listen and learn from Bowen, and you'll be fine," Captain Casey told me. Casey was a big guy and was constantly smoking or chewing on a cigar. With his Army-issue reading glasses on the end of his nose, he looked down at me and said, "Bowen is the best damn platoon sergeant I ever met." High praise from a battle-tested Vietnam veteran infantry officer.

I took the advice, and I believe to this day that no other person in the company could have had the same impact as Wendell Bowen. As a young female soldier, my reception could have been awful. But Sergeant Bowen commanded respect from his troops. My transition was seamless and receptive because he made it clear to everyone that he believed in me. He treated me with deference as he would any other new lieutenant, man or woman. NCOs are the unsung heroes of the military—everyone talks about majors and generals. As a 2nd lieutenant, I was higher in rank than Bowen and, technically, his boss. But the unspoken word in the military is that NCOs are there to train the incoming new lieutenants. Men like Wendell Bowen would be crucial to rebuilding an Army damaged by the Vietnam War, a vicious cycle that unfortunately continues whenever we are at battle. NCOs pick up the pieces after war. They break down and rebuild soldiers into leaders. They train war fighters despite often not having adequate resources for professional development and sufficient funds for essential training and equipment. Unlike commissioned officers, NCOs typically don't have a college education. But there was no greater teacher than Sergeant Bowen.

As a leader, I was responsible for writing evaluation reports. They became part of a soldier's permanent file. When a soldier went before a promotion board, the words used in the evaluations really mattered. Sergeant Bowen taught me that "outstanding" was viewed differently from "excellent," and "excellent" was different from "exceptionally well." I had a two-star boss who routinely used the phrase "precious few like this one" in his evaluations. The first time I read it I thought, "Wow, this is wonderful. I must be pretty good." As it turned out, he used that phrase in far too many reports to give it any credence. I also learned that being short and concise was better than long and flowery. The reports were vital to helping my subordinates understand their strengths and shortcomings. I learned to underwrite an honest mistake. Making a distinction between sins of omission and commission was crucial. Most important, I learned how to reward and encourage good, high-achieving soldiers and discipline and challenge others.

In 2005 I gave a young captain a General Officer Memorandum of Reprimand (GOMOR) for driving under the influence of alcohol. I was the senior commander on Fort Lee, Virginia, and the incident took place on the post. The captain was attending the quartermaster career course. Quartermasters are the supply experts in the Army. Driving under the influence of alcohol was a problem in the Army, and there really had to be extenuating circumstances to not take the strongest actions against offenders. The official report said he'd been weaving across the center line into oncoming traffic, luckily without tragic results. I reviewed the evidence and talked with the offending officer. He was contrite and regretted his actions, but I wasn't sure he fully understood the seriousness of the offense. I decided that the official reprimand would remain a permanent part of the officer's military record.

After I had retired I received a letter from his current battalion commander and a brigade commander asking that I consider recommending that the GOMOR be removed from the officer's official file. The officer had been promoted to major, and both his battalion commander and brigade commander thought he had matured into one of their very best officers. He had the potential to command a battalion. They believed the rebuke had served its purpose and that the officer had proved to be an outstanding leader. They sent me copies of his officer evaluation reports, which were impressive. I thanked them for reaching out to me in retirement and for believing in this officer and sticking up for him. I wrote a letter supporting removal of the reprimand from his file. I do believe people can learn from their mistakes. This young man obviously had. I hope he comes out on the battalion command list, an accomplishment that would have been unlikely had the reprimand remained.

I cannot stress enough the importance of getting to the root of a mistake. It can determine success or failure for any command or business. Some mistakes are made because people care and want to make a difference. I've made many mistakes and performed below the standard in my career. Recalling again my inadequate first award ceremony, my battalion commander could have easily derailed my career mobility after my epic bout of stage fright at Fort Sill forty years ago. It would have been easy for him to conclude that "If she can't even read a basic 'Attention to Orders' and an awards citation, then how is she going give marching orders during war?" But my boss knew I wanted to do right; I just hadn't adequately prepared for the task. He encouraged me and gave me hope by telling me I'd get it right next time. His support made me work harder. I was no longer afraid to fail or to take chances.

Employees trying to do the right things for the right reasons usually have to take risks to achieve great results. Creativity and innovation should be rewarded. New ways of doing things can lead to better efficiencies and greater effectiveness. Occasionally you'll have to rein in your colleagues' creativity, but that's a good problem.

Other lapses of judgment are flat-out criminal and unforgivable. Leaders should show no weakness in fixing the problem by taking appropriate disciplinary action. Never reward bad behavior. Everyone takes notice when you ignore such actions, and it inevitably undermines your authority and your respect. It also can lead to financial and professional ruin.

My stint as Sergeant Bowen's platoon leader lasted two years. Midway during our time together the supply platoon leader/property book officer and his NCO were relieved of duty for fighting over a CB radio and several knives of a soldier who had committed suicide. In the mid-seventies CB radios were a big deal and expensive, but there is no excuse for how the property book officer and his NCO handled the situation, and the soldier's belongings should have been inventoried and sent home to his family. Again, this was during a dark period for the Army. The selfish and childish act of trying to steal from a dead comrade wasn't an aberration; many soldiers had lost their way. The property book officer and his NCO were in obvious violation of Army regulations. Pressure and greed got the best of them. But their crime opened a door for me and Sergeant Bowen. Captain Casey selected me as the new supply platoon leader/property book officer and allowed Sergeant Bowen to move over with me to clean up a property accountability mess.

Over the next several months Sergeant Bowen and I worked days, nights, and weekends accounting for nearly a million dollars'

worth of equipment, including vehicles, tools, mobile field kitch-
ens, space heaters, and generators. Normally such audits would take
less than thirty days, but this one dragged on for several months as
we located misplaced items and documented losses and reported
hundreds of items unaccounted for or stolen. It was tedious but important work. It was an experience that made a profound impact on
me early in my career. Accountability—whether it involves people,
property, or actions—would become a founding principle of every
assignment I had, from 2nd lieutenant to four-star general. It would
drive my priorities and strategy at every level of command.

At the end of our second year in the company, Sergeant Bowen
was reassigned to South Korea for a one-year "short tour," as they
were known. I reported up the street to be the battalion adjutant,
working for the battalion commander. To me adjutant meant paper pusher, and I wasn't really excited about the move. On day
one I met Sergeant Lester. He had the reputation for being the
absolutely best technically qualified personnel NCO on the installation. And that was a good thing because I knew very little about
the personnel business.

Sergeant Lester looked like a bookworm. He had a slight frame
and was barely taller than me. He wore thick, dark-black army-
issue glasses, with slicked-back brown hair, parted on the side.
Like Sergeant Bowen, I hung on his every word about how to run
the personnel shop—what worked, what didn't work, and things
that could get us in trouble, such as late Officer Evaluation Reports (OERs). Back then we had mimeograph machines, IBM Se-
lectric typewriters, and Wite-Out.

Wite-Out is a quick-drying goo that comes with a finger-
nail-polish-like applicator and was used to blot out mistakes on
correspondences and forms. Some administrative types were really
expert at using Wite-Out, and that saved retyping many a letter.
But Wite-Out wasn't allowed on the OER form, so once an error
was made, the clerk had to start over and retype the entire form.

This put additional pressure to get them done perfectly and ahead of schedule. My battalion commander expected me to write reviews for all the officers he was responsible for rating. Here I was, only a lieutenant writing evaluations on majors, captains, and my fellow lieutenants. It seemed strange, but I learned over time that it wasn't that uncommon.

I remember thinking, as I started to get in my routine in this new job, that even though I dreaded leaving the company and my platoon, this job wasn't that bad and I really was learning a lot. Sergeant Lester and I hit it off very well. He knew everything about personnel accountability and all the forms required to track people and get them paid—the myriad tasks that we now call human resources (HR).

Sergeant Lester wasn't the healthiest guy. He was fidgety, and he constantly coughed and sneezed. He blamed it on horrific allergies that often required special shots at the hospital. His condition was often debilitating and forced him to miss work.

One morning I came into work, and he was not there. He had called in sick because of his allergies. I didn't give it much thought because it was a common occurrence. Plus my second NCO always filled in admirably, and she was someone I could rely on. When Sergeant Lester returned to work the next day, he said he was feeling much better. He was a good guy and incredibly talented. I wanted to make sure we were doing everything possible to get him healthy.

A couple of days went by, and Sergeant Lester told me he had to leave at about 1500 hours to get his allergy shots. This became part of his routine that I just accepted. Every other day he had to leave early to get his allergy shots in order to function. I also automatically assumed that if he was under a doctor's care, that this was acceptable behavior. I guess I had rationalized that it was a tradeoff to keep talent. If he had been a low performer, I might have been more inquisitive about the doctor's appointments and missed duty time. But he was a star player with an impeccable reputation.

When his absences became more frequent, though, I became worried. I called the hospital to check with the doctor about his condition. The hospital had no clue what I was talking about. There was no record of regularly scheduled visits or allergy shots. I was shocked. I sent my assistant over to his house to check on him. He answered the door in his bathrobe. His hair was messed up, and he looked out of it—he was addicted to painkillers. He hid it so well. No one could believe it. He was humiliated when we discovered the truth. He needed help. I went to the battalion executive officer and, ultimately, to the battalion commander to remove him from his position and get him enrolled in the drug and alcohol program. I don't know where he is now, and I don't know whether he ever kicked the habit.

Fortunately most of the NCOs, and particularly the command sergeant majors, that I served with over the years were much like Sergeant Bowen, all bringing years of experience and talent to the team. They all took the time to mentor me. I learned to understand and cherish the power of the command team—the unspoken but sacred relationship between the commander and the senior NCO. Sergeant Bowen taught me that. I just didn't know it at the time.

In May of 1978 I was offered a chance to become a maintenance company commander—something no other woman had done at Fort Sill—or most other places, I suspect. I needed a first sergeant and knew exactly where to turn. I called South Korea and asked Sergeant Bowen whether he would consider the position upon his return. He said, "No, ma'am, I wouldn't consider it. . . . I would be absolutely delighted to do so."

So I took over the maintenance company and continued to benefit from the experiences and wisdom of Sergeant Bowen for the next year. Instead of peppering him with questions, I was now in the position of laying out my thoughts and asking what he thought. Our interactions had changed. Now more than ever we were a team. I was in charge, and he was my right-hand man.

Our year in Company Command passed too quickly, and this time I was the one with the orders: I was Germany-bound. In July of 1979 we had a brief change of command, and our partnership was over. I received a Meritorious Service Medal, pretty rare for a brand-new captain. When the adjutant said, "Attention to Orders," I had a quick flashback to that dreadful day when I was the adjutant reading the citation. This time there was no reason for stage fright, though, because I had my battle buddy, Sergeant Bowen, sitting right there in the front row. He was trying not to smile while standing at the position of attention, but both of us were smiling with our eyes. After the ceremony he came up to me and said, "Damn, ma'am, I am so proud." I still didn't know whether I'd stay in the Army, but I knew I'd take the lessons I'd learned to my next assignment and be a better officer for it. The last time I saw Sergeant Bowen was in the office. We had a brief beer call and Wendell had a few smokes. When it was time to go I was sad. "Sergeant Bowen, thank you for teaching me what right looks like. Thank you for teaching me how to be a good officer." I hugged him. We don't say good-bye in the Army because that sounds too final. So I said, "See you later." We left it there and didn't add "until next time." It never occurred to me that I'd never see him again.

As I progressed in my Army career, Sergeant Bowen and I lost touch. When I received my four-star nomination my husband said we needed to track down my mentor and invite him to the Pentagon for the ceremony. What began as two-year adventure turned into a thirty-eight-year decorated career that he helped launch. Other than my father and my husband, no one was more deserving of taking part in my celebration than First Sergeant Wendell

Bowen. Without him I never would have advanced from butter bar to four-star. I had to find him.

I really didn't know where to start. I knew he retired to Tennessee, but then I'd get busy and not think about it for a few days. I Googled him in hopes of finding some clues—no luck. Finally on a whim one day I called the operator. I asked whether there was a Wendell Bowen listing anywhere in Tennessee. I fully expected her to tell me she'd need more information, but she didn't. She said she had a listing and gave me the number. I had butterflies as the phone rang. When I heard "Hello?" I said, "Wendell, is that you? This is Ann Dunwoody."

"No, this isn't Wendell. This is his brother." He told me that my most significant military mentor had passed away a year earlier of cancer. My heart sank. Regret filled my soul. For years I had told people what a tremendous impact he'd had on me, but I never told him. I talked with his brother for a few minutes and explained who I was. I told him what a profound impact his brother had played in my professional development. I recounted how he planned on making the "best platoon leader in the United States." Finally I told him I was going to be promoted to four-star general and that I had just wanted Wendell to know and to be there if he could. After a moment of silence his brother cleared his throat and with that familiar Tennessee twang and Southern graciousness and said, "Wendell would be so proud." His words brought me to tears.

three

★ ★ ★ ★

THE ENEMY WITHIN

"Leaders Aren't Invincible—Don't Try to Be"

THE MILITARY BUILDS warriors to protect and defend. If you are not prepared to serve, to kill, or to be killed in combat—or even while carrying out routine tasks on a military post or in a mess hall—then don't apply.

How's that for a job description? Male or female. GED or PhD. The second a civilian takes the military oath of enlistment and crosses over into the armed forces, that becomes his or her reality.

As soldiers, we are reminded of this every day. While writing this book I lost a good friend and great officer who had worked for me. On August 5, 2014, Major General Harry Greene was ambushed and killed, not in typical combat but by someone who was supposed to be an ally. He was making a regular visit to the Marshal Fahim National Defense University in Kabul, a military training academy, when he was shot and killed by an Afghan soldier. Fourteen NATO and Afghan service members were wounded in the attack.

Harry was serving as the Deputy Commander of the Combined Security Transition Command and was responsible for helping transfer security control to the Afghans. I visited this operation in 2010 when my friend and high school classmate, Lieutenant

General Bill Caldwell, was in charge of the camp. The professional training program was designed to empower the Afghan Army to stand on its own two feet. Bill brought an incredible amount of energy, growth, and visibility to the program. It was a great transition for the US Army—a transition from doing the heavy lifting and leading the fight to training the Afghan Army and supporting the fight. Four years later Harry Greene was assigned as second in command for this mission.

The attacker was trained by us, but he had hidden his true allegiance. He wanted to kill, and he succeeded. General Greene was part of the Acquisition Corps, not a vocation where you'd expect to find yourself in harm's way. But he was a soldier first, and soldiers know the deal. When he was a one-star general I knew him and his performance of duty very well. His primary focus was research and development of better equipment for soldiers. He was energetic, brilliant, and compassionate. Even though he was a diehard Red Sox fan and I was a Yankees devotee, we were proud upstate New Yorkers who recounted brutally cold winters and amazing summers around the Finger Lakes.

When he worked under my command, Greene had split his time between Aberdeen Proving Grounds in Maryland and Natick Laboratory's Soldiers Systems Center in Massachusetts in the 2009 to 2011 timeframe. His staff gently teased him by creating life-sized cardboard replicas of Harry in uniform so he could be in all places all the time. He cared deeply about the military. He eventually was promoted to two-star general. I reached out to offer condolences to his former boss and a mutual friend of ours, Heidi Shyu, the Assistant Secretary for Acquisition Logistics and Technology.

In her e-mail response, she articulated best what Major General Greene stood for:

This is a devastating loss for ASA (ALT) and the entire Army. As you know, he was a fierce advocate for the soldier. I saw him in Afghanistan in March and said to him that it must be tough to be there. He replied that there is nowhere else he would rather be than with Soldiers.

Major General Greene's service and ultimate sacrifice saddens yet inspires me. He died doing what he loved for a country he loved. He was the highest-ranking member of the US military to die in the line of duty since September 11, 2001, when we lost a three-star general, Tim Maude, in the attack on the Pentagon. He wanted to be in Afghanistan with his soldiers. He probably could have been at the Pentagon at the time of the ambush, but he was where he felt most at home: with soldiers.

My heart hurts for Major General Greene's family. I truly understood their pain.

My father graduated from West Point and joined the US Army just in time for World War II. Even seventy years ago he enlisted for the same reasons most soldiers do today—to be part of the ultimate team that protects this great nation from the constant threat of war and terror. The year Dad graduated, 1943, there were two graduating classes at West Point: January and June. The new graduates were immediately sent off for advanced training and either shipped to Europe to fight the Germans or the Far East to fight the Japanese. America was at war, and every American knew it. The nation was fully mobilized, and our industry was squarely focused on cranking out the instruments of war—airplanes, ships, tanks, trucks, ammunition, and anything you can imagine to support a war. Rationing was common—rubber, gasoline, sugar, and more. It wasn't just the Army and Navy's fight; it was America's, and in 1943 the outcome was in doubt. Themes of the day included Rosie the Riveter because women were vital to the defense industry. Uncle Sam wants "You" because everyone was in the fight. And war bonds were being hawked all over the country to help the government fund the military effort.

It didn't take long for Dad to become battle tested. In 1945 he led a group of young soldiers while serving with the 14th Armored Division along the French-German border. Many of the troops under the command of my twenty-six-year-old father were just teenagers. Dad was severely injured during combat when his tank took a direct hit from enemy fire. Doctors told him his leg would probably need to be amputated. A stubborn war fighter, my dad's response was priceless: he told the doctor he was going to keep his leg long enough to kick the doctor in the ass with it. He was awarded the Purple Heart and continued to serve after his recovery, both legs intact.

In 1951 Dad was back in the battlefield leading the 3rd Battalion, 17th Infantry Regiment during the Korean War. By the time his tour ended, he was awarded the Distinguished Service Cross with Valor during combat operations and received a second Purple Heart after suffering another leg injury while on a mountaintop in Korea. Luckily it was his "good" leg and the gunshot wound left no lasting damage. He again recovered and continued to serve.

Twenty years later Dad commanded the 5th Mechanized Brigade in Vietnam. He is a proud three-war veteran from what we now refer to as the Greatest Generation. The first two names that come to mind when I hear the term coined by Tom Brokaw are Mom and Dad. They, along with all the extraordinary men and women born around 1920, survived the Great Depression and willingly signed on to serve and protect their country through World War II. They did so without question because they knew it was the right thing to do.

This selfless generation literally changed and—in my patriotic opinion—saved the world. Had the Axis powers not been defeated, the United States would have lost its independence, our people would have lost their cherished freedoms, and without the United States as a superpower to it, the world would have been under the heel of the Nazis. Our national survival was at stake. When soldiers deployed there was no midtour vacation, no rest, and no peace in sight. They joined for the duration of the war, knowing that they might not return home. Many of those who did come back often did so severely wounded. Most of the dead never returned to the United States; they were buried in cemeteries in France, Germany, and Belgium, often close to where they fell. While hundreds of thousands of soldiers sacrificed their lives overseas, their wives, girlfriends, and sisters took on more responsibility at home. The Greatest Generation paved the way for America's prosperity and status as a global leader. Most impressively, it never sought credit in return. These heroes fought the most abject adversity and won.

Today's soldiers and leaders like Major General Harry Greene are no different—they serve for the greater cause. Country is more important than self. For some, my husband and I included, it starts as an economic solution. I decided to join the Army because they were going to pay me $500 a month during my senior year. I saved that money and bought a Plymouth Duster for $2,000. For Craig it was economic as well. Football and ROTC paid the bills for his college education. When he graduated he was married and expecting his first son; being a lieutenant in the Air Force sounded like the fastest way to financial stability.

But for many of us service becomes a calling and a passion for a variety of reasons. You train for the fight, and when you are in the fight you fight like you were trained. You fight for your brothers and sisters in arms. You fight to the death for them. No one enlists without being acutely aware that he could die in a training exercise, from friendly fire, or in combat. Despite the dangers, soldiers are trained to be fearless, brave, and indestructible. That's the biggest blessing and curse of being a war fighter. The air of invincibility can lead to heroic acts or cripple a soldier and be counterproductive. Everyone knows Superman has his Kryptonite. Soldiers brace themselves for the ultimate Kryptonite—terrorist threats and weapons of mass destruction. But as soldiers, we aren't prepared to battle the enemy within. It's often tough to admit we need help; however, dealing with weaknesses head-on can be the ultimate strength. Or, as G.I. Joe said, "Knowing is half the battle." No one is immune—the boss who is always late, the colleague who spends too much time by the water cooler gossiping about other people's love lives, the coworker who stresses out about everything and can't make a decision or a deadline.

It's impossible to turn on the news and not see something military related. Many are feel-good stories—soldiers surprising their families at schools, offices, or sporting events while home on mid-tour leave, a brief and necessary respite from the rigors of battle. Others are more somber—a dozen soldiers killed in an ambush, a star athlete killed in friendly fire, or thirty-one lost in a tragic helicopter crash. Others are 60 Minutes–type exposés that point to the shortcomings of soldiers from entry level to the top of the food chain. Soldiers are convicted in the rape and murder of a teenage girl and her family in Afghanistan. A married general officer has inappropriate sexual contact with several subordinates. A senior leader misuses government funds for lavish trips. Although these are not the norm, they are part of the reality of the military. They can destroy a promising career, ruin a marriage, or leave one questioning his existence from a jail cell at Fort Leavenworth.

I WAS FIRST confronted with my personal vulnerabilities early in my career. It rocked me to my core and made me question everything in my life—my marriage, my career choice, my faith, and whether my family would support me in a time of crisis.

It was 1980, and my days at Fort Sill were coming to an end. I was leaving there as a captain and was hooked on the Army. I had worked hard and had been recognized for my dedication and accomplishments. Company Command had been great, and I loved my job and leading soldiers. I loved the little house that my first husband, Ken, and I bought four years earlier. My marriage was going okay, which is a terrible way to describe matrimony. Ken and I were developing different interests. We had been high school sweethearts, but after high school graduation he spent a year at the University of Texas before enrolling at West Point. That year was a year of independence and different interests. Our long-distance conversations switched from the military and sports to existentialism, religion, and philosophy. When he decided to attend West Point it made me think that many of his new ideas were just temporary musings. Sticking to our long-term plan, we got married when he graduated in 1976, but it was destined to be a short-lived marriage. While at Fort Sill it was clear that I thrived in Army life more than Ken did. The one constant joy in my married life was my bubbly and faithful English Springer spaniel, Gypsy. I wanted the marriage to work, but the possibility of a breakup was in the back of both of our minds.

Ken was notified that he was going to the Artillery Officers Advance course, an early-level advanced training school to prepare officers for increased responsibility. He was reassigned to Germany. I had enjoyed attending high school in Belgium, so the thought of going back to Europe was appealing. I called my assignment officer and told him I would be seeking a joint-domicile assignment. Joint-domicile assignments were a relatively new trend in 1980, but the Army was committed to trying to keep married couples together at the same location. My assignment officer then informed me that I too would be going to the Advance course that summer at Fort Lee, Virginia, but assignments beyond that were unknown. I had already done a bit of homework and knew that the parachute rigger detachment would probably change commanders while I was in Germany, so I asked for a slot to rigger school. I loved jumping out of airplanes and knew it would be the perfect job. Completing rigger school now would be ideal, so when the time came I'd be fully qualified to at least compete for a rigger position. But my assignment officer thought differently.

He called me later that week to tell me that I didn't have time to attend rigger school when there were no rigger positions coming open. He also said there were no quartermaster jobs coming open. If I wanted a joint-domicile assignment, it would be in my secondary career choice of personnel. He then gave me the worst news possible: I had been projected to get a job as the community adjutant in Wiesbaden, Germany. I was crushed. Fortunately the head of the Quartermaster branch disagreed with my assignment officer and overturned his decision about rigger school. Unlike my assignment officer, he agreed that any training I might need in Germany should be done now to save the travel expense of getting the training later. As a result, I would be allowed to attend rigger school before heading off to Germany. But I was still heading overseas as the community adjutant—and dreading it.

Have you ever gone through a time in your life when just about everything went wrong—spiritually, romantically, emotionally, and physically? That's how I felt almost the second I landed in Germany to meet Ken, who had been assigned as an artilleryman in Wiesbaden. My entire job as community adjutant—the "welcome wagon" of the Army—would consist of presenting the introductory briefing to newcomers. It was a sissy job in every aspect, and just thinking about it put me to sleep. The only bright point was that with so much free time on my hands, it seemed like the perfect time to start our family.

It was 1981, I was twenty-eight years old, and, as they say, my biological clock was ticking.

Ronald Reagan was the new president, and there was a new optimism in the air. The Army was in the process of recovering from the neglect it had suffered after the Vietnam War. The focus had returned to Europe, and at this time, during the Cold War, the threat of the Soviet Union was very real. It should have been a good time for me, but it wasn't.

I dreaded the monthly newcomers' briefings and wearing my plastic Corfam shoes, skirt, and blouse instead of combat boots and fatigues. I quickly became bored with presenting the introductory slide shows for new soldiers and their families:

> The commissary is located over here, and the post exchange is over there. Here's what you need to have to get a driver's license. This is where you go to get your gasoline ration cards, and here are the rules for using your ration cards. Don't break the ration card rules or you'll lose you ration card and have to pay German prices at the local petrol stations.

I know it was an important briefing, and I tried to inject enthusiasm into my presentation. Like most of my assignments in the Army, I worked with great people and great bosses who were trying to make a difference in the community. I wanted to help them.

Home was worse. Ken had rented a tiny, one-bedroom apartment with a kitchen barely big enough for a coffee maker and a bathroom that made an airplane lavatory seem spacious. Whenever I talked about having a family, Ken stared at me as if I were from Neptune. It never crossed my mind since I started dating Ken as a seventeen-year-old that we wouldn't have kids. I wanted picket fences on military bases around the world with a few military brats of our own. I mean, who marries a Catholic girl in the seventies or eighties and doesn't expect to have kids? But, amazingly, the subject of family never came up in ten years of courtship or marriage. I was devastated. He had never wanted kids, which is probably why he never mentioned the topic. I always assumed he did, which is probably why I never raised the subject. The timing stunk.

I hated my apartment. I wasn't happy with my job. My marriage was falling apart. It turned out that all the stress was literally destroying my body. From the moment I'd wake up I felt like throwing up and would gag a few times before the nausea subsided. One morning I noticed some blood as I coughed up a little phlegm and immediately went to see the doctor. He ran some tests and then asked me whether I had been under any stress. Under normal circumstances I would have laughed. Stress? As the community adjutant? Of course not. Then it hit me: the stress I was experiencing was the cumulative effect of my marriage, my job, my house, and my separation from my family. The medical diagnosis was a bleeding ulcer. He prescribed Maalox but told me I had to find ways to reduce the stress and heal my body or I'd be on a collision course to an honorable discharge. Here I was, welcoming every new soldier to Germany, and I felt like the most unwelcoming person alive.

Ken and I legally separated. I found a new place to live. We decided that officially divorcing in Europe would be a real hassle and mutually agreed on finalizing the divorce once we returned to the States. Even though it was the right thing for both of us, the divorce only made me more miserable. My Catholic guilt kicked in. Though I was much happier with my new house, with Gypsy as my faithful sidekick, my stress and ulcer were not in check. Not only was I a flop in the eyes of God, I knew I would be a failure in my devout mom's eyes. Because I idolized my mom, in my mind this was a fate worse than disappointing God, and neither confession nor communion could make it right. Her tough soldier who rarely cried now sobbed regularly in her darkest moments. I cursed, chastised, and doubted myself.

All my life I was taught not to quit. I didn't win every cheerleading competition, gymnastics tournament, or tennis match, but I always battled to the end. I agonized over how to tell my pious mother. I knew she would see it as her daughter committing a sin in the Church that she held as near and dear as her own flesh and blood. It was a long and emotionally charged flight home.

Frankfurt to New York City, a connector to Buffalo, and then an hour car ride with Mom and Dad to our home in Randolph. My parents had been married for thirty-five years, enduring deployments, wars, and long-distance separations. Even through the occasional tough times my parents stuck together. I spent almost every moment in transit contemplating how I would break the news to them.

When we reached the house I scurried upstairs to my old room to unpack. It was almost 5:00 p.m. Since Dad had retired, happy hour started at five o'clock on the dot. After we toasted my temporary homecoming in the kitchen, I just blurted it out: "Mom, Dad, Ken and I are getting divorced." To my total surprise and relief, my saintly mother and old-school father could not have been more understanding and supportive. For the first time in months I could breathe. Over time the stress subsided, my ulcer abated, and my smile returned. I switched back to my maiden name—I was Ann Dunwoody again.

Our vulnerabilities come in all forms. It doesn't have to be physically debilitating like mine, but often it's self-inflicted. Imagine my surprise when my parents told me they never really thought Ken and I were a great fit.

A failed marriage wasn't my Kryptonite, nor was being stuck in a mundane job or living in a crummy place. But stress and how I deal with it was—and still is—my ultimate undoing. Stress can be hazardous in every job. No occupation is immune; it's not just the military. Pilots, police officers, CEOs, first-responders, even schoolteachers, clergy, and professional athletes are subject to pressures unthinkable years ago.

The military encourages you to ignore the emergency flares—be macho, suck it up. That's the typical reaction internally and externally. But that type of response can have devastating consequences, as evidenced by increased posttraumatic stress, suicide rates, divorce, and domestic violence. Holding everything in was the worst thing I could do. I had to find ways to reestablish a sense of balance in my life.

The Army teaches you to be hard-core. We want our soldiers to believe in themselves, to believe in each other. We want them to think that they can do anything and everything. And when a man or woman joins the Army we want to make them bigger, stronger, faster, and more self-assured than they were the day they joined. This training, this confidence building, this testing of your inner will power never ends.

As an example of the physical demands that come with an Army calling, one of the requirements of being in the 82nd Airborne Division back in 1988 was that every soldier had to be able to complete a 12-mile road march in combat boots, battle dress uniform, Kevlar helmet, weapon, gas mask, load-bearing equipment (a shoulder harness and waist belt to attach ammunition pouches, canteens, knives, and first aid pouches), and a thirty-pound ruck sack on your back—in three hours. Sound easy? Go out and walk 12 miles without any of that equipment and tell me it's easy. I had run the Marine Corps Marathon of 26.2 miles in three hours and thirty-three minutes just two years earlier. I was in excellent physical condition, but there's still no comparison between these two physically demanding activities.

Once again my belief in myself and my belief that I could do anything that anyone else in the division could do had me fired up for this challenge. The twelve-mile route had been briefed. We assembled on schedule at 0630—it was going to be hot. We started the process of weighing everyone's ruck sack to ensure it met standard; there were rumors of past soldiers who had tried filling their ruck sacks with inflated air mattresses to give the appearance of a full and heavy ruck.

A new field grade major in the division, I had never really talked to anyone about preparing for the ruck march, and no one offered any advice. I assumed it would be another test of physical endurance. But I was wrong. I showed up in my starched battle dress uniform, pants bloused (tucked into boots), and spit-shined Corcoran jump boots, ready to go.

When the ruck march started and the timers said "go," I was off and moving out, thinking to myself, *I'm in great shape and this should be no problem.* Well, about an hour into the ruck march the back of my heels started to hurt. I had brought a clean pair of socks to put on once the ones I was wearing got sweaty, but the pain had nothing to do with the sweat and had everything to do with the boots I was wearing. I noticed everyone else was wearing their well-worn and broken-in G.I.-issue boots, not their "prepared for inspection" highly spit-shined jump boots. Theirs looked like bedroom slippers on their feet, and mine might as well have been high heels.

About two hours into the ruck march the pain in my heels intensified, and my feet were killing me. An ambulance followed the formation, picking up the casualties—those who were dehydrated or were just unable to make the distance. Unforeseen things always happen: twisted ankle, someone didn't drink enough water, or someone had too much fun the night before. The unit was always prepared to collect them and treat them if necessary. As tempting as it might have been to climb into the ambulance and ride home, in my mind I knew there was no way I was going to get into that ambulance without dropping dead first. The thought of not making it, the thought of being a "fall out," the thought of not finishing before most others made me that much more determined.

Forget the pain—focus on finishing. I did just that. I got to the finish line ahead of most soldiers and then almost collapsed. I had to get my boots off. My socks were soaked in blood. I struggled into a vehicle and went to the medical clinic to have the doctor take a look at my feet. It was awful. The doctor looked at me in disbelief that I had worn my Corcorans on the road march. As he was examining my feet, he had me roll over on my stomach so he could focus on my heels. He took a tongue depressor, wrapped it in gauze, and stuck it my mouth and told me, "This is going to hurt—bite down on the tongue depressor." There were two huge blisters, larger than silver dollars, one on each heel. He had to cut the loose skin off each blister and then pour on iodine to clean the area. *Holy ouch— did that hurt!*

He ordered me not wear boots or running shoes until my feet healed. *Great,* I thought, *I have to wear flip-flops around in uniform for a week—how embarrassing.* That week I did my morning physical training in a secluded area where fewer people could see me walking in flip-flops. After that, before anyone in my unit ever went ruck marching for the first time, I shared my story in hopes that they could learn from my mistakes: Wear comfortable boots and two pairs of socks. Don't get overconfident. Be prepared mentally and physically. Some might say that our determination to never fail can be a weakness as well as a strength.

The concept of comprehensive soldier fitness entered the Army in 2008 when the Chief of Staff, General George Casey, determined that the Army was too often deployed and out of balance after almost a decade at war. The program had five components: physical, family, social, emotional, and spiritual. We had long been an institution focused on providing the tactical and technical skills needed to fight battles; "Be All You Can Be" and "Army Strong" were our calling cards. No soldier came to work thinking they would be anything less than all they could be. Now, for the first time in my career and probably in history, we were viewing a soldier's health in a different way from just blood pressure and heart rates—we were looking in a holistic way at a soldier's well-being.

I have a dear friend who I worked with at Fort Bragg. My husband, Craig, also knew him from the Rangers years earlier. He was a great soldier. Ranger school is one of the most demanding in any branch of the military. During months of training it's common for healthy men with minimal excess body fat to lose twenty, thirty, and even forty pounds. If you were overweight when training began, you either quit or emerge from it in the best shape of your life. Sleep deprivation and starvation are critical elements of the training because they test the mental toughness of these future war fighters. In some cases you're given mere seconds to eat a meal; in other cases you're too exhausted to eat a bread crumb. Ranger school pushes you to the brink.

Our friend was notorious for working ridiculously long hours to get the job done. His typical dinner was leftovers in the microwave long after his children had turned in for the night. When he was passed over for brigadier general on his first look, no one could believe it. We were dumbfounded. He had been promoted ahead of his peers so often that everyone assumed his hard work would be recognized again. I agreed that he deserved to be promoted, but it also drove home with me that working longer hours doesn't necessarily equal better performance. Working harder doesn't mean working smarter. Longer hours mean less sleep, fatigue, ulcers, compromised decisions, and a lack of balance in one's life.

The following year our friend was promoted to brigadier general, and it was richly deserved. He was given a new assignment as an assistant division commander and spent the next year fighting the war in Iraq. At one point his boss went on a two-week leave, so our friend was now the boss. His eighteen- to twenty-hour days turned into twenty-three-hour days—his only rest came from brief catnaps. This went on for more than a week. People urged him to rest, but he was in charge. He thought he had to keep going because he loved his soldiers and they were in harm's way. He also admired his division commander and would never do anything to let him down. People depended on him, and the work wasn't finished. But the truth was that it would never be finished.

He was overwhelmed and didn't know it—until he cracked. One day he went to his bunk and told someone, "I need some help." He was immobilized, and he couldn't think. He was done. He didn't know how to stop. He didn't know how to take care of himself. He couldn't say, "I'm calling it a day, and I'll get back in a few hours."

He recovered physically and mentally but not professionally. The same people who train soldiers to never quit and never give up wouldn't give him another chance. They gave up on this man, and it was the Army's loss.

If you aren't aware of your weaknesses, an enemy or even a so-called colleague may use it against you. The senior Army leadership discovered my friend's fatal flaw before he did. No one is indestructible, and no one should aspire to be unbreakable. When our friend was home, recovered, and ready to resume his life, he wanted to explain to his brothers and sisters what had happened. After confiding to his older sister, who teaches theology at a major Catholic university, she offered the following advice: "You have to use this event to teach other people about this. Let yourself be a lesson to others."

My friend isn't alone. Even in my post-military career I still have a fear of public speaking. I have given hundreds of speeches since my infamous meltdown as a lieutenant in the auditorium at Fort Sill nearly forty years ago, but nothing has remedied the nervousness, the stress, and the fear. It's just not a natural thing for me to stand up in front of a large audience and discuss leadership, building a winning team, being a woman in the Army, logistics, or any other subject I've been asked to talk about. I recently gave a speech on leadership and creating high-performing organizations to General Hugh Shelton's leadership conference at North Carolina State University, with General Shelton in the audience. I prepared for months, even though the general was a close friend and I was speaking on topics that literally were my job for two decades. I can answer questions all day on logistics, on challenges of being a woman in the military, and on leadership lessons, but a thirty-minute speech takes real work and requires time and effort. My speechwriter used to tease me, and now my husband does the same, saying, "No Dunwoody speech is finished until it is delivered." I'm constantly rewriting and tweaking until I'm at the podium. The night before any speech is a restless one as my nerves work overtime. My public speaking phobia has also led to some imagined ones as well.

I love listening to music, but I can't carry a tune. Listening to me "sing" is a painful experience for anyone within earshot. I love to put the top down on my Thunderbird and sing along to Jimmy Buffett, the Eagles, or another favorite blaring on the radio. Anyone who's heard me during those drives would attest to my tone deafness. Fortunately this has never been a requirement for senior officers; if it had been, I may not have made it past 2nd lieutenant. I once had a nightmare about reading the citation at an awards ceremony as battalion adjutant. As I stood on stage, the tape playing the National Anthem broke and the battalion commander asked me to sing it instead. I almost had a heart attack in my sleep. Talk about self-induced stress.

Although public speaking and singing have never been my strong suits, some of my biggest strengths also come with caveats. When I took over AMC I had to manage my Kryptonite nonstop. I'm a big-picture person: I like strategic thinking and planning and prefer not to dwell in the nitty-gritty detail unless it is necessary to do so. Knowing this, I would bring in people who were good at working the finer points for all the strategic ideas—people who complemented my strategic proclivity and excelled at rolling up their sleeves and digging into the minutiae.

My military deputy at AMC was a three-star general who also was a strategic thinker. This was potentially a poor fit and redundancy. I needed a deputy who could turn my vision into a detailed reality. I told him my concerns, and he adopted an approach that was outside his comfort zone. He learned how to execute the vision deftly rather than create it. This illustrates the fact that a subordinate's duty is to accommodate the needs of the commander or boss, even if those needs are counter to one's natural way of thinking. We've all had to do it in our careers.

I'm always trying to improve things. I never run out of ideas, which drove my staff batty. To keep things running efficiently, I made sure I had people who would tell me when my new ideas were unrealistic, ridiculous, or counterproductive. Though the wheels are always turning in my head, at some point even the best ideas aren't helpful if they aren't timely. As my husband once told me, "You need a good idea cutoff point."

Big-picture thinkers always have ideas—Walt Disney, Steve Jobs, Henry Ford. I recently read a book that's a darling on Wall Street, *The Outsiders: Eight Unconventional CEOs and Their Radically Rational Blueprint for Success* by William N. Thorndike Jr. I received an autographed copy from one of the subjects in the book, Bill Anders of Apollo 8 fame. He was the pilot of the lunar module for the 1968 mission that circled the moon for the first time and paved the way for the first lunar landing and famous moon walk that made Neil Armstrong and Buzz Aldrin household names. Bill's most impressive accomplishment, however, might have been the turnaround he engineered at General Dynamics in the early 1990s. Bill was a big-picture, strategic thinker extraordinaire—I'd like to think he picked up a lot of those traits during his days at the Naval Academy and in the Air Force. As Thorndike observes, some of the greatest CEOs, like Anders, are visionaries and not micromanagers. They know their Kryptonite and surround themselves with people who complement them and help execute their vision.

Shortly after I retired, the chairman of the Joint Chiefs invited me to sit in on a discussion with active military leaders about an ethics crisis plaguing the military, from the Pentagon to the service academies. There had been an unusual spike in the number of high-profile incidents perpetrated by senior officers, and the Petraeus resignation from the Central Intelligence Agency was still fresh in the news cycle. "What the heck is going on here?" could have been the name of the forum. Perhaps the most damning form of Kryptonite that I and others on the panel observed was hubris.

Some people grow with a self-confidence that spurs their success and fuels their ambition. But that confidence can also be destructive. Promotions and praise often lead people to think that they are untouchable and above the law. Whether it's the obnoxious screamer who gets pleasure from belittling others in public or the boss who thinks sexual advances toward subordinates are acceptable, hubris has been the downfall of too many leaders. Friends, family, and colleagues see it, but they're afraid to tell you and feel your wrath, whereas some believe in you and think you really are that special; they buy into the mystique. But they also know that you can make life unpleasant. I truly understood the pride and arrogance that hubris represents and had seen it deleteriously affect the lives of several of my military colleagues during my career, but I never knew the self-destructive implications of the word itself until that chairman's meeting.

Some professional officers with distinguished careers seemed to get to a point at which they felt entitled to do whatever they wanted, despite their oath to the military and their country. Even more shocking was the occasional spouse who reveled in the success and demonstrated the same bad behavior. I remember an incident in Europe years ago in which a general's wife drove her husband's official US government armored car to the golf course for her usual round. She left the keys in the ignition and the car was stolen. The inappropriate use and loss of the car was bad enough, but the loss of sensitive communications equipment installed in the vehicle could have been serious.

Similar betrayals of trust occur at government institutions and in corporate America every day. Some elected officials parlay their power and authority for special favors, all in the name of serving the people. In the military manifestations of hubris are found in toxic leaders who abuse subordinates for their own aggrandizement, spend tax-payer money for their own benefit, or sexually abuse subordinates for their own gratification. These are all the result of hubris. The military is not immune from it—no institution is.

For a great leader, colleague, friend, or parent to be his best, he has to acknowledge his worst. Throughout my life I've met plenty of superheroes, but the strongest and most effective among them were the ones who were simply human and knew they weren't perfect. They were the men and women who, like my father, believed in their duty to country and sacrificed for others without hesitation. They all had their strengths and weaknesses. They excelled at times; they stumbled at times. But the great ones always made sure they could walk tall by recognizing their own enemy within and confronting it.

four

* * * *

DOOR KICKERS
"Believe in Yourself"

AS I WRITE THIS, the US military has been involved in active combat for more than thirteen years, the longest protracted period in modern history. When I joined the Army the Soviet Union, North Korea, China, and Vietnam were the hot-button topics. In the 1990s we were at war in the Middle East after Iraq invaded Kuwait. The combat zone included some very familiar places: the Persian Gulf, the Red Sea, Iraq, Kuwait, and Saudi Arabia.

After 9/11 the landscape changed. Since then American combat forces have been deployed in Afghanistan and Iraq. We have also sent war fighters to Islamabad (Pakistan), Dushanbe (Tajikistan), Bishkek (Kyrgyzstan), Tashkent (Uzbekistan), and Djibouti City (Djibouti), as well as Yemen and Somalia. We also have troops in West Africa trying to help combat disease instead of enemy forces while also monitoring unrest in Eastern Europe and a nuclear threat in North Korea. Most Americans could not identify the continent where these cities and countries are located.

With the emergence of ISIS, just as we were scheduled to withdraw troops from Middle East, we find ourselves facing several more years of drawn-out combat. But one victory has already been achieved. Lost among the headlines of the ISIS situation is the role of a female soldier from the United Arab Emirates (UAE) helping to lead the charge against terrorism.

Major Mariam Al Mansouri is her country's first female fighter pilot. In an October 2014 interview with CNN she said, "At that time, the doors were not open for females to be pilots. So I had to wait almost ten years for the decision to be taken." She persevered and refused to give in to sexist myths about the role of women in war. I haven't had the privilege of meeting Al Mansouri, but she is a kindred fighting spirit. Part of me is also proud the story didn't grab more headlines because I believe the military should be gender blind.

There are no longer traditional battlefields as we used to know them. Even as late as the Gulf War of 1991 the battlefield lines were clearly drawn. Combat troops and scouts, predominantly male, were on the front lines, where combat operations would take place. Support personnel, male and female, were behind those formations in relatively benign areas. They would push their supplies and other support requirements forward to the front lines in anticipation of need or in response to calls for specific equipment or supplies. Today, particularly in terms of combating terrorism, there are no front lines. Cities and neighborhoods are the battlefields. September 11 was a harsh reminder of this new reality.

As Al Mansouri said, "We are in a hot area so that we have to prepare every citizen. Of course, everybody is responsible of defending their country—male or female. When the time will come, everybody will jump in."

Prior to 9/11 the policy on women in combat was pretty clear: women were not allowed to be assigned to units where their primary duties would subject them to direct ground combat action. When the battlefield changed, however, the way we fought had to change as well. It was relatively easy for leaders to work around the language in the policy. Particularly with combat medics, women were frequently "attached" to combat units that were going into harm's way. "Attached" meant they were on loan for an unspecified period of time and were then routinely used in the more dangerous combat actions.

There are many arguments made for and against women being permitted to train and perform in direct ground combat roles. For me there is one primary question: Can a woman meet the same standard required of her male counterparts? If she can, then there is no reason why women shouldn't be able to do the job. The underlying question is whether the standards have evolved in a way that wrongly discourages otherwise qualified applicants from completing the training regimen.

Historically there have been many instances when women have participated in combat by hiding their gender and enlisted disguised as men. Deborah Sampson served for three years in the Revolutionary Army. During that time she was injured twice and was almost killed when a musket ball shredded her thigh. She bravely refused help, treating her own wound out of fear of having her identity revealed. When she fell unconscious, however, a doctor treating her for malignant fever discovered her gender. She was quietly discharged. She was later awarded a disability pension of four dollars a month for her service. Nearly a century later Sarah Edmonds, aka Franklin Flint Thompson, joined the Union Army as a male nurse during the Civil War. She later became a spy in the Union Secret Service. She was a master of disguise, infiltrating groups as a man or woman, black or white.

Over time it was not uncommon for women to follow behind the men of an Army. Some were wives who wanted to be close to their husbands, and some were women who just wanted to make a living by cooking, doing laundry, and, yes, even the oldest profession. When needed, because of casualties, women were known to take up arms and fight. Who doesn't think of Joan of Arc when they envision female war fighters?

Mary Hayes was a legendary soldier's wife from the American Revolution who, and when her husband was carried off the battlefield, she took his place at the cannon and continued to fire. In more modern times women were used in combat roles such as air defense artillery and in espionage.

Today countries around the world are increasing the opportunities for women in the military. Australia permits women to train and perform in combat jobs but has had few takers. Canada has no restrictions on females. In Israel 90 percent of the jobs are open to women. In New Zealand there are no restrictions, but it's also noteworthy that as of this writing no woman has yet qualified for their Special Air Service (SAS), our equivalent to Special Operations Forces like Navy SEALS, Army Special Forces, or Air Force Combat Controllers.

When Secretary of Defense Leon Panetta announced in 2013 that the restrictions for women in the US forces were going to be lifted, it was handled in a very thoughtful way. Instead of saying *just do it*, the services were given time and parameters for implementing the new policy. If, after careful review, the service chiefs or combatant commanders did not think women could perform a specific job, then they would have to explain why not. To date, all of the services are working their way through the new policy. Even the most demanding training pipelines—SEALs, Rangers, and other specialties—are looking for female candidates.

One of the real drivers for opening more combat roles for women is the perception that women can't ascend to the highest levels of the military without the opportunity to command in combat. When I attended last year's retired four-star conference, one of the attendees went on a rant about women in combat. He argued that the military and the Army were making a big mistake by opening more combat roles to women. He further commented that every time we open another door for women, we lower the standards. All eyes darted to me when he finished.

I cleared my throat and made my case. First, I agreed with the assembled audience that lowering standards just to accommodate women in these new roles would be a serious mistake. Second, I emphasized that I trusted Army leadership to do a prudent review of the standards to ensure that we had the right criterion. I concluded with my own story.

When the Army opened Airborne School for female officers in 1975, it was not a popular decision. I was one of the first to attend. I was more than capable of meeting the exact same standards as the men, both physically and mentally. Completing Airborne School opened doors for me, including my eventual assignment to the 82nd Airborne Division. Without that opportunity my career would have been dramatically different, and I certainly would not have earned a seat at the retired four-star conference. When I was finished telling my story, I looked around the table to broad grins, nodding heads, and several thumbs up.

I can't say how many female Navy SEALs, Army Rangers, or Air Force Combat Controllers we will have in five or ten years. Perhaps, like now, there will not be a single one. I only know that if there are some women who want to and are qualified to compete for these tough assignments, then they should have the opportunity.

I'm proud that I served in a military that has often led the way in breaking barriers. Not only did I benefit from this during my personal journey, but I also witnessed the military challenge de jure and de facto cultural barriers that were prejudicial and oppressive to Americans. Some are even hard to imagine today. The integration of blacks into the military after a nearly two-hundred-year history of countrywide discrimination, the acceptance of women into the regular Army after years of being second-class citizens in the Women's Army Corps (WAC), the implementation of Don't Ask, Don't Tell (DADT) as an interim measure before gays were allowed to serve openly, and, finally, the current review of the ban on women in combat.

None of these changes happened overnight. But in every case it took whites, blacks, women, and gays who were willing to kick down doors and demonstrate that they were capable and that their integration would not lead to the demise of this trained and ready Army.

I joined the WAC and never had any illusion as to what I was getting myself into. I never wanted to be Rambo, never thought about fighting for the opportunity to join the combat arms. All I really wanted was to find a career that would allow me to do my job in both peace and war. Fortunately for me, the transformation that would begin integrating women into the regular Army was just beginning. The only all-women trainings I ever attended were my initial training as part of the college juniors program and my first Basic Officers course. But transformative change is never easy and rarely quick.

When I joined the Army, old-school folks assumed that all women enlisted for one of two reasons: they wanted to be a man or they were trying to get a man—many wives of male soldiers hated the prospect of women in the Army, as they were afraid it was their man the women were out to get. I remember telling my mother that I was going to pin a picture of my boyfriend on my uniform so everyone knew I wasn't on the dating block. She just shook her head, not knowing what to say but probably wondering where she had gone wrong with her middle daughter.

Fortunately the climate had changed by the time President Obama abolished DADT. Instead of shoving it down the military's throat, there was an implementation period that helped the services deal with the very real and sensitive challenges that the change would present. In about twenty years it had essentially became a nonstory. Of course there were howls from some corners, but quite honestly, we were mentally prepared to accept the reality that gays were already serving, many with distinction, and the law needed to be changed to keep pace with reality. Some of the most respected retired military figures (Colin Powell, John McCain) and the highest-ranking active members of the establishment—including the chairman of the Joint Chiefs of Staff, Admiral Mike Mullen—championed the change. Just a few decades before, this was more unthinkable than women joining a coed military. But the military again took the lead in a country that still allows most states to fire employees based on their sexual orientation.

The military's acceptance of such groundbreaking policies isn't part of a democratic process that allows soldiers to vote. (If that were the case, change could have been much longer in coming.) The military is the only institution in America that can be told to do something and the instant response will be, "Yes sir. Yes ma'am. Aye-aye sir. Aye-aye ma'am." The US government and our president can tell the military to desegregate, integrate, or allow people to be openly gay, and it will get done. And that's what the military does, albeit sometimes begrudgingly and stubbornly slowly.

It's hard for millennials to even fathom an all-woman WAC, an all-male West Point, or ROTC programs that excluded women. The disestablishment of the WAC and the integration of women into the regular Army helped facilitate a major diversification of our ranks. Policy change, however, didn't necessarily mean an immediate change in mindset. Biases and prejudices persisted. By 2010 the number of women on active duty had grown from 55,028 in 1973 to 202,070.

I've walked, crawled, and skipped through many open doors and even had to kick in a few. With each opening comes the challenge of proving I can handle the job. In my case the media tended to focus on the fact that I was the first female to do this or that. Although it's a natural response, one that brought greater awareness of the importance of women in the military, for me it was never about becoming the first anything; it was about being able to make a difference and being respected as a soldier and a leader.

One of the realities of being an Army brat is that your family usually moves every few years. Whenever Dad received a new assignment, I was always excited about the new adventure. One of my top subordinates and closest friends had a similar path.

Lieutenant General Pat McQuistion is an Army brat. Her father was a 1st sergeant in the Korean War. She has six brothers and sisters. I remember telling her at her promotion ceremony to LTG that I came from a big family as well. "I don't know about you," I said, "but I joined the Army to get a little peace and quiet." Her husband, Leif, is an Army officer who retired as a colonel from the Medical Corps. They have three children, all college graduates. Not having had children of my own, I always marveled at how she was able to do it all. When I joined the Army pregnant soldiers were automatically discharged. That policy changed for good shortly thereafter.

Pat has one of the broadest portfolios of tough assignments of any logistician. From the Sinai, Egypt, to Kuwait, to Germany; from Fort Hood, Texas, to Washington, DC; from Tobyhanna, Pennsylvania, to Rock Island, Illinois, commanding at every level, from maintenance company, battalion, brigade, one-star, and two-star. She has had remote year-long tours, where families are not allowed to come along. She was in charge of running logistics and supporting coalition forces for an entire country. Pat is a very attractive woman with big brown eyes and a Hollywood smile. She's about five-foot-seven and for the bulk of her career had much longer hair than I did, almost down to her waist. I don't know how she managed to keep it up, but she always looked *strac*—Army lingo for sharp. When she found out she was going to Kuwait for a year as a one-star general, she finally cut her hair chin-length just to avoid the hassle of messing with it while deployed, especially while wearing a helmet.

I knew of Pat through brief encounters and by reputation in her early years in the Army. General Sullivan used to always ask me, "How is Pat doing?"—she was his speechwriter when he was Chief of Staff of the Army. "You know she is a terrific officer," he'd say. "I really think she has great potential."

I always agreed with him, "Pat is doing fantastic, and all of her bosses tell me the same thing. She's about to head over to command 21st Theater Support Command now."

General Sullivan nodded his head in approval.

Pat actually worked for me three times once I became a general officer. This was not by chance—I wanted Pat on my team. When I was a one-star, she worked for me as a colonel in the Sinai. There she served as the chief of logistics for a multinational force charged with maintaining the peace treaty between Israel and Egypt. Later, when I was a three-star and the Army's senior logistician in the Pentagon, I brought her in; by then she was a colonel promotable, meaning she had been selected for brigadier general but had not yet been promoted. But not wearing a star did not slow her down one bit. She was responsible for strategic planning and plotting the future of logistics for the Army. There are so many general officers in the Pentagon that colonels are plentiful. Even though Pat hadn't "pinned on" her new rank, it never stopped her from walking the halls of the Pentagon with confidence and authority. She did not take "no" for an answer. When I was a four-star, she worked for me first as the commander of Army Sustainment Command, a two-star position, and she replaced my deputy commander, a three-star position. I watched Pat perform in all of these extremely tough but critical positions. She has an engaging leadership style that makes people want to be on her team. She is a visionary leader who can anticipate future challenges while connecting the dots across global organizations, and she is a gifted communicator. As the commander of Army Sustainment Command, she produced an animated video that provided a simple but compelling explanation of why the Army needed to consolidate our supply activities and establish AMC as the lead materiel integrator (LMI). It was very powerful, and it worked.

With each of these moves I would always call Pat and tell her what the Army had in mind for her and get her thoughts. She was always positive and always ready for the next challenge. The toughest phone call I had with her was when she was finishing up her two-star command in Germany. Again, she had done an exceptional job. She was ready for promotion to three stars, but the Army didn't have any positions available. I told her I needed her to run Army Sustainment Command. I assured her that this was an important assignment that probably should be a three-star position.

We needed Pat there to push through some major initiatives while waiting for three-star openings. We were in the middle of transferring seventy Director of Logistics organizations, located all over the United States, from Installation Management Command to AMC. We were also transforming the way we contracted services for the Army. Instead of having multiple contracts—literally hundreds—each with its own overhead costs for maintenance, dining facilities, and supply activities, we were consolidating the contracts and creating competition for the bids. This would not only save millions of dollars but would also allow for increased opportunities for large, medium, and small businesses. I told her that it would probably last for only a year. She would also need to move from Kaiserslautern, Germany, to Rock Island, Illinois, and then possibly relocate again. She and Leif ended up loving Rock Island and really didn't want to leave, but a three-star deputy position in AMC came open ten months after her return to the States, and she was the best person for the job.

I recently asked her how she felt when she earned her third star.

"I was humbled, overwhelmed, a bit anxious, and excited—in that order," she recalled. "I knew a lot about AMC, but I also had a pretty good idea about how much I still needed to learn. Knowing I was coming into such a great team, with you in command, made me feel better about leaving a job and a place we loved. I knew you'd make the transition as easy as possible for us."

I also asked Pat what it meant being a woman in a position of power. I would pass along her words to any woman thinking about enlisting:

> Women continue to do very well in the Army, but in many ways I think it's been more challenging for them to achieve balance because of the numerous deployments over the past fourteen years. I'm in awe of our younger generation. They will have more opportunities that weren't open to my cohort—they can compete for combat arms positions, go to Ranger training, lead a greater variety of units and missions. But they will need very good support structures and voices that continue to tell them they can achieve things they might not know they're capable of. No one knows when they enter the military what their full range of contributions can be. But women can learn very quickly to stretch their horizons and challenge themselves to overcome ever-increasing challenges. That's pretty exciting.

Soldier, mom, wife, community volunteer, and exceptional leader—Pat does it all. There's no doubt she was four-star worthy.

WHEN PEOPLE FIND OUT I'm a four-star general they often ask whether it was a difficult ascension, invariably assuming that it was. In other words, how did you do that as a female? Rarely do the questions have anything to do with my job responsibilities or competence. My rise wasn't much different from other successful leaders. I was fortunate that it happened, but it could have just as easily not happened, as there are many opportunities to stumble along the way. For me it never seemed as difficult as people try to make it out to be because it was never anything that I had set out to do. The Army constantly provided me with opportunities to grow as a soldier and a leader.

The Women's Officer Orientation course in the summer of 1974, before my senior year in college, at Fort McClellan, Alabama, was a life-changing experience for me. I thought I was a pretty disciplined person—growing up on military bases and being a multisport athlete—but I quickly discovered a new meaning of structure, order, and regimen. We were up late every night shining shoes, pressing uniforms, waxing floors, and cleaning latrines as we prepared for the morning inspection. I certainly didn't like waking up to barking drill sergeants who were put on earth just to make our lives miserable. But they were teaching us values and principles.

Up at zero-dark-thirty every morning for physical training (PT), we dressed in the goofiest outfits: light green collates (a skirt/shorts kind of getup), with a light green blouse and white Keds tennis shoes. It was the most impractical and ludicrous training outfit. We would do the dirty dozen exercises: two-mile run, jumping jacks, situps, pushups, squat thrusts, and so forth. Being a physical education major, I didn't mind the fitness drills, but I didn't know why we had to do them in the dark before the sun even came up. We also used to run in formation in our fatigues and G.I. boots. The boot thing made even less sense to me. Much later there were studies done that revealed how bad running in boots was for your knees and ankles. But I ran hundreds of miles over many years in boots, and I have the aches and pains to prove it. Today technology has made military boots as comfortable as running shoes.

After PT it was back to the barracks for more manual labor. We scrubbed floors on our hands and knees with old toothbrushes. We made barrack beds with flawless hospital corners. *Who needs this?* I thought to myself. No TV. No free time. They managed to fill every second of the day with a chore or training.

Even though I had these thoughts and observations, I kept them to myself. I wanted to excel at everything. The women in the orientation were juniors from colleges all over the country. They were very talented and competitive, and many of them were more committed to joining the Army than I was at the time. I loved getting to know this dynamic group of women. Even though I really didn't know whether I wanted to join the Army, I still wanted the final decision to be mine. When I got my acceptance letter I was confronted with my first career crossroad: Should I coach and teach or should I stay in the military? I thought about my dad's career, our family legacy of four generations of West Point graduates, and my sister Sue's Army experiences. Another door was opening. I just had to have the courage to go through it. In June 1975 I was commissioned as a Reserve (2LT) officer.

Although the first two female enlisted soldiers graduated from Airborne School in late 1973, it was 1975 before the Army allowed female officers to attend Airborne School. In fact, being allowed to attend became a key factor for me in deciding to accept my commission as a 2nd lieutenant. When it was time to select your branch specialty—your career field—I asked each branch representative whether they had any jump school slots. Some of the branch reps looked at me as if I were crazy. A quartermaster representative was the first who looked me up and down and asked, "You really want to go to jump school? I'll send you to jump school." From that day forward I was a quartermaster. Later in the process other branches such as Ordnance (maintenance) and Signal (communication) also sent women to Airborne School. Not only was I getting paid $500 a month during my senior year in college, I was also going to learn how to jump out of airplanes. Where else could I have gotten an opportunity like that?

Not everyone at Fort Benning, Georgia, was excited to see 2nd Lieutenant Dunwoody show up for training. The "Black Hats," as the instructors were known, didn't like girls crashing the club. The first day I showed up at the Training Company there was a large recruiting poster behind the clerk. It showed a big, tough paratrooper with a parachute on his back. The poster read, "Paratrooper: last step to becoming a man."

I just smiled, knowing what I was up against. They tried to force me to cut my hair, even though I was in compliance with the regulations. They claimed the bobby pins that held my hair in place were a safety hazard. It was pure nonsense. The next day, instead of a haircut, I used a small cocoon of masking tape to hold my hair in place. I looked ridiculous, but they had nothing else to say.

Once the training began, things improved, and the few women in the class trained right along with the men. We had slightly modified physical training standards than the men, like fewer pullups, but the graduation standards were identical: Pass each phase of ground week and you move on to tower week, then complete tower week and it's on to jump week, where, if you successfully complete five jumps from an aircraft in flight, you're an Army paratrooper.

I'll never forget my first jump. As I moved toward the door to exit the airplane, one of the Black Hats smacked me hard on my rump with what came to be known as a five-finger tattoo. That was the only time that happened to me, and I never saw them do that to anyone else. After that they made me a stick leader, meaning I'd get to jump first. I thought, *Wow, a promotion already. I must be really doing well.* Later one of the Black Hats told me that they chose me to go first so that any male jumper behind me would be too embarrassed to chicken out. At graduation they announced that I was selected as one of 4 honor graduates out of a class of 264 new paratroopers. The officer in charge pinned the wings to my uniform above the left shirt pocket without the backings, then punched the wings into my chest. I was startled and knocked off balance but very proud of my "Blood Wings." My diploma says US Army Infantry School, Airborne Course for Women. I often wondered how long it was going to take them to drop the "for Women."

During my first duty assignment after serving as a platoon leader and battalion adjutant I was offered company command. This is a big deal for a 1st lieutenant. It is an officer's first opportunity to lead and be in command of soldiers. Although I was honored to have the opportunity, part of me wondered why I would take on such a responsibility while knowing I likely was getting out in another year. However, turning down a command limits one's future potential because commanding a company is a basic leadership requirement for every officer. I took the command, and it was one of the best decisions of my life. I enjoyed it so much that I decided to extend my commitment in the Army.

Fast forward seven years to 1987, a watershed year for me. By May, Craig and I decided we were all in and would be married when we could finally work out an assignment to the same location—that ended up taking two years. I had commanded two companies, earned my master's degree in logistics management, completed the Command and General Staff Officer course (CGSC), and was promoted to major. At this point I was a senior parachutist, a parachute rigger, and a fully qualified jump master—I was particularly pleased with my jump master status. As a certified jump master I was qualified to supervise and complete the safety inspection of every trooper's parachute to ensure they had donned it and fastened it correctly and, ultimately, to be responsible for an entire planeload of paratroopers, day or night. It is a critical skill and one the Army doesn't take lightly. It is also one of the most exhilarating and exciting things a soldier can do.

I had new orders to report to the 82nd Airborne Division at Fort Bragg, North Carolina. I was fired up. I was joining "America's Guard of Honor," the "All-Americans" of the 82nd Airborne Division. Unfortunately it was too good to be true. When I arrived at Fort Bragg, instead of being welcomed with open arms, it felt like the division was pushing me away. Clearly the senior leadership must have thought the Army had lost its collective mind when it assigned a female field grade officer to the division.

I found myself in limbo as closed-door meetings were held to determine what to do with me: accept me into the division or send me across the post to the Corps Support Command—a good job but not part of the 82nd. After weeks that seemed likes months, the decision was made that I'd be allowed to stay. I immediately became the highest-ranking woman in the division.

My excitement was tempered when I was informed that the most coveted jobs were already taken. Instead of becoming the division parachute officer (DPO) or taking on some comparable job, I was assigned as the division property book officer. None of my male CGSC friends and counterparts would have been offered a job they clearly were overqualified for. The culture of the "Division" was not quite ready to put a woman in a critical position. Rather than take me at face value for my credentials, they named a really nice guy, who wasn't nearly as qualified, as the DPO. He was a long shot to ever be promoted again and had never been selected for CGSC. My assignment, meanwhile, required no advanced schooling. My predecessor had not been selected for promotion to the next grade. He decided to retire, and I begrudgingly replaced him. I was disappointed because the new job was not commensurate with my qualifications. It was an easy job, I liked my colleagues, and it was a job I knew a lot about because of my early experience of running a supply room with Sergeant Bowen. Instead of running the property book for a company of 220 soldiers, I was now running a property book for a division with 14,000 soldiers.

Still, I had my reservations. For the first time in my thirteen-year career I started considering options outside the Army. Before making a decision, however, I vowed to give this job and these knuckleheads my very best. I wanted to show senior leadership that not only could I do the job but that I was also ready for tougher assignments.

After a week or so my new boss, a colonel and the commander of the Division Support Command, asked me to meet him and the other new field-grade officers for physical training the following morning. We met behind his headquarters at 0630 hours for an orientation run. It was the colonel's way of getting to know his six new majors and finding out what kind of physical shape we were in. As we ran along the fire-break dirt roads of Fort Bragg, the colonel showered us with questions. Are you married? Kids? How many jumps you got? (This is a technique I adopted in my later assignments. What better way to get to know people than with a grueling, gut-check run?)

During the run our boss also told us about the "Griffin Mile." It's named in honor of one of the premier support battalions in the 82nd, the Golden Griffins of the 407th Supply and Transport Battalion. The Griffins rig all the parachutes for the division—personnel parachutes, heavy equipment rigging, and airdrop—along with supply. I was really enjoying the colonel's banter, but my new peers weren't looking as happy. By the time we hit the six- or seven-mile point, we'd been running for close to an hour. That's when we lost the first of the majors. He couldn't keep up with the pace and fell several hundred yards behind. Another mile up the road another major dropped from the pack and started to walk. And then another and another. Before long it was just the colonel and me. As we crested a hill I figured we had run twelve miles, with no end in sight. About a quarter-mile later I spotted a Jeep and a driver. As we arrived at the Jeep the colonel looked over at me and smiled, "Jump in, Dunwoody. Those boys should be able to find their own way back." I thought to myself that I just might have a chance in the 82nd Airborne Division after all.

When a paratrooper exits the side door of a C-130 Hercules aircraft, the first thing he or she feels is the powerful blast of the aircraft's propellers. It comes before the falling sensation and before the vigorous jolt of the static line breaking the rigger tape that holds the parachute in the bag. On February 16, 1989, I was officially "prop blasted" into the 82nd Airborne. It was a long-time ritual to indoctrinate the newly assigned officers of the 82nd.

Paratroopers did not gain full acceptance until they were prop blasted. It was hazing in its purest form—ceremonial torture that featured twelve straight hours of physical and mental abuse. I hated it. It was painful, but I had to do it.

The "certified prop blasters" (torturers) served as the "black hats" for the day. Starting at 0630 you began a rigorous physical training program that included rope climbing, pushups, situps, jumping jacks, running, and anything else you can think of. But more than anything, we did pushups. Hundreds of them. "Dunwoody, drop and give me more pushups! Now!" Thankfully I was not alone. There were about twenty of us, including one other woman, a young lieutenant. We all received the same treatment, us "miserable blastees" not yet worthy of being in the division. We carried litters with our teammates as patients on a stretcher for the sick and wounded down Manchester Road toward the drop zones. After several miles we'd change places and continue on.

Later we were taken to the sixty-four-foot-high jump training tower, just like the ones they have at Fort Benning for Airborne school. We suited up in the training rigs with the heaviest combat load possible and waited our turn to jump. Our protagonists squirted us with a water hose, threw eggs at us, and made us lay down and do the log roll in the sand in the training pits. They laughed and told us they were making sugar cookies. Having been in the division for more than a year by then, I knew full well what a tradition the prop blast was and how important it was to pass the test and receive your highly coveted, laminated prop blast card:

> Be it known by all troopers that Ann E. Dunwoody MAJ HHC DISCOM, having engaged in the ancient and honorable ritual of the Prop Blast and having successfully completed same and having entered his name in the book of honor is hereby proclaimed a qualified trooper, 16 FEB 89.

It was signed by the presiding colonel. Yes, my laminated card says "his." But I consider that progress from a few years before, when I received my Airborne Course for Women diploma.

No one wanted to go through this ordeal again—to be "recycled." Everyone stuck together to make sure all of our jump buddies made it through. It was the truest of team-building exercises, and I still remember some of my "blastee" buddies. Lieutenant Colonel Rick Ross was a short, fit Quartermaster officer; Major Sam Deford, a tall, good-looking helicopter pilot, was the operations officer for the brigade; the other female was Lieutenant Jamie Jones, about my size and with short brown hair and glasses; and Captain Emick commanded the parachute rigger company. He had previously been an enlisted soldier and was short with a crew cut and a forceful personality not very popular among his peers.

Toward the end of a grueling day, with the sun long set, we began the formal portion of the ritual. We were in a dilapidated World War II–era, single-story building. At one end of the building was a mock jump door, replicating the one you'd find on a real aircraft. We were suited up as if it were a real jump. In front of the mock door was a long table where the board of five senior officers, in this case one colonel and four lieutenant colonels, would sit and pass judgment. They would decide whether your conduct and performance were worthy of a thumbs-up and entry into the club. A thumbs-down meant you retreated to the back of the line, waiting for another chance to exit the jump door, join the team, and save face.

Behind the panel was the audience of honorable past blastees. They were swilling beer and smoking cigars, a raucous bunch indeed. We all noticed that next to the jump door was one of the black hats holding wires that were attached to the metal door along with a car battery. We also noticed black hats with buckets of water and small limbs from real trees. We weren't entirely sure how the electricity, water, and tree branches were going to play into the scenario, but we'd find out soon. We were lined up by rank order. I was a major. Because there were two lieutenant colonels (LTC) in the class, I was the third in line to face the panel and the crowd. My eyes were as big as tennis balls as we peered out to watch the first miserable blastee. A black hat barked, "Stand in the door." The first candidate, LTC Ross, took a proper airborne exit position and waited. As he held the side of the door, the black hat connected the wires to the battery, giving the jumper a jolt of electricity, and then commanded "Go!" The jumper made a vigorous leap out the door, assumed a tight body position with his head down, looking at his reserve parachute, and shouted at the top of his voice, "One thousand, two thousand, three thousand, four thousand! . . ." He descended the two feet to the floor below.

In a normal airborne operation these are the procedures a paratrooper would execute. If by the time you yell "four thousand!" you have not felt the jolt that would indicate that your parachute is inflating, then you would assume a malfunction had occurred and deploy your reserve parachute. For our first blastee, once he hit four thousand and looked up as if to check his inflated parachute canopy, one of the black hats screamed, "Prepare for a water landing!" at which point the blastee was drenched with a bucket of water. Then another black hat yelled, "Prepare for a tree landing!" at which point the blastee was smacked to and fro with several branches. After those slaps subsided, two more black hats moved in to push the jumper around, spin him in circles, and otherwise try to disorient him.

I received only a few tips on how to survive this ritual and pass the drill on my first attempt. The first was to memorize the instructions you are given on how to report to the president of the board or else I would automatically be sent back to the end of the line.

Sir, Major Ann E Dunwoody, Social Security number XXX-XX-XXXX, respectfully reports to the president of the board and very meekly and humbly requests consideration for acceptance into the ancient order of prop blast jumpers.

The second piece of advice was to have a couple of good jokes ready, as they could be your salvation. Our intrepid LTC reported to the president of the board accurately, reciting the scripted greeting while presenting a sharp salute. From there the panel peppered him with questions about the division's history, told him to sing "The Division Song," and asked more questions about anything and everything they desired.

What is the largest drop zone on Fort Bragg? (Sicily)

What is the diameter of a fully deployed MC1-1B parachute? (thirty-four feet)

Who was the first American general to jump into combat? (Maxwell Taylor)

(People have told me that Ann Dunwoody is the correct answer to prop blast questions that are used to this day. Who was the first female division parachute officer? Who was the first female to command a battalion in the division?)

The president canvassed the board and heard hooting and hollering from the crowd. The first blastee, not surprisingly, received a unanimous thumbs-up. He was then rewarded with a celebratory swig from the Miley mug (ceremonial mug made from an artillery shell) and officially signed into the book of honor. The ritual brew was a toxic mix of champagne, vodka, lemon juice, and sugar, with some dry ice to give it a mysterious cultish appearance. Over time folks would be more creative in making the magic punch—more ingredients and a more colorful description:

whiskey representing the fuel in our vehicles, sugar representing the fuel for our bodies.

The next blastee in line wasn't so lucky. He fumbled while reporting to the president and was greeted with chants of "Recycle! Recycle! Recycle!" He was sent to the back of the line. Then it was my turn. It started as I expected. First, the jolt of electricity hurt and the ice-cold water was brutal. I barely noticed the tree branches. I properly reported to the president and began fielding questions. I missed one before I was to sing the division song. Argh. There were a couple of recycle chants. I sang the song accurately. My lifelong tone deafness and fear of singing publicly caught up with me. Because I can't carry a tune, there were those who ignored my enthusiasm and resumed the recycle chant. At this point I started to panic. I was exhausted and wanted it to be over. So I asked the president for permission to speak. Permission granted. I asked the president whether I might offer a joke to prove my worthiness.

I will not tell the joke here, but suffice it to say it was one of crassest jokes ever told and would have made the saltiest of sailors hoot and holler. The crowd roared its approval, five thumbs immediately raised from the board, and it was done. My mother would have died if she'd heard that joke—in fact, it was only years later that I confessed my lewd tactic to her. But it worked. I downed the alcoholic punch in the Miley mug in one long slug, then demonstrated that I had done so by turning the mug upside down on the top of my head, sounding off with a loud and thunderous "AIRBORNE!"

Despite my incredible reception, all I could think was: *Whew, I made it!* It was finally over. I was now able to join the honorable blasted members for a beer and then cheer my fellow blastees on. I won't tell you what happened to Captain Emick, but it was a long night for him before he finally made it.

Little did I know how physically demanding the Prop Blast would be. I had scheduled an early flight to see Craig, then my fiancé, in Fort Walton Beach, Florida. When I awoke the next morning everything hurt. Even my eyelids ached when I blinked. I hurt worse than I did after trying out for gymnastics in college. When Craig picked me up, all he could say was, "Ann, you look pathetic." Not "Hi Honey, how are you? Congrats. So happy you're here." I think he was truly stunned that the prop blast had almost virtually "done in" his little paratrooper. All his visions of celebrating were gone. It was a slow recovery weekend.

I can't believe they actually allowed someone to videotape the proceedings. Today it would be all over YouTube, and heads would roll. But for me, I was fired up. I had proved once again that I could hang tough with the boys. I showed my dad the video—big mistake—because I thought he would appreciate it. I was wrong. He did not think this tradition was honorable or appropriate. He could not believe they sanctioned such hazing. But it was just part of the culture back then.

IN THE SPRING OF 2008 President George W. Bush nominated me for my fourth star. Since the announcement the Senate had unanimously confirmed my nomination. We were now just waiting for November, when the official ceremonies would take place—my promotion in the morning and the change of command where I would replace a friend and mentor as the commanding general of the AMC. That was still a few months away, but I was granted a surprise sneak preview. I was shocked when my boss told me I was invited to the Army Four-Star Conference; after all, I wasn't officially a four-star yet. But apparently the Chief of Staff of the Army, General Casey, had reasoned that all the wickets had been passed and the nomination had been confirmed, so why not include Dunwoody? Suddenly I was sitting at the far end of the table, attending my first four-star general officer conference.

When the eleven four-stars arrived I greeted each with a firm handshake and, in some cases, a hug. I knew everyone in the room, some very well and others just casually. General Dave McKiernan, a friend and comrade who had a daughter at West Point at the time, said, "Congratulations, Ann. I am so proud of you—you earned it." General Dan McNeill said, "Blackjack"—he still calls me Blackjack, my call sign from Fort Bragg—"You did it! Welcome to the big leagues." These senior leaders were stationed not only in critical locations in our country but also in key locations around the world, like Afghanistan, South Korea, and Germany. But as we sat down and started discussing the pressing business at hand, it struck me: these same men had sat around this table earlier this year and evaluated me and my career. Ultimately they made the decision that I was going to be the one, the next commander of AMC, that of all the potential candidates, Ann Dunwoody was their choice to forward to the Secretary of the Army, then on to the Secretary of Defense, and ultimately up to the president. But it was here that the real decision, made by the people who know the most about what is best for the Army, was made. And now, here we sat, talking about two-stars who we thought should be three-stars and where they would serve.

So when people ask me why I was the first female four-star general, I feel like saying, "I don't know—ask them." They weren't selecting the first female four-star general; they were selecting the next commander of AMC and decided I was going to be the one. I was now their equal. I truly felt like part of the team, part of the band of brothers. It was finally okay to think of it as a band of brothers—and one very proud sister.

five
★ ★ ★ ★

COURAGE
"Do the Right Thing for the Right Reason"

MY BROTHER BUCK STILL makes me laugh with a tall tale from his days at West Point. He sat down for his final exam for a philosophy class to find that the professor had only one question: "What is courage?" After pondering for a few minutes, my boundary-pushing brother wrote, "This is."

He then stood up, turned in his paper, and marched out the room. When he returned the next day for the final grade of his academy career he found a manila envelope with his masterpiece inside. There was a big "F" written in bold red ink along with a comment from the professor: "That wasn't courage. It was stupid. See me. ASAP." It was a joke to be sure, but it illustrated a point: everyone has their own definition of courage. It could be bravery on the battlefield, fighting against social injustices, or standing up to a bully.

Although not as glib as my brother's example, I have a simple definition of courage: *Having the guts to do the right thing for the right reasons.* It sounds straightforward, but it's not always easy. Often people do the right thing for the wrong reasons or the wrong thing for the right reason. The motivations vary, but sometimes it's because they are uncomfortable with being different. I have seen perfectly well-deserving people promoted not because of their stellar track records but because they happened to mirror their bosses—same race, gender, school, upbringing, and so forth. I have also seen people advance through the ranks, with barely adequate skill sets, just because they were part of the good ol' boy network. There are examples of soldiers hitting ceilings or not being allowed to fight for all the wrong reasons—perhaps most notably the Tuskegee Airmen. These brave African American heroes had to fight just for the right to serve their country during World War II. I have had the pleasure of meeting many such great patriots during my career, and their bravery has always inspired me.

By the summer of 1990 I had really found my footing in the 82nd Airborne. I had just completed my tour as battalion executive officer (XO). My outgoing battalion commander and his family would be friends forever. Before his change of command it was announced that the division parachute officer (DPO) and I were going to swap jobs under the next commander. My professional career and experiences had been building to the point where this was my ideal job, a perfect fit.

When Saddam Hussein invaded Kuwait in August of that year, the 82nd was the first military unit to be alerted for a deployment that would come to be known as Desert Shield and, later, Desert Storm. When we huddled in the battalion to get the new commander's guidance, I was stunned. He announced that the XO, the operations officer, and the command sergeant major would be the first to deploy with an advance party, followed by him and the rest of the battalion. As the DPO, I would stay back and push the battalion out. In my mind this was completely illogical—according to deployment doctrine, the XO stays behind to push the battalion out.

It is critical in such deployments that the DPO be forward deployed to be in place in case there is planning for airborne operations. I was furious, but I obeyed orders without objection. This was the real thing, and there was a lot for all of us to do. Plus, at the time I had no evidence to suggest that gender bias was the underlying factor in the decision. As events unfolded, however, I gained a better understanding of the biases and prejudices that existed at the time. I never wanted to be an airborne ranger, but I did want to do my job. We couldn't have policies that allowed women to serve in positions in peacetime but not in war. Three weeks later I jumped on an airplane headed to Saudi Arabia. No one gave me orders to report. I had pushed the battalion out, so I went down to the deployment center and signed up for a manifest slot. Off I went.

When I touched down in Saudi Arabia it was reminiscent of my first days at Fort Bragg. People gave me that look: *What is SHE doing here?* When I linked up with my unit, it wasn't a happy reunion. I could tell that my commander wasn't looking forward to letting his boss know I had arrived. There was talk that I would be sent home. I don't often get angry, but now I was livid.

Sometimes you get lucky, however, and this would be one of those times. As I waited in limbo, the Army released its new list of lieutenant colonels. Guess who was on the list? Better yet, I was below the zone, which meant I had been promoted a year earlier than my peer group.

The personnel officer briefed the division commander, who was now aware of my presence in Saudi Arabia. He summoned me to division headquarters. When I reported to him, he offered his hand in congratulations. He was much nicer and far more hospitable than I had imagined. He asked me how many other Transportation officers were selected below the zone for promotion. I told him that I didn't know because I was a Quartermaster officer. (Quartermasters focus on supplies, whereas Transportation officers focus on distribution.) When he learned that I was the only Quartermaster officer selected below the zone, he just stared at me. I still don't know whether he was mad, confused, or just speechless.

Strong leaders I had known during my career always treated everyone with dignity and respect. Army leadership had put me in a critical position after already serving two years in the division. But now that we were going to war I felt that they didn't really want a female in the job of DPO. This was probably the one time in my Army career when I felt as though I lacked an advocate. I had a new battalion commander and a Division Support commander who either shared the same unenlightened view as the division commander or were afraid to stand up to him.

That day was a turning point. My unique early promotion ensured that I would not be shipped home from Saudi Arabia. My track record validated my presence, and I refused to be belittled or bullied. That same month I became part of the division commander's secret operations cell responsible for planning future airborne missions. This well-meaning man, who had clearly not been so keen on women in *his* division, became and remains cordial and engaging to this day. I often joke about him being a revisionist historian. He now tells me that he always supported me and is my biggest fan. At least he finally found the courage to give me a chance, and I'm grateful for that change of heart.

IN 1992, SHORTLY AFTER I took over battalion command in the 82nd, I was surprised to discover that the inventory of parachutes and air items that we maintained for the division did not meet requirements. The division consisted of about fourteen thousand soldiers, and we had only about nine thousand parachutes. I don't know whether it was a result of parachutes being lost, damaged, or destroyed after our airborne operation in Panama for Operation Just Cause, the lack of attention while we were deployed for a year in the Gulf War, or whether we just had a larger than usual number of chutes reach their twelve-year service life limit.

I suspect that all of these factors played a role in the critical shortage. We had enough parachutes to drop just three-fifths of the division. Had the division commander been called upon to do a larger airborne operation, we would have been courting disaster. I knew that I had to report the shortfall to my boss, and ultimately to the division commander. I really didn't care at that moment whether we got more money for more parachutes; I just wanted the leadership to know what capability it had to execute an air operation, so I included the information in my readiness report to the division commander. Normally the division commander gets briefed monthly by his staff, but this particular month the division commander had other commitments and was taking the monthly report only for the most urgent situations. I told my boss that I planned to let the division commander know of this critical shortage. Much to my surprise, he told me I didn't need to report it and not to worry about it. I couldn't believe it. *What now?* I thought.

I debated my next move. The following day I told my boss that I was going to see the division commander about the parachute problem. He told me to do what I needed to do, but he would not be going with me. Apparently, he didn't believe it was a significant enough issue. For me it was a significant issue, and I wasn't going to endure another sleepless night. I made the right call. The division commander didn't have much time for extended conversation, so I quickly told him we were short five thousand parachutes. After explaining the situation I could see his look of surprise and then deepening concern. He thanked me for bringing the matter to his attention. He made the necessary moves to get the funding to bring the inventory of parachutes back into compliance.

Even though my gut proved correct, my boss seemed to be unhappy with me. Despite what he may have perceived as an act of defiance, I did gain a measure of respect for him when he later put his ego aside and gave me a good officer evaluation. Even more pleasing was that I received a glowing evaluation from the division commander. "In sum, a superb commander with warrior skills who has what it takes to go all the way to the top!"

When I deployed with the 82nd Airborne Division to Desert Shield/Desert Storm in August of 1990, I witnessed America's incredible reach of Army logistics, and it is stunning. The ability to provide sustainment of Army equipment halfway around the world for a major fighting force is uniquely American. And yet at the time our systems for doing so were not even close to perfect. Thousands of items started flowing into the three operating ports we established in Saudi Arabia: one port for containers, one for ammunition, and another for equipment. But we did not have a modern system to track all the supplies and equipment entering the country from multiple destinations, and bookkeeping inventory was secondary. Our military understandably wanted to make sure our soldiers had what they needed when they needed it; they didn't care whether it was being accounted for accurately. Organizations at all levels—tactical, operational, and strategic—were ordering supplies, ammunition, and equipment to make sure there would be no shortfall when the order was given to go to war. We had to be prepared to expel Iraqi forces from Kuwait and reestablish the borders as they existed before the Iraqi invasion.

Historians and politicians have credited the massive deployment of supplies and equipment for the swift defeat of Iraq in what we now call the 100-Hour War. As a young field grade supply officer, I was responsible for receiving the supplies and equipment earmarked for the 82nd Airborne Division. Remember, this was 1991—we didn't have the online tracking systems that are now common to UPS, FedEx, and other shipping and logistics companies. Instead, we had to rely on responsible NCOs and officers to watch for inbound pallets and equipment at the seaports and airports. The situation was so bad that we placed orders for the pallets and containers to be marked with large colorful placards bearing the 82nd patch. But even that still didn't prevent other units from stealing or "borrowing" supplies and equipment for their own organizations. We used to call people who were rewarded when they brought home "bootie" to their respective units "junkyard dogs."

Though the Desert Storm operation was successful, the supply chain was a mess. We had containers upon containers of Lean Cuisine spaghetti meals. This was fine if you wanted spaghetti three times a day or were on a carbs-only diet, but the meals were never prearranged to provide food suitable for breakfast, lunch, and dinner. It was just massive quantities of ready-to-eat TV dinners.

Ammo came in by the ton. Like everything else, it arrived in containers that were not part of an organized tracking system. Aviation units received artillery shells, whereas artillery units ended up with spare helicopter parts. It became a scavenger hunt trying to figure out what had arrived at port and where it belonged. Containers stacked up, and pallets stood still. The accumulation of containers became known as "Iron Mountains." At the end of the war more than twenty thousand containers were returned to the United States unopened. Yes, we had what we needed, but at what cost? Imagine the price of shipping twenty thousand twenty-foot containers from the United States to Kuwait and back to United States with the contents never having been touched.

After the war we vowed to never build Iron Mountains again. We created In-Transit Visibility (ITV) technology, allowing us to track supplies and equipment from start to finish. Unfortunately, however, the leaders in charge of allocating resources had different priorities. The Army didn't want to invest in systems that automated the logistics community; instead, it continued to invest in systems that gave commanders real-time intelligence, real-time operational pictures, or sexier war-fighting tools and high-powered guns and tanks. The decision makers discounted the value of systems that would help us track, distribute, and manage invaluable equipment. It's inconceivable that Walmart, Kroger, or Amazon.com wouldn't be able to track millions of items, stored in warehouses around the world, in seconds. But in 1991 the Army couldn't. Development and deployment of such a capability would take more than another decade, but that is another story.

Property accountability had become one of my passions since my days as a 2nd lieutenant serving with Sergeant Wendell Bowen. Together we helped regain accountability and document every item in the 226th Maintenance Company. We accomplished our mission with stubby pencils and mounds of paperwork.

As I have previously mentioned, as a major in the 82nd Airborne, my first assignment was working as the division property book officer. The division property book was a five-inch thick binder listing every piece of known equipment. It was an archaic system that required visual inspections to verify equipment on hand and a dated checkmark in the property book. In the old days units would hide excess equipment by loading it in trucks and driving it around while the inspection was taking place. The manual accountability system rewarded hoarding of supplies.

But our world had changed since the days of pencils and property books. After the deployment to Desert Shield/Desert Storm it was obvious that we had to fix the broken system of fighting a $250 billion war with pencils, paper, and blind trust. When the Army didn't deliver an appropriate solution, its various organizations took matters into their own hands. Information technology was coming to the forefront, and smart people at the unit level were devising their own systems just to survive. The 82nd Airborne developed their own automated spreadsheets for tracking their equipment, while the 1st Corps Support Command (COSCOM) developed its own—but different—automated spreadsheet to track their equipment.

Commanders and senior staff could no longer stand the consequences of not knowing where and how much stuff they had.

Boutique—or individualized—systems were developed based on the needs of the unit that designed them. Spreadsheets popped up all over the place. Predictably, these systems didn't interface with each other. The units had basically digitized the same old information and entered it into a computer program as opposed to developing an interactive and modern system that would actually allow us to share information. We needed to be able to do more than just see the same old paper information on a computer. The Army still hadn't come to grips with funding and creating a system that would prevent Iron Mountains from happening again.

When I returned to Fort Bragg in the summer of 2000 to take command of the 1st COSCOM, I became the first female general officer in that storied post. Nearly a decade had passed since Desert Shield/Desert Storm, yet in the aftermath of 9/11, we soon found ourselves deploying once more, and again without the technology needed to track and manage our equipment. As the 18th Airborne Corps started to deploy to Afghanistan, we ran into the same issues with supplies flowing into the country by air, sea, and land. We had no way to track what was being delivered to specific units. At one point we had mountains of food at a location in Uzbekistan with very few troops, and at Bagram Air Base in Afghanistan we had too little food where we had thousands of troops.

Company commanders were transferring equipment between deploying and nondeploying units so quickly that the dinosaur paperwork process made it almost impossible to keep track of the equipment. It was so bad that some of the commanders put away a month's pay into their savings account, knowing they would be held liable when they changed command and couldn't account for equipment. It was impossible to keep track of all the movement with these outdated systems.

Radio frequency identification (RFID) tags were in their infancy, but we started using them. We set up tracking systems so we could follow equipment and supplies as they moved along the supply chain. The new systems were often unreliable, but it was a start.

In 2005 I became the G4 (deputy Chief of Staff for logistics) of the Army and vowed to make the modernization of the military's tracking system my mission. During my first briefing with the Chief of Staff of the Army, General Pete Schoomaker, he told me, "I need you to tell me what's really going on. Everyone wants to tell me the good stuff. No one wants to tell me the ugly stuff."

Next he added something that probably helped me keep my sanity and my job: "Ann, two things can happen in this building. You can let the bureaucracy wear you down, or you can wear it down."

Working in the Pentagon was unlike anything I'd ever experienced. Hardly anyone ever said hello as they walked the hallways from meeting to meeting. I remember telling my XO to shoot me if I ever acted that way. Thankfully, he didn't listen. After my first thirty days in the Pentagon I found myself taking my work home with me, slogging through the lobby with my head down as I walked toward my car. I had to slap myself out of this funk and get back to being positive about the work ahead.

I turned my focus to getting an automated enterprise system that would make it easy for commanders to account for their property. The Army, Army Reserves, and Army National Guard would use the system. It would provide visibility to the senior leadership of the Army so they could have an enterprise-level system to manage of all of their equipment and assets.

The technology was there. The system, called Property Book Unit Supply Enhanced (PBUSE), had been designed, but no one had been successful in gaining funding for the project—the cost of the system was $53 million. That's a lot of money, but I was certain that it would easily pay for itself in a short time. Such a system would eliminate most redundancies, reduce fuel costs, and make a more productive workforce from the warehouse to the foxhole. My staff and I prepared a briefing that outlined our past failings, touted the value of PBUSE, and articulated the cost and consequences if we didn't invest in this system. It was compelling. The thought of not implementing it was scary.

The briefings were well received at every level. We always left with every indication that we would be given the resources. But then the story would change. When you are at war, I was constantly told, the Army can't afford to spend that kind of money on the "Logistics tail." I would correct them every time: "You mean Logistics muscle!" Every time I got a *no*, my team and I went to the next level in the ladder of command. For those in the Pentagon, it's easy to exercise the power to say no. Very few people can really say yes, and many folks give up after the first door is slammed in their faces. This was one of the most frustrating periods of my career. I was trapped in a maze of bureaucracy, and I realized the challenge of changing the culture.

My hopes were waning as I tried to get funding approved. To me it was a no-brainer. I honestly thought I had more power and authority as a colonel than I now did inside the Pentagon as a three-star general. As a last resort I gained an audience with the "Three Kings"—the real decision makers, a council of three-star generals that the Army Chief of Staff trusted and relied upon to make the final resourcing decisions. They were also friends of mine who clearly would appreciate the merits of PBUSE and support funding it. The briefing went very well. They asked good questions and acknowledged that PBUSE was sorely needed. Then they told me their recommendation: "Sorry, Ann, but we just have too many higher priorities right now and cannot fund this." I was shocked. I was dumbfounded. But mostly I was pissed off!

I was so mad that I actually thought this might be a red line for me, an unacceptable way ahead that might compel me to leave the Army. But I was conflicted. On the one hand, I was prepared to step down if I couldn't convince Army leadership to fund this critical program. On the other hand, if I didn't fight for it, I feared that no one else would. The people who would suffer most were the soldiers on the battlefield.

Without PBUSE it would continue to be difficult to verify what equipment our deployed soldiers had or needed. When in doubt we would requisition more inventory and ship it over. Naturally every commander wanted the latest version of night-vision goggles, protective flak vest, boots, uniforms, GPS, and radios, but when you have a million-man army, you can't field everything for everyone at once. The Army has to prioritize the distribution of new equipment. Soldiers who were deployed multiple times and were assigned to different units between deployments would end up with ten pairs of boots, five sets of wet-weather gear, four sets of goggles, and three backpacks. Without a system to account for items given to a soldier prior to deployment, the procedure was to issue a full set of gear each time. I remember telling the issuing team that I didn't need another set of boots before one deployment, only to be given one anyway.

I thought hard about my next step. I reflected back on what General Schoomaker said when I became his G4: "When something's wrong, come see me. Don't let the bureaucracy get you down." Then I thought about what Major General Tom Burnette told me: "If something is bothering you and you can't sleep at night, come see me." And I thought about the support I received from Major General Hugh Shelton for doing the right thing for the right reasons when I came to him with news about the parachute inventory. My mentors had reinforced the importance of courage: when in doubt, do what's right.

I had a long talk with my husband. I told him I had to let General Schoomaker know that we were not getting the support to fund PBUSE. The thought of going over the heads of my fellow three-star generals on the Army staff tormented me, but the consequences of not getting PBUSE funded were far worse.

The next day I sent an e-mail to General Schoomaker:

Chief, I've been in the saddle for three months now, and we have been working hard to get the funding for the automation program that will help the Army see and manage its equipment more efficiently and effectively. The importance of this program had increased tenfold with the transformation to a modular Army, where people and equipment were in constant motion. We continue to try to track equipment using toilet paper and spreadsheets. We cannot continue to operate this way—you remember the Iron Mountains we had during Desert Storm. We are still stuck in the past. I have been to every level and every organization inside this building to try to convince them we need to get on with this. All understand the need, but none will support the funding. The last straw was a rejection by the Three Kings. I defer to you. I know the Army's funding requirements exceed available money. If you believe we cannot afford this program at this time . . . I will sit down, shut up, and color.

Very Respectfully,

Ann

The Chief responded within hours. He asked the director of the Army staff to set up a meeting with all the three-stars—including the Three Kings—to address the issue. I remember standing outside the Chief's office waiting for the meeting when a three-star asked me whether I had any clue what was going on. I told him I thought we were there to discuss PBUSE. The meeting was a one-sided conversation between the Chief and the three-stars. In short, he told us that the Army needed to come into the twenty-first century and spend the money for an automated system to manage our equipment. Make it happen. End of meeting.

Commanders in the field thanked me because it made their job easier. The logisticians were also grateful, as they now could best manage and account for the equipment in their units. Finally, it was part of the operational backbone of our eventual Global Logistics Enterprise Network being established to track readiness and prioritize resources necessary to do so.

My fellow three-stars—many of whom remain good friends—weren't as appreciative. I suspect they thought our stand-alone Standard Army Management Information Systems (STAMIS) were good enough. But these systems didn't interface with one another, and they couldn't provide real-time data. Latent data in logistics is about as relevant as reading yesterday's newspaper. Armed with the Chief's support, my team continued our pursuit of PBUSE.

The automated program eventually came online. We started fielding the system to the Army divisions within a few months, but it took a couple of years to issue the program to the entire Army. Once the system was completely implemented and up and running, we could track equipment from the Midwest to the Middle East. We knew our inventory levels at all times and in all places. Ultimately our entire suite of information technology systems were all aligned.

In 2010, when the decision was made to surge forces in Afghanistan, we were able to shift more than 50 percent of the required equipment from Iraq to Afghanistan rather than sending other equipment all the way from the United States. That action alone easily paid for the initial investment in PBUSE and demonstrated that AMC had arrived. We had matured from a command that used hundreds of IT systems to track readiness information into a centrally connected command that had one large IT enterprise system. Instead of guessing what equipment needed to be fixed based on historical data or buying equipment based on historical data, we could repair and buy based on real-time data.

Without conviction and stubbornness, I'm not sure how long it would have taken for our leaders to implement and embrace PBUSE. The good Army leaders who I admired and respected were men and women with courage, people with the guts to do the right thing. Through the years I found that the higher you go in rank, the harder it is to fight for what's right. Counterintuitive, right?

Once you achieve the rank of general, you may think that whatever you say goes. In reality the higher your rank, the more political your decisions. You compete for limited resources, and not every battle is worth fighting. You have to pick and choose when you are willing to put your stars on the table. What are the consequences of not doing something? In the case of PBUSE, the consequences of not buying and delivering the program were too severe, too costly. Once the Chief gave the green light, I went to Congress to discuss the reprogramming of dollars to fund the program with the Defense Appropriations Sub-Committee. It was an easy sell. In fact, Congressman John Murtha, the chairman, said he was surprised we didn't already have this technology and asked what we were we waiting for!

The reality is that every senior leader in the Army, particularly four-star generals, have to make tough decisions every day. As General Gordon Sullivan once told me, by the time you make four stars, all of the easy decisions have been made. Whether the Army is at war or during peacetime training for war, for me prioritizing resources was at the top of the list of challenging decisions. I witnessed personally the sad, cyclical way our army is funded. Funding peaks at the height of combat operations and declines as the end of conflict approaches. Some politicians are anxious to take the "peace dividend" from the army, as if to pay back the funding it used to conduct the war that the nation had sent it to fight. This cyclic nature of resourcing our military leads inexorably to a state of unpreparedness to fight the next contingency, and it is extremely short-sighted, in my opinion. There is no doubt in my mind that this short-sighted way of resourcing our military costs lives and endangers missions.

This historical practice has had devastating effects. At the end of World War II the budget cuts resulted in an army unprepared and untrained, as evidenced by the embarrassing employment of Task Force Smith to Korea. Task Force Smith was the name given to a small battalion-sized fighting force that was sent to Korea to stop or at least delay the advance of the North Korean Army and was the first American-led fight of the Korean War. The result was a disaster, as the poorly trained, outgunned Americans were swiftly defeated and retreated. After the conclusion of the war in Vietnam, the budget cuts were so severe that the Army was unable to man, train, or equip its forces. I still remember reading a letter from my brother Buck, who was an Army lieutenant stationed in Germany. They had golf carts to simulate tanks and broom handles for rifles, and that was how they trained. We were a broken Army, and it took almost ten years to recover and rebuild.

Today we see a similar budgeting pattern. The reality is that after the "announced" end of these wars, the Army remains committed, with boots on the ground. We are a touch-and-stay Army. After the 1978 Camp David Accords brokered by President Jimmy Carter, a treaty signaling peace between Egypt and Israel, a multinational peacekeeping force for the Sinai Peninsula was put in place—an American Army force is still there. After the Armistice was signed in 1954 we are still on the ground in Korea. Even with the promise of technology, it will not replace boots on the ground. The nature of our business doesn't allow us to unplug; it requires a continuous presence and resources.

The draconian nature of the budgeting process forces Army leadership to figure out ways to best articulate risks and fight for resources to preclude another Task Force Smith or Hollow Army. The formation of the Three Kings was an attempt to do just that.

What I learned by watching and participating in the process is that the best way to fight for resources and articulate risk is through diversification of the team—having subject-matter experts who understood other service capabilities, experts who understood other countries' capabilities, experts who understood the requirements of the entire Army force, not just the combat arms.

Sustainment of a global force is complicated. It is so intricate that it is hard to put in layman's terms without minimizing the difficulty of sustaining forces in a land-locked country with forward operating bases on remote mountaintops while being shot at, blown up, or hijacked. So as the task becomes more complex, the group responsible for advising and recommending must be able to understand and articulate all aspects of the issue, including the needs of activities and services other than their own. People need to check parochialism at the door. We can no longer afford discussions to be about what's best for my service, my branch, or my program but rather what's best to support and defend the nation.

If it were publicly listed when I took over in 2008, with its $47 billion budget, AMC would rank forty-seventh on the Fortune 500 list, between Lowe's and Time Warner, but obviously the AMC and US Army aren't for-profit companies. The things AMC does are not about making money for shareholders but about supporting soldiers on the battlefield and being responsible stewards of taxpayer dollars. Regardless of the mission, any CEO dealing with that kind of budget has massive responsibilities. Greedy people will look for loopholes and ways for personal gain. Even in the nonprofit world there are those stealing money for their personal gain. While I commanded AMC, I was concerned about stealing and selling equipment or information, trafficking in the black market and taking bribes before awarding contracts. I initiated many investigations to discern whether the bounds of propriety were crossed. Fortunately, during my time at AMC there were no big cases of impropriety. But there are many such cases in military history. Remember when the CIA's Robert Hanssen was caught and convicted of selling information to the Russians or when Darlene Druyun, a former principal deputy undersecretary of the Air Force for acquisition, was convicted of upping the price of a new Air Force tanker aircraft, knowing full well that she intended to work for Boeing, the contract winner, after her government service ended?

If you compromise your integrity and principles on minor issues, it gets easier to make bad choices on the big issues. Every day individuals and organizations fail to do what's morally or legally right—political scandals, sports leagues turning a blind eye to criminal behavior, CEOs abusing their authority. The fallout inevitably costs even innocent people their jobs and reputations because no one had the courage to speak up. In both the military and the civilian world it becomes challenging to blow the whistle when the bad behavior you witness is coming from your boss. But I can personally attest that you will never soar to new heights like the Tuskegee Airmen without summoning the courage to fight for what's right.

six
★ ★ ★ ★

THE MAN
BEHIND THE CURTAIN

"Recognize Your Advocates,
Janus-Faces, and Detractors"

THE WIZARD OF OZ is one of my all-time favorite movies. I love how it transitions from black-and-white to color. I adore the singing and dancing. I love the contradictions: tornadoes and rainbows, humor and sadness, and wickedness and goodness. As I got older this classic went from being a scary movie with a happy ending to an entertaining masterpiece filled with lessons about leadership, revealing perspectives on the human condition.

When Dorothy, Toto, and the troops arrived at the Emerald City to see the great Wizard, they thought he was going to fix everything. He was intimidating and demanding. He also turned out to be a big phony—just a little old man behind a curtain making promises and demands while trying to continue his ruse with the good people of Oz, showing that the black-and-white, pedestrian life of Kansas beats fraudulence in color. In the real world there are people who can actually help you make it and then there are those who make life miserable without you ever knowing. This is true in the Army as well.

The Army has a formal process for helping assign and professionally develop its officers. Each officer has an assignment officer who is responsible for matching the Army requirements to individual preferences, with the understanding that the needs of the Army come first. This process takes care of the majority of assignments on a daily basis. It's productive, but it's not perfect.

There is also an informal process, one that's less publicized and certainly not institutionalized. This unofficial practice allows leaders to weigh in on the decision-making process. Just as in *The Wizard of Oz*, people are working behind the curtain to influence decisions. Throughout my career I had more people working behind the curtain who helped me than hurt me—though I only found this out after the fact.

I was unaware that leaders were working behind the scenes to influence several of my key assignments and talking up my reputation. When I became a general officer, I also enjoyed using these informal channels to champion my own subordinates.

Although *The Wizard of Oz* may have given "the man behind the curtain" a bad name, that reputation isn't always the reality. Many proven and effective leaders work behind the scenes. It is a necessary practice because our normal business processes can be too cumbersome to get it right every time. They're not flexible enough to take into account extenuating circumstances. Good judgment and effective intervention are often required to get the job done.

Be it the Army or any other large business, organization, or bureaucracy, there will always be people who operate behind the curtain. These are usually senior people who want to operate outside the norms to wield power and influence without leaving their fingerprints on the outcome, the rainmakers who pick up the phone and say, "I don't want excuses. I want results."

For every highly effective action that is accomplished from behind the curtain there is equal potential for misdeeds and harm. That's why it is so important for us to recognize our advocates, Janus-faces, and detractors. We all have them. We need to know how to spot them, deal with them, and mitigate how and why they negatively affect us.

> **Advocate:** a person who supports you for all the right reasons with no ulterior motives.
>
> **Janus-face:** someone who is duplicitous and will say all the right things to your face while stabbing you in the back every chance he gets.
>
> **Detractor:** a person who openly undermines you, often for no good reason.

In a perfect world every leader would provide honest and constructive feedback to their subordinates when dealing with the realities of individual strengths and weaknesses. Strong performances that achieve a higher standard would be praised, encouraged, or otherwise rewarded, and those who fall short of the standard would be counseled and provided the means to improve or correct whatever deficiencies have been identified.

I view advocates as leaders who intercede on behalf of others. This advocacy can take many forms, including job recommendations and defending colleagues. For me the most obvious interventions by advocates took place during the assignment selection process. On several occasions I received assignments that I was perfectly happy with, only to see them mysteriously change. The new assignment was always for the better but never came with any explanation.

One advocate that I will never forget who worked from behind the curtain was Major General James Wright, affectionately known as Chicken Man. He was a people person who almost everyone liked, and he liked almost everyone. He was a Quartermaster, a senior soldier who oversees supplies and the logistics business of the Army. He lived for everything Quartermaster and was the Corps' staunchest advocate. He believed in the war-fighting aspect of the Quartermaster Corps long before most understood the concept. Normally we assume that the infantry and the combat arms officers are the war fighters; branches like Quartermaster and Ordnance were considered technical supporters. Chicken Man understood that Quartermasters had to be able to survive and fight on the battlefield in order to provide support to the front lines.

He was a great mentor to me, his enthusiasm a welcome change. When he came to see you, he'd leave your left arm sore because he would always deliver a firm punch just below the shoulder while he stared into your eyes with his infectious grin. It was Chicken Man who sat as a member of my battalion command selection board, and knowing that I was at the top of the order of merit list guided the members of the panel to select me in the category of Supply and Transportation (S&T) battalion. Chicken Man was probably the one board member who knew that the only S&T battalion that was going to be looking for a new commander that summer was in the 82nd. There was one other S&T battalion, but the commander there was not departing until the following summer.

The announcement of the first female to command a battalion in the 82nd raised eyebrows throughout most of the Army. Fortunately I had been in the division for four years and my reputation was secure. When people ask me what job I liked most, the answer was easy: hands down, battalion command in the 82nd—commanding in this elite Airborne Division, jumping out of airplanes, supporting and supplying the division with beans, bullets, fuel, and parachutes. Chicken Man called me after the announcement. "Dunwoody," he said, "congratulations! I am so damn proud of you. I'll have to share the 'Paul Harvey' rest of the story next time I see you." I could tell from his voice that he had a hand in pulling it off.

In 1995 I was preparing to graduate from the Industrial College of the Armed Forces (ICAF). ICAF was one of several War College alternatives available to students. One afternoon I received a message to call a one-star general I'd known from the 82nd Airborne Division. He wanted to know whether I would be interested in coming to the Pentagon to be part of his transition team for the new Chief of Staff of the Army. I told him I would love to be part of the team. He said he would work on getting me an assignment to the CSA initiatives group, a select think tank for the Chief. As my first assignment at the Pentagon, this would be a great opportunity to see our senior leaders in action and learn firsthand how the Army runs. Imagine working at Facebook and one day someone asks you whether you'd like to be part of a select group that will help Sheryl Sandberg plot the future of the company. That's what I felt like.

By the spring of 1996 I had been selected for promotion to colonel and was awaiting notification for a brigade command assignment. There were several possibilities, but anytime you're in the running for a Division Support Command (DISCOM), you'll gladly take whatever you get. It really is the premier colonel-level command for a logistician because the DISCOMs provided direct support to the combat brigades. We were still a linear army back then, and divisions were on the front lines, with support units in the rear areas providing support. Think about the Civil War: two armies online, face to face, one attacks and the other defends. It's straightforward, albeit messy. That's a linear battlefield. Higher-level logistics units that belonged to the Corps were even further back on the battlefield and often provided indirect or secondary support to combat units.

After 9/11 all that changed. Today's battlefield is no longer linear; it's asymmetric, and there is no front or rear boundary on the battlefield. In the military, when we say "asymmetric warfare," we mean battles fought between opponents whose relative military power or whose strategy or tactics differ significantly. We can bet that wars will continue to follow the asymmetric pattern, as terrorism and non-nation-states continue to wreak havoc either for religious beliefs or economic necessity. These insurgents or terrorists avoid massing their forces because they know we would destroy them.

While working for the Chief of Staff, General Dennis Reimer, in the Pentagon I was amazed by how many of my former bosses or colleagues would come by to say hello. My close proximity to the Chief was a natural draw—who wouldn't be honored to "run into" the Chief in the hallway or my office? One day a one-star general stuck his head in the door to see whether I was alone. He was my former boss, so we had a good relationship. As he came into my office, he gave me a big smile and started a hula dance. "Can you spell aloha?" he asked me. He had seen the assignment slate and told me I was Hawaii-bound. Confidential information, of course. Sure enough, a couple of days later I received a request for orders from personnel command (PERSCOM) saying I would be headed to Hawaii to command the DISCOM as a colonel-level logistics brigade responsible for providing logistics service and support for the 25th Infantry Division—a two-star general command. I was ecstatic. It was my dream job in my dream location. It also quickly became a dream deferred.

The man behind the curtain stepped in. Within a week I received new orders to report to Fort Drum in upstate New York to take the DISCOM of the 10th Mountain Division. I now would be heading to one of the coldest, snowiest locations in the United States. I called PERSCOM to try to figure out what happened. After some hemming and hawing, a branch chief finally told me about my good fortune. His boss had been given specific orders to keep me within the 18th Airborne Corps (ABC), the higher headquarters for 10th Mountain Division. I was dumbfounded. He went on to explain that the only DISCOM in 18th ABC changing commanders that year was Fort Drum. Turns out, my advocate knew that the 18th ABC would receive priority funding and training dollars (resourcing), even at a time when budgets were tightening. The very nature of contingency response was training and equipping the light forces. The 10th Mountain Division was the epitome of a Light Infantry Division. Though it was hard for me to see the big picture at that moment, my advocate was keeping me in the spotlight, in the middle of the fight, instead of waxing a surfboard in Hawaii.

In 2000 an eerily similar thing happened as I was awaiting orders for a new assignment following my selection for promotion to brigadier general. It didn't surprise me to know that the very same advocate intervened. There were two Corps Support Commands (COSCOM) coming open, and I had my fingers crossed that I'd get one of them. Sure enough, I got a call from someone asking whether I had been practicing my German. I was excited, but not nearly as excited as Craig was. He began researching the ski areas in Germany and Austria and was confident that his dream golf excursions to Scotland and Ireland would soon be a reality. Not so fast, my dear.

When the formal orders arrived, I was told to report to the ski oasis of Fort Bragg, North Carolina, as commander of the 1st COSCOM. In terms of assignments and prestige, this was a logistician's Super Bowl. 1st COSCOM belonged to the 18th ABC, and this meant we'd be on the cutting edge of whatever contingencies would come down the road. Contingency missions are short-notice missions that include the full spectrum of operations, from disaster relief, peacekeeping, and stability operations to full-fledged combat. The 18th ABC was the Contingency Corps for the Army, with rapid-response capabilities. Although the job overseas would have been incredible, the American presence in Germany was waning and resources were limited. Once again I was thrust front and center into the logistics spotlight.

IT WAS A BEAUTIFUL Tuesday morning in September at Fort Bragg. It was warm but not as oppressive as the normal summer day. Craig had already walked out the door to meet the ladies at Iron Mike at the end of the street for their daily four-mile run. I was right behind him, heading for the office to do physical training. As I drove by Iron Mike, a famous statue and popular gathering place, we all waved, as they were still in the stretch-and-gab phase. By 7:30 we were both home for breakfast, and I was doing my normal quick turn to clean up and put on a uniform in order to be back to the office by 8:00. Craig lingered in running clothes, only changing his shirt, as he would go to the gym behind Ryder Golf Course to do exercises, lift weights, and do a stint on the Lifecycle stationary bike. Retired life was good. But he never made it to the gym that day.

I was in my COSCOM headquarters office, fourteen months into a two-year tour. I was doing routine paperwork at my desk with the TV on but the volume down. I heard someone from the front office yell out, "Turn on the TV!" I looked up and saw the tower burning from the impact of the first airplane. I got up, ran over to turn up the volume, and just stood there in front of the TV . . . and then there was the second impact, this one broadcast live for all to see. *Oh my God! Get Craig on the phone, please!* "Unbelievable!" Craig said. "Ann, we are under attack." I couldn't get the thought of someone killing all of these innocent people out of my mind.

When American Flight 77 hit the Pentagon I had the feeling that life at Fort Bragg and the rest of the Army had just changed forever. That morning was just a blur, as the damage intensified and the new realities of the day sank in. Fort Bragg came to a virtual standstill. No one knew whether there would be more attacks or where they might occur. Fort Bragg was on lockdown, as we tried to protect the installation and our soldiers from the real or imagined threats that surfaced on such a devastating day.

Fort Bragg covers 251 square miles and has boundaries on four North Carolina counties—Cumberland, Hoke, Moore, and Harnett. Since its inception it has been an open post, meaning that civilians could visit and drive through and were only restricted from certain headquarters buildings, Special Operations units, and the airfields at Pope Air Force Base and Simmons Army Airfield. The post was dissected by a number of roads that soldiers and citizens shared. From Fayetteville the quickest way to Pinehurst or Southern Pines was to take Manchester Road through the heart of this storied military reservation. There was Plank Road, Morganton Road, and Bragg Boulevard (highways 24 and 87), all key arteries, not just for the post but also the entire region.

That all changed on 9/11. The first order of business was to secure or prevent access to Fort Bragg's seventy-mile perimeter—restricted access, armed soldiers at makeshift check points, 100 percent identification checks, closed roads, and ready reaction forces poised to respond to problems. If you weren't a soldier or didn't live or work on Fort Bragg, you could not enter. For civilians, that meant no more easy access on the post or across the region. It was a mess. My headquarters was three miles from my on-post quarters (residence) and on the opposite side of Bragg Boulevard. At the end of the day I tried to go home. I arrived eight hours later.

September 11, 2001, marked the day that America lost her innocence. No longer could Americans deny that we lived in a dangerous world where people were willing to go to extremes, even sacrifice their own lives to attack us, to hurt us, and, most importantly, to terrify us. Many Americans refused to believe that we were under attack when the US Embassy was overrun in Tehran in 1979 and 52 American diplomats and citizens were held hostage for 444 days. Embassies in Islamabad and Tripoli were also attacked that year. We refused to believe we were under attack when the Marine barracks in Beirut were attacked in 1983, killing 241 Americans. Subsequent attacks or plots to attack embassies—American sovereign territory—in Kuwait, Jakarta, Rome, Lima, Paris, Tanzania, and Kenya barely lasted a news cycle despite the loss of American lives and property. Those events happened over there, not here. September 11 changed all that. Americans were forced to admit that we were at war, and the priority became to protect the homeland and deal with the problem over there before they can attack again over here.

Across America roads were closed, barriers constructed, and fences built, and the growth in all things intended to provide security blossomed. New businesses were formed, new government agencies created, and new directives issued, all to ensure that Americans could feel safe again. The airlines reeled as they tried to figure out how to prevent their planes from being used as the latest and deadliest terror weapon. Rules were changed, cockpit doors were secured, and security lines grew long as the fledgling Transportation Security Administration (TSA) tried to figure out how it would do business in this new reality. Americans kept their televisions on, not wanting to miss the breaking news of the next attack.

In the military the situation changed as well. The myth of a "peacetime" military was shattered. Money was immediately available for whatever was needed. The newest buzzwords became "supplemental funding." Forces were ready to go—but where? Who had done this? Where were they? How would we recognize them when we saw them? The reality was that we couldn't really answer these questions and were on the verge of discovering a new kind of enemy, one with no obvious state sponsorship or recognizable uniform, an enemy willing to use any tactic, any means at their disposal to kill, disrupt, and achieve their goals, whatever they might be. There would be no battlefield per se; cities, neighborhoods, villages were all on the map. There would be no safe area. Business, crops, livestock would be collateral damage at the least—and often targets themselves.

The fighters themselves—the enemy—were bound by their faith and objectives. They had no rules, and we were slow to figure out their culture. Where we as Americans would go out of our way to protect, save, or spare noncombatants, particularly women and children, this new enemy saw them as a means to be used, exploited, and even employed as shields. We didn't understand these people, and we probably still don't.

The combined leadership at Fort Bragg knew immediately that the initial response to 9/11, the first units to deploy to Afghanistan, would be Special Operations Forces, followed shortly by elements of our very own 18th Airborne Corps. When the Special Operations units were deployed from Fort Bragg, they normally were accompanied by a very small logistics capability. As operations expanded, the 18th ABC was tasked to provide a three-star-level joint task force at Bagram Airfield. As their mission expanded, so did the requirements for logistics support.

Secretary of Defense Donald Rumsfeld placed a cap on the number of people who could be deployed into Afghanistan, and that really caused problems. Of course, commanders and planners wanted to maximize combat power on the ground, and as frequently happens, the logistics to support those forces wasn't getting the necessary consideration. With the manpower cap we had to figure out how to provide food, ammunitions, clothing, fuel, and supplies from someplace outside of Afghanistan.

We selected a location in Uzbekistan that had an airfield that could handle large cargo aircraft bringing in equipment. It also had a rail line that could be used to bring in supplies by train. Although the Task Force commander's staff was somewhat leery of us establishing a logistics base in Uzbekistan, we made a compelling case. Before we deployed our logistics task force, logistics operations were piecemeal, with every unit fending for themselves. We were able to consolidate the logistics capabilities in Afghanistan, provide a single command headquarters from our industrial base in the United States, and coordinate the distribution of supplies to match the requesting unit's requirements. This eventually led to the establishment of a Joint Logistics Command that coordinated support for all services (Army, Navy, Air Force, Marines, and Special Operations Forces) in Afghanistan.

General Dan K. McNeill became the commander of 18th ABC shortly after I took the helm at the 1st COSCOM. A native North Carolinian, General McNeil was sneaky smart, could run all day, and had done every tough war-fighting and combat job in the Army. He never served a day in the Pentagon, and there should be some sort of a special medal just for that. He was cool, calm, and cautiously suspicious of the unknown. Some people trust people immediately, but with Dan McNeill you had to earn his trust. It was a tough call for him, but he approved our request to establish a logistics task force in Uzbekistan when others were naysayers.

A year later, when the 18th ABC joint task force returned to Fort Bragg, General McNeill, known to his friends as DK, said, "Blackjack, standing up the log task force in UZ was absolutely the right thing to do. It allowed me to focus on the fight while the logistics task force focused on making sure all American forces had the supplies and equipment they needed when they needed it." I thanked him with a handshake and a salute. The "go to" 1st COSCOM had succeeded in a very demanding environment. DK continued to quietly mentor me in casual conversation ever since, giving insights on what to expect during a four-star conference or how best to tackle a problem or sharing his evaluations of senior logisticians. He and his wife, Maureen, are still great friends today.

I remember the McNeills inviting us over for a backyard reception in honor of General Hugh Shelton, who was then the chairman of the Joint Chiefs of Staff. Of course we would go, but in this case we were really looking forward to the event, as General Shelton and his wife, Carolyn, were two of our favorites from over the years. We RSVPed yes, and it was on the calendar for Saturday night. We decided to invite another couple over on Friday night to grill some salmon, and all of a sudden we hear the 82nd Airborne Division Chorus singing, and it's coming from the direction of the McNeills' home. My first thought is they are rehearsing for tomorrow night's reception. What followed was uncertainty, then panic, then regret, then embarrassment. We put the reception on the calendar for Saturday, but it was in fact taking place on Friday night as we were serenaded in our own backyard. Yikes.

In 2004, as a two-star, while serving as the commanding general of the Combined Arms Support Command at Fort Lee, Virginia, it was clear to me that all potential job openings for three-star logistics positions had someone else pegged. No one was talking to me about the future, and no one was talking to me about retirement either.

Out of the blue I got an e-mail from the General Officer Management Office (GOMO), saying that the new CSA, General Pete Schoomaker, wanted to nominate me for a three-star position in the building. I was shocked because I had been told that all the three-star positions already had other general officers nominated for them. These general officers were senior to me, and all fully capable. Because of the CSA's intervention, I was promoted to three stars and became his director of logistics for the entire US Army. He later told me he would like to see me get a four-star assignment with AMC, which would make me the first female four-star general. It was a holy-cow moment for my career. Never had I thought that becoming a four-star was even possible. Me? Really? It was the first time in my life that anyone had mentioned four stars and my name in the same sentence. I was humbled. Unfortunately General

Schoomaker was also set to retire well before that final decision would be made.

In 2007 General Schoomaker's successor as Chief of Staff, General George Casey, was sworn in. My potential four-star assignment was suddenly in limbo. Like every Chief—and rightfully so—he came in with his own ideas. He had some different thoughts on who should be the next AMC commander. I'd never served with him before, and he didn't know me from an empty chair. It would have been very easy for him to go in another direction, and I expected that he would. Once again I found support from an advocate, this time the vice Chief of Staff of the Army. During the first four-star conference with the new Chief, a lively discussion about future general officer assignments ensued. New names were being tossed around as potential candidates for the AMC. At some point during the session my advocate asked the rest of the four-stars why they were back-peddling and putting their preferred candidates back in the mix. What changed? His lobbying and the support from the then-AMC commander put me back on the path to four stars. If not for them, I probably would have retired happily as a three-star. It takes guts and courage to stand up for what you believe in. No words could express my admiration and gratitude for their faith and trust.

The advocates in my life were the leaders who went out of their way to help me. It often happened behind the scenes. In some cases I didn't know about their actions until years later. They were opening doors for me and providing me with exciting and rewarding opportunities that I would never have enjoyed under the formal system. The job of senior leaders is to develop other leaders. It requires senior leaders to weigh in on key decisions. Leaders who don't weigh in lose their vote. All of these decisions could have gone another way. Had no one championed me at this juncture, I might never have made four stars. Advocates are the easy leaders to talk about. They were my coaches, mentors, and influencers. They are leaders who believe in a person's potential and find ways to weigh in at critical points in someone's career.

Not everyone I served with was a "Dunwoody" advocate. In simple terms, I found that leaders who weren't advocates were either back-stabbers or, even worse, detractors. Janus-facers come in many forms and have a variety of characteristics. Most of them are patronizing or condescending and treat you as though you aren't good enough to be on their level. There is an element of danger when dealing with them. Many appear friendly and say the right things to your face. They might even offer assistance. Rest assured, help or support from a patronizer is insincere and rarely if ever helpful. In an institution that's built on trust, the person who pretends to befriend you is usually sticking a bowie knife squarely between your shoulder blades. I dealt with my share of these misguided souls during my journey to four stars. The funny part is that they later trumpeted my success and took their share of the credit.

I found that you can win two-faced people over, and when you do, there is nothing more satisfying. After a year of good performance in the 82nd Airborne I had people telling me I needed to interview for a battalion XO job. This is the number-two person in the battalion and generally runs the day-to-day staff operations. Normally the commander, XO, and command sergeant major work very closely to oversee all the battalion actions. When I interviewed for a battalion XO job in the 82nd with a projected vacancy, the leaders were noncommittal.

The battalion commander acknowledged I was qualified, but it turned out he had another plan in mind. I later learned he wanted to extend his operations officer for a year and move him up to be his XO. This would have meant extending him for a fourth year in the 82nd and deferring him from going to Command General Staff College (CGSC). That could have put him behind his peers, as he would have been a lieutenant colonel by the time he graduated from CGSC at Fort Leavenworth. It was a head-scratcher for me, but that's what they ultimately decided to do.

That's when an unlikely ally stepped in. The assistant division commander for support, a stern-looking brigadier general in the 82nd Division headquarters, heard I was leaving the division. Like most senior leaders in the division, he had not thrown out the welcome mat when I arrived. I had a lot of interaction with him during my first year in the division because he had overall responsibility for support and equipment readiness. I had briefed him on several occasions, and over time I believed he really did see me as a quality officer and paratrooper. He expressed how well I'd done my job and handled the "difficulties" of being a woman in the 82nd. As far as he was concerned, I had proven myself and belonged in the division. When he found out I was leaving to be an XO for the battalion outside of the division, he called my chain of command to find out why. He wanted to know who had been selected for the XO jobs in the division. The rest is history.

I ended up staying in the division while the other officer went off to school as he should have in the first place. Somehow the world didn't end. Today I am still very good friends with my then battalion commander and DISCOM commander, both of whom went on to be multistar generals. We still chuckle about the phone call from the "Prince of Darkness," as the assistant division commander for support was fondly known. No one was trying to do anything evil; they were making a decision that made perfect sense to them and involved minimal risk. The officer had been in the division for the three years he had been the battalion's operations officer, and therefore his knowledge of the battalion would have made for an easy transition to the XO position. I had only been in the division a year and had not served in the battalion. It's a natural thing to go with the ones you know.

In extreme cases Janus-facers can abuse their power in criminal ways. This was the case among drill sergeants running basic training at Aberdeen Proving Grounds, Maryland, in the early 1990s. These so-called professionals had been entrusted to train America's sons and daughters. They were expected to instill Army values, teach soldier skills, and foster trust and confidence in the chain of command. Instead, they threatened new recruits with elimination if they didn't perform sexual favors as part of their basic training. They harassed, assaulted, and raped young recruits, some of whom were trying to escape economic disadvantage or unhappy homes. It was clearly a leadership failure and an abuse of power and authority counter to the very professional culture and standards that the uniform stands for. They showed a complete disdain and lack of concern or respect for new recruits. They went beyond being patronizing and instead evolved into felons.

At the time this occurred, I was at Fort Drum. I had just left an assignment working for the Chief of Staff of the Army at the Pentagon. The Army was beginning gender-integrated training for new soldiers, and this was a case in which the leadership failed to set the conditions for success. When Aberdeen made the news, there was a lot of discussion about eliminating gender-integrated training. The Chief of Staff was deeply concerned about the incident but also looked at the larger issue of sexual harassment as an Army-wide problem. My personal thought was that we needed to train as we fight. Integrated training was a reality, and it also served as an equality benchmark. Training together meant building trust, confidence, and teamwork. It also meant overcoming long-held prejudices and sexist views. We had to figure out how to measure success and how to make integrated training work. At the time I did not believe that sexual assaults were part of the Army culture but instead that this bad behavior at Aberdeen had been tolerated in an organization with a subculture that clashed with Army values. I had been in the service for twenty-one years and had never encountered any direct form of sexual harassment or assault. Although in my early years I was exposed to questionable language, inappropriate comments, and jokes, these were a reflection of the Army in the 1970s. I did believe, in this case, that our junior enlisted women had become the easy targets because they were young and less experienced. This was a failure by the chain of command to enforce standards.

The Chief instituted what was then called the "Consideration of Others" program, Army-wide, to intensify his focus on the Golden Rule: Do unto others as you would have done unto you. As with most difficult situations, the Army learned a lot from the Aberdeen case and took action on multiple fronts, coming out stronger as a result. Fortunately the Army didn't eliminate gender-integrated training, which could have been the outcome; instead, the Army convinced Congress and, ultimately, the American people that this behavior was unacceptable and not part of our culture and that leadership would take appropriate action.

When I was a major I had a boss who always complimented me on my work and praised me in public, but when I received my officer evaluation report from him the words were underwhelming, such as "Promote ahead of Peers" or "Select for battalion Command." These sound like great comments, but in the Army remarks on evaluation reports are typically inflated, particularly for "fast track" officers, those selected below the zone, or promoted early. The potential comments are more important than the performance comments and usually address an officer's promotion potential four to five years out.

One of the senior civilians in the Army was the most egregious Janus-facer I had ever met, praising and acknowledging our partnership and my leadership in public forums only to talk badly about me behind closed doors. One of my subordinates came and told me, "Careful, ma'am, there are sharks in the water." One of his friends was privy to the inside conversations.

What was most frustrating to me was that I had gone out of my way to try to build a trusting relationship with him. I brought him to my headquarters for briefings, I called to keep him informed of issues, and I even took him on a trip to Iraq and Afghanistan. I was disappointed in myself for not being able to build a trusting relationship with this man. After about three months of trying, I realized that he was just a two-faced person and I wasn't going to change that. I felt used. When others caught on to his ways, he came under fire and ultimately resigned.

Detractors are often capable of anything. If your boss counsels you about your job performance and not all the comments are favorable, that doesn't make him a detractor. Detractors try to criticize or demean you without any knowledge or reason. Detractors can be motivated by a seemingly endless number of prejudices, biases, or insecurities.

Detractors also can be formidable. Many are not coy or pretentious; they just don't like you. It could be for any number of reasons. Some of my detractors felt the Army was going to go to hell because of women; they felt obliged to limit our participation and our roles. Maybe they didn't believe I could meet their standard. Some believed there was real "man work" and real "woman work"—with no room for overlap. I'm certain some simply felt threatened, either by me or fearing that I might perform better than them. Some people are afraid of being outperformed by anyone; others are terrified of being outperformed by a woman.

Take, for instance, my first division commander who wouldn't let women jump out of the same aircraft he was on or monitored the percentage of women being assigned to the division. "1.2 percent and holding, sir," was the division personnel officer's response when asked about how many women were in the division.

They probably hadn't noticed I was in the room. I had one boss who didn't talk to me unless he absolutely had to—avoidance behavior.

Most of us have worked for or with someone who saw you as a threat to their own career progression. Inevitably that person tries to derail you at every opportunity. They can do it through anonymous 360 evaluations, in closed-door sessions, or by subtle comments on promotions panel discussions. The higher in grade or rank you become, the number of officers selected for each sequential promotion gets smaller and smaller, and the playing field becomes more competitive, driving some to fight for their own interests and advancement at the expense of what's best for the Army and the nation. The detractors invariably believed that every good job or assignment I received was because I was a woman, not because I was best qualified. Competition obviously doesn't have to be based on gender. Though I've never worked for a woman, some of the harshest comments I've ever heard concerning detractors have come from women who worked for other women. For some I was just an easy target. Or so they wrongly thought.

I have found some people to be very territorial and protective of their mission. I don't know whether they're suspicious by nature. It's frustrating when you identify a problem, only to be rebuked when you offer your organization's expertise. Detractors don't want your help for fear of appearing needy or weak.

As the AMC commander, I had a very challenging situation with a patronizer who became a detractor. He convinced his three-star boss whom I had served with in the Pentagon when we were both three-stars that my command was invading his battle space during Operation Iraqi Freedom (OIF).

Their headquarters was to facilitate the reception of new units deploying into Iraq and Afghanistan and the redeployment (return) of units back to their home station at the end of their deployment. It was an extremely challenging mission, complicated by pressing presidential mandates, timelines, and uncertainty of the threat. We offered an innovative solution to an enormous logistics problem he had in Iraq. I was prepared to offer my own people to help, but he was insistent that I should butt out. He refused to listen to our solution and was confident that his deputy had it under control. I was disappointed.

I believe the deputy was really more interested in who was going to get the credit for the mission accomplishment. Someone once told me that "if you don't worry about who gets the credit, you will be amazed how much you can get done." Both presidents Truman and Reagan said essentially the same thing.

When it was announced that the commander's tour was about to end and another three-star general was going to replace him, I reached out to his successor before he deployed and invited him to visit our headquarters. I laid out our concept and walked him through the benefits of our support. Unlike the outgoing commander and his deputy, the incoming officer appreciated our collaboration and embraced the idea. He welcomed our people and assistance into his battle space. The exact same idea that the detractor had rejected was seen as a solution by the advocate.

While working with advocates, Janus-faces, and detractors, I have learned that people can change and grow. Detractors are the hardest to convert, but they could become a staunch advocate once they believe in you. That being said, there are some people who will never change. That's okay too—you just need to know and understand who you're dealing with.

seven

THE MIRROR, MIRROR SYNDROME

Leverage the Power of Diversity

ONCE YOU RETIRE FROM the Army the first few days of rest are a godsend. I never realized how truly tired I was until I was freed from the 0500 alarm that announced the beginning of every new duty day. After the first week of late sleep-ins I was able to establish a more comfortable up-with-the-sun routine. Nothing bugged me more than the get-up-in-the-dark, run-in-the-dark ritual that was my life all those years. After a few weeks of rest and a more comfortable routine, I started to wonder whether my cell phone still worked. That was okay with me—for the first time in my adult life I knew that everything I did would be on my own terms and in my own time. At least that's what I expected for my transition to civilian life—walking on a beach near you. But as soon as word of my retirement spread, the recruiting began—phone calls, letters, and e-mails from headhunters, corporations, universities, and defense contractors: *Would you be interested in joining our team? Have you considered being a consultant? You would be perfect for our PAC.*

We're looking for talented female leaders with diverse and accomplished backgrounds.

The overtures were part-flattering and part–kissing up. I wasn't ready to jump into academia or corporate America. I wanted some me-time and long-overdue QT with my family and friends. Immediately joining another company full time after thirty-eight years in a demanding business was a nonstarter. I didn't want to get back on the same treadmill I just got off. No one becomes Bill Gates or Donald Trump by working in the military. Few people know that salaries are capped after you make two stars and that you have to sell or divest any defense stocks you may have purchased for investments. We even had to get rid of one of my all-time favorite stocks, Disney, because they did business with the government. Apple stock had to be sold as well. If folks joined the Army for the money, we would be a much smaller army. However, I am not ungrateful for the exciting, challenging, and patriotic life I led in the Army, and I am grateful for the retirement benefits I have. I appreciate the health care provided by the military until Medicare kicks in, access to military facilities such as commissaries and base exchanges, and a pension for the rest of my life. Additionally, four decades in the ultrarigid structure afforded some financial flexibility and freedom. However, the point is still one worth considering: we pay our military "CEOs" far less than concomitant business leaders receive . . . that is the price of service. I wouldn't trade the lifetime of service to our country for a higher paying job—there is no better job than service in the military!

The phone keeps ringing. My husband always takes the call and jots down a message. He'll Google the company calling and then peek into my office. "Hey babe, looks like another board of angry, old white dudes," he'll joke.

That's his code for another executive calling to see whether I'd be interested in interviewing for an advisory board spot or a consulting agreement. It was amusing to me when they wanted an association with me but didn't want to alter their board composition. I would always research the company and follow up: "Hello, this is Ann Dunwoody returning your call." Inevitably the male voice on the other end would say, "Hello, General Dunwoody, this is so-and-so from so-and-so, and we're interested in you for such-and-such." Because I was in the very early stage of my retirement, I would always say, "I would love to come meet you and your team so I can find out more about you and what you would like me to do."

I never said no, and I always flew out to meet the CEO.

I know most people think they are the one being interviewed, but for the first time in my life I could pick and choose who I wanted to work with, so I always went out to conduct my own personal interview. In February of 2013 one of my former mentors, then working as a senior VP in a Fortune 500 company, called. "Hey Ann, it's Dick. I want to recommend you to our CEO to join our board of directors."

I responded with, "Really? That sounds great."

Dick: "Let me work it out and get back to you."

Craig and I did some research on the company and discovered that several more of my former mentors were on the board. I flew to New York City and had lunch with Dick, the CEO, and the head of the Nomination and Governance committee. It was the first time I had a glass of wine with lunch in years.

We talked about what I did in the Army, and Dick shared some of my accomplishments. The CEO was just as personable as he could be. I said to him, "I saw that you used to be the head of the company's ethics committee, and that makes you and this company very appealing to me." I felt very comfortable, like I had known all of them a long time because we had values in common. Alan, the chair of the Nomination and Governance committee, was a very nice gentleman and seemed to want to recommend me for the board. I asked the CEO what he thought I could bring to the board. He said, "I'm impressed with your background and in managing global logistics for the Army, foreign military sales experience, acquisition process, and your leadership experience, and quite frankly, I don't think you're going to be on the market very long. I'd like you to consider joining our board." I blushed at his invite. Of course this was just step one in the process.

A few weeks later I flew up to New York City to have dinner with the other board members and key members of management. This felt a bit more like an interrogation than the first meeting. It's a big decision for the future of a company and shareholders, so board members are usually very inquisitive. They all knew I was the first female four-star general, and my allies on the board had filled them in on my background before the nomination. "What exactly did you do in the Army? Did you really jump out of airplanes? Are you married? Do you have kids? Where are you living now? What do you think about our company? What can you add to our board? Are you considering any other boards? "

Later that night Dick jokingly told me that he and the CEO had arm-wrestled any naysayers in the hallway and were ready to move forward. The next step was a board meeting on June 5, 2013, with key shareholders to get their buy-in. I was not invited to this in person but was told to call in after the CEO had the discussion and support of the entire group.

I sat at home waiting to call in at 10:00 a.m. per the instructions e-mailed to me. My first attempt to call in failed. Where is my secretary or aide-de-camp when I need them? Oh, that was my last life. I tried again. Now it's 10:05. I join the meeting by conference call. The CEO says, "Congratulations, Ann. Welcome to our board."

"Thank you, Chairman. I am honored and excited. I look forward to joining your team." I hung up and immediately ran into Craig's office to tell him the news.

I now serve on the boards of two Fortune 500 companies; one defense, L3 Communications (LLL); one nondefense, Republic Services Group (RSG); and a third not-for-profit company, Logistics Management Institute (LMI). On the two Fortune 500 boards I am the only female sitting at the table. Fortunately I serve on boards that are committed to changing the status quo. Each is rethinking what makes a board most effective and reflective of its consumers' and shareholders' interests. Our boards are looking beyond the traditional CEO/general counsel/CFO roles. Experience in those roles is central to the success of any board, but different backgrounds and fields—marketing, logistics, communications, technology—are equally important in a globally connected business universe.

WHEN THE EVIL QUEEN looks into the magic mirror and asks the fateful question, "Who's the fairest of them all?" she really just wants confirmation of what she already believes. When the magic mirror tells her something she doesn't want to hear, well, all hell breaks loose. In our daily lives I call this misguided need for affirmation and tuning out other perspectives the Mirror, Mirror Syndrome.

Interest in diversity, especially in the military, is a relatively new focus area. It is too easy and convenient for folks to view it as the continuation of affirmative action and quotas for minorities and the disadvantaged. Policies established to promote equal opportunity and equal employment were often viewed as forced inclusiveness rather than recognizing that prejudices and biases existed and we needed policy in order to move forward.

Historically, all organizations of every demographic—military, political, or corporate—have traditionally taken on the senior leaders' characteristics. Once established, it's a difficult paradigm to break. What I'd found in the Army—and I suspected that it wasn't much different in corporate America—was that conservative, older, white males were making the primary decisions. That was just a fact. They were not evil people. Much of what I'm describing is a result of traditionally accepted roles for males and females. By force of habit they surround themselves with what they like to see: people to whom they can relate. They have the same education, the same mission focus, and the same experiences, and they look at problems through the same color lens. So it should be no surprise that they naturally have a tendency to agree. These leaders are often wildly successful. But in my view their organizations will never realize their full potential without leveraging the power of diversity.

I saw this firsthand in the corporate world when I met Ted Childs, the lead diversity officer at IBM, in the late 1990s. IBM is an organization that was at one time a clear reflection of the Mirror, Mirror syndrome: all white males, dark suits, white shirts, black shoes, and black ties. How does a white male know what a female likes or dislikes in personal computers? How does this guy know what a person from China likes in a personal computer? Or a Japanese or Hispanic consumer? They don't. Childs, an African American, set out to demonstrate the power of diversity. He hired the best of the best—white males, females, Chinese, Japanese, African Americans, Hispanics, and other minorities—to help customize IBM's products to best support the customer. Not surprisingly, revenues increased.

Although the power of diversity is sometimes hard to quantify, Childs definitely got my attention. His success revealed a few points: (1) diversity wasn't about numbers or quotas—having one of these and one of those—it was about diversity of thought, and not just anyone's thought but the best-of-the-best thoughts; and (2) these folks had to have a platform from which their ideas could be heard and implemented.

I have experienced the horrible feeling of being the lone voice in all-male forums when it was very difficult to be heard. A new idea could easily be dismissed by a few heads shaking or simply by deft silence in the room. If I felt strongly about something, I would repeat it, and if I really felt strongly about something, I would have to raise my voice or throw out a four-letter word to get their attention: "You guys are coming up with the same old shit solutions that haven't worked in the past!"

I remember specifically one heated discussion in the Pentagon concerning whether we needed to put a major logistics services contract supporting the war effort in Iraq and Afghanistan back out for bid, known as recompeting. At the table was the senior leadership of the Army; the highest-ranking uniformed generals along with the political appointee civilians who are the inner circle for the Secretary of the Army. The generals knew how difficult a recompete would be for continuity in the war zone, but the political appointees were adamant that the Army must recompete the contract. One official stated emphatically that if we don't, "The Army will get a black eye." I couldn't believe my ears! The General Accounting Office, Army Audit Agency, and our business case analysis all supported extending the in-place contract. Because it was my contract to manage, I had talked to the senior commander in Iraq and asked for his thoughts, and he said, "Ann, if we don't get to keep the same contract, we'll risk meeting the presidential mandate [timeline] for exiting Iraq." I also had a copy of the operational impact letter he had sent to the Chief and the Secretary outlining the risks associated with not extending the existing contract. So when the conversation continued toward directing a new contract initiative, I was mad. I straightened up in my chair and told the assembled group, "If you are going to demand we recompete this contract contrary to the analysis and against the advice of your senior commander in Iraq, then we better be prepared to tell the president that we may not make his deadlines to get our equipment out of Iraq." They just stared at me, but in the end we extended the contract.

What I witnessed during my military career was a steady effort by leadership to better understand and appreciate the power of diversity. I watched the doors continue to open. When I joined the Army women weren't even allowed to serve in the 82nd Airborne band, attend West Point, serve in units whose primary mission was direct combat, fly fighter planes, or serve on a tank.

While corporate America was discovering the value of diversity in winning over shareholders, the military was realizing the importance of diversity in waging and winning wars. In the midst of the longest period of sustained combat in American military history, General George Casey had the vision and courage to champion diversity. As troops continued to serve in Iraq following the capture and execution of Saddam Hussein, Casey unveiled a new task force charged with building on what should be the Army's greatest strength.

> The purpose of the task force is to increase awareness and to inform ourselves about how we need to adapt what we're doing so we can sustain awareness and focus on diversity. I will tell you that I firmly believe the strength of our Army comes from our diversity, I started getting a sense, that because of everything going on, because of the war, because of how stretched we were, that it caused a perception that we were done, that we had licked this already, that people weren't paying [diversity] the attention that is due. So we need to do something to energize folks and change the focus of folks on diversity.
>
> Army News Service, November 30, 2007

With this announcement the Chief of Staff of the Army created the Army Diversity Office. Prior to the creation of this office the term *diversity* was not even part of the Army lexicon. This new office, in working with the Recruiting Command, found that the Army was not an accurate reflection of the face of America. There were growing numbers of Hispanics in America, but the Army did not reflect that growth. The task force also learned that work-life balance issues made it difficult for trained Army females to continue to serve after having children. Finally, the office discovered that the Army was not doing enough to attract the best and brightest from diverse communities around the country.

Progress has been made. The percentage of enlisted women has grown seven-fold since the end of the draft in 1973. As of 2010, 14 percent of the enlisted force are women and 16 percent of the commissioned officers are women. Female minorities are finding greater opportunities. Black females (31 percent) and Hispanic females (16.9 percent) represent nearly half of the females on active duty, while the same categories of males make up less than 30 percent.

Today the Army has a publicized diversity definition: "The different attributes, experiences, and backgrounds of our Soldiers, Civilians, and Family Members that further enhance our global capabilities and contribute to an adaptive, culturally astute Army." The complete strategy and roadmap are public record.

Change takes time, and recruiting and developing leaders takes time. Without a balanced representation of soldiers from different backgrounds in the Army ranks, our ability to grow diverse leaders is challenging. There is far too often a tendency to surround ourselves with people who mirror us and to promote people in our own image. In reality, however, this approach provides a false sense of security that you are spot-on in your decision making. The best way to have healthy debates and find the optimal solution to very complex problems is to have the best and brightest group of people who can offer diverse perspectives. I came from a middle-class, military background. My family and social circles shared similar views. Had I only sought people with the same upbringing, my teams wouldn't have been as successful. But being inclusive—leveraging the different attributes, experiences, and background of our soldiers, civilians, and family members—helped me look at things in ways I probably would never have considered. That's the power of diversity of thought.

I first met Coca-Cola Chairman and CEO Muhtar Kent when he visited the Pentagon as a guest of the Chief of Staff on November 8, 2010. The Army has long looked at business and industry in an attempt to stay current with best business practices. During our first meeting Kent, a Turkish American educated in London, shared that he implemented an aggressive program to increase the number of women on his senior management team. Through a market survey of customers Muhtar learned that women make more than 70 percent of the purchasing decisions when it comes to his product lines. Yet when he looked around the table at senior management meetings, only a couple women were in the room—less than 20 percent. He initiated a career development program for women with the stated goal of ensuring that half his leadership team be female by 2020.

On March 18, 2012, Muhtar invited my husband, Craig, and me to Atlanta to meet with his team and give a presentation on leadership and the power of diversity. When Craig asked Kent whether the men in his organization were feeling left out, he just chuckled. He responded thoughtfully and emphasized that talented people never have to worry about finding opportunity. Coca-Cola Company ranked No. 33 on *DiversityInc*'s Top 50 Companies for Diversity for 2014, up five spots from 2013. This marks the company's twelfth consecutive appearance on the list." Anyone who visits the Coca-Cola headquarters will see diversity in action. You see diversity in action by seeing a variety of people from different backgrounds with different experiences in leadership positions across the organization. It is the knowledge that your leadership team will be more effective if it has diversity of thought in the decision-making process. It is not just about diversifying the employer for the initial-entry work force; it's about embracing diversity of thought in management and in key leadership teams. When employees can look up and see themselves in the leadership team they will see hope and opportunity.

When I joined the Army many of our organizations were designed by function—infantry units, supply units, aviation units, transportation units—making diversification of talent more challenging. On a larger scale I would say it was similar to the parochial and cultural differences between the services—Army, Air Force, Marines, Navy, and Coast Guard. Today we have less functional units and more multifunctional, and we have less single-service operations and more joint operations—all leveraging the power of diversity of thought and experience.

By the summer of 2002 I was expecting a new assignment. I called Craig as soon as I hung up the phone: "I just got the call—we're going to the Military Traffic Management Command" (MTMC). That was all I knew; I couldn't answer any of his questions: "Where is that located? What do they do? Who will you work for?" He called me back in fifteen minutes. "I think it's located at Fort Eustis near Virginia Beach," he said. "Wouldn't that be a nice change?" He also said, "It's hard to tell, as they have some sort of facility in the Hoffman Building inside the DC beltway. I'm not sure who they work for, but it's either Army Materiel Command [AMC] or the United States Transportation Command [TRANSCOM]. I'm still not sure what they do, but it sounds like some sort of military police or transportation business."

I thought this was a mistake. *Traffic management?* I couldn't stop thinking about the scene from the movie *Patton* when George C. Scott is standing in the middle of a muddy intersection in Italy. Traffic is at a standstill, with convoys of military trucks all blasting their horns, trying to cross the intersection, no one yielding, everyone trying to be first. There's General Patton, with riding crop in hand, directing truck after truck to stop or go, finally getting the convoys moving. Is that what my life has come to, directing traffic?

When I assumed command of MTMC as a brand-new two-star general in September of 2002 I was the first Quartermaster officer ever to be selected to command this outfit. This was the premier and most highly coveted two-star command for the Transportation Corps (TC), and every commander in its history had been a transportation officer. MTMC was the Army component of US TRANSCOM, a joint Combatant Command headquarters. MTMC was responsible for all surface transportation of commercial trucks, rail, and seaborne vessels along with the seaports to support them. The Air Force component of TRANSCOM controls all military and commercial airlift operations, and the Navy component of TRANSCOM controlled the military supply vessels. We were a nation at war in the aftermath of 9/11, and these component commands were extremely busy moving the military forces, equipment, and the steady flow of supplies to the war. Between December 1, 2002, and May 31, 2003, MTMC shipped 112,064 containers on commercial vessels. Lined up end to end, the containers would have equaled 448 miles, or a round trip between Washington, DC, and New York City. We shipped more than 18,000 shipments of ammunition, using 6,168 rail cars and 108,500 trucks. We loaded more than 50 million square feet of vehicles and equipment on 331 vessels, or the equivalent of 1,036 football fields.

I still couldn't figure out why they had selected me for this command. If I couldn't figure out why I had been selected, you can imagine the reaction from the Transportation community, particularly the retired senior officers. At the change of command ceremony I felt as if I were on display like a rare exotic animal at the zoo. I received few of the normal congratulatory hugs and handshakes. A couple of weeks later I ran into the then Chief of Staff of the Army, General Eric Shinseki, at a reception at the Fort Meyer Officers Club. I thanked him for putting his trust and confidence in me to run MTMC. He smiled and shared that he had been blasted with e-mails from the retired generals from the transport command community. He had reached out to several of the active-duty transport command generals, asking them whether they could quiet down the retired generals. No luck, the protests continued. Finally General Shinseki sent a note to several of the loudest complainers and told them that he had personally reviewed the potential candidates and that I was the clear top choice. "We have a tough fight in front of us [mobilizing for Iraq]," he said, "and I selected the best-qualified general officer for the job. If they knew of someone better qualified, then speak up." Crickets.

In this situation the diversity issue was more about the questioning of qualifications to do the job. I wasn't a transporter by trade; I was a muddy boots, multifunctional supply officer. They thought I was in their rice bowl, their area of expertise, which was no place for outsiders. They are the same people who will say, "Because that's the way we've always done it."

Later, in October of 2005, I earned my third star and was named director of logistics for the Army, becoming the first female officer to serve in that position. This was a three-star post that reports to the Chief of Staff of the Army and provides guidance and oversight in logistics, sustainment, and maintenance. The Chief of Staff heads the military side of the Department of the Army.

The Chief of Staff also has a four-star vice chief, a three-star director, and a primary staff of three-star generals who are called deputy chiefs of staff and then the name of their functional specialty. These specialties include personnel, intelligence, operations, logistics, communications, budget, and resources. I was the deputy Chief of Staff, logistics. I was the only female, and the deputy Chief of Staff, personnel, Lieutenant General Mike Rochelle, was the only African American. We were a testament that the Army was taking diversity seriously, and there are many more such examples. But it didn't take long to realize that there was work ahead. That's when I officially met the Three Kings.

At any given time there are right around fifty lieutenant generals in the Army. The most prestigious jobs are commanding the Corps War fighting headquarters like the 18th Airborne Corps. But arguably the most powerful and influential of the three-stars are the Three Kings. Although I was aware of the Three Kings, I had few dealings with them until I arrived at the Pentagon. The Three Kings made all the critical budget recommendations. They consisted of a trio of three-star generals: the Army director of operations, the Army budget officer, and Army director of resources. Each was West Point–educated, usually a combat arms officer. And, of course, each was a white male.

They were the right hands of the Chief of Staff of the Army and his vice Chief of Staff, advising them on important resourcing decisions. They were good friends. But on the surface there was nothing diverse about the group—same academic background, same training, same combat focus. Same old, same old.

The Three Kings were assembled shortly after 9/11 in response to the need to make rapid financial decisions based on the fickle availability of supplemental funding provided by Congress to support the war. The Pentagon is a massive bureaucracy, and the Three Kings were designed to cut through the red tape and make rapid and responsive recommendations to the Chief. They very well represented the fighting force of the Army, the combat arms. Staff members such as myself rarely had a chance to voice our opinions or concerns.

Once, they decided to cancel the distribution of equipment after we had already spent money on the repair, modifications, and upgrades of the equipment in favor of buying new equipment. Another time they reduced funding for depot-level repairs after we had already paid to transport the equipment to the depots and had the workload scheduled. Trust me, the Three Kings were great leaders, colleagues, and friends. They excelled at making crucial real-time decisions in an ever-changing and highly politicized environment. But I am convinced that had the triumvirate been a more diverse and larger group, it would have made even better decisions, particularly in important noncombat areas.

By the time I arrived, the Kings had built their sheltered, three-tiered fiefdom. First, you had to go see the Three Wise Guys (three colonels). Next came the Three Wise Asses (my term of endearment for the three brigadier or major generals—it was really Three Wise Men). Finally came the Three Kings. We always had to start with the Wise Guys, regardless of our rank. The Three Wise Guys could summarily veto high-ranking leaders, with their concerns never even reaching the Three Kings. It was infuriating and insulting.

Because of their combat mindset, the Three Kings focused on military muscle such as tanks, helicopters, and precision-guided munitions. They were less concerned with sustaining these systems or the needed automation to manage or track them. We still did not have a modern system to track and manage all of our equipment. We once discovered seventy tanks on Fort Hood, Texas, that no one in the Army, except a few folks on Fort Hood, knew were there. If you are the Three Kings and you can't see it and you need it, you buy more. It was a very expensive and ineffective way to do business.

When subordinates—not even the Kings themselves—had told me *no* one too many times I turned to the Army Chief of Staff for guidance. First, I told him the moniker was arrogant and absurd. *Three Kings—really?*

The Chief laughed. "You know my wife always picks up on those things. It never occurred to me that the name of the group was exclusive or even offensive or that it lacked any diversity of thought." Even the vice Chief of Staff, General Cody, joked later, "Ann, maybe it should be called the Three Kings and a Queen." I'm sure there were a few other suggested names like Witch or another one that rhymes with it. I suggested he add new voices and perspectives to the decision-making process to guarantee that multiple options were presented to him and that potential unintended consequences of these decisions could be discussed.

I was insistent that my voice be heard on issues of equipment repair and sustainment. Who in the Three Kings could be objective enough to recognize that their views might be myopic? It was classic Mirror, Mirror Syndrome. Intentional or not, this homogenous group told the boss what they thought he wanted to hear because they were trained to think the same way. The Chief ultimately changed the unofficial moniker from Three Kings to the Budget Review Process, but his boys' club didn't alter much. High-level preparation sessions, however, became more inclusive of the specific stakeholders affected by big decisions. It was a small but important step in diversifying the thought process and makeup of Army leadership.

The Three Kings didn't have a monopoly on lack of diversity. My very own logistics team was guilty of the same offense. When I was appointed director of logistics, I was surprised to find that for the first time I had a different diversity issue: most of my senior leadership team, around ten people, was white and *female*. A few months later I had a key vacancy due to a retirement. I needed a new civilian deputy, a two-star equivalent job and a really important hire for me. I hoped to go through the normal civilian personnel process of advertising, interviewing, and selecting the most qualified candidate while hopeful that I could alter the makeup of what most perceived as the logistics girls' club. When the slate of candidates was formed, the clear best résumés were women's. I wasn't going to settle for a lesser-qualified candidate for the job, as I've always lived by the practice of hiring the most qualified person for any position.

I decided to call my former deputy from my previous job as the Combined Arms Support Command (CASCOM) at Fort Lee, Virginia, Tom Edwards, to discuss my dilemma, and see whether there was any chance he might want a change of scenery. I was pretty sure he would have little interest in leaving Fort Lee, some ninety miles down Interstate 95 from my office at the Pentagon. Tom Edwards was an icon on Fort Lee. He had been the civilian deputy to what must have seemed to him like an endless succession of CASCOM commanders. He truly was the institutional continuity on Fort Lee in regard to every logistics issue facing the Army. He had been there so long that he knew more about the organization than anyone on the installation: what worked, what didn't work, what had been tried and tested, and what had failed. He was smart, articulate, and a genuine people person.

"Tom Edwards speaking."

"Tom, this is Ann Dunwoody."

"Hey, General, how are you?"

"I'm doing great . . . except that I'm up here inside this five-sided building!"

We continued our small talk, catching up on the current thoughts of the day. Finally cutting to the chase, I said, "Tom, I'm calling to ask you whether you would consider being my deputy. Don't say anything yet. I know you have no desire to move and probably don't think you have any reason to move, but hear me out. Listen, I know you have never been up here, but I've only been here a month, and all I know is that *you* are the one I need to be my civilian deputy."

"But General, I've never even been in the Pentagon before."

I got on a roll—and turned into a headhunter.

"Tom, I know that, and that's probably what makes you such a great candidate for the job. You're not a bureaucrat, and you know more about logistics than anyone I know. Tom, folks up here respect you, and you could really help get things done. You can certainly help take on the logistical challenges we have up here at Army level, and they are tough."

I'm sure he wished he had never taken this phone call. Turning down a request from a former boss and friend is hard—and I expected he would. But I had to try. The good news was he didn't say no and hang up. Convincing his wife, Susan, would be the real test. She was thriving in her own successful career, and a move north was not part of her plan. It was not an easy sell, but after much consideration and discussion, they figured out a way they could make it work. Touchdown!

It was a great hire, and I now had one of most astute professional logistical minds ever helping me collaborate with the rest of the Army and other military services on the difficult issues of the day. His accomplishments were recognized when he was named one of the Department of the Army's top Civilians of the Year by receiving the Meritorious Civilian Service Medal by the Secretary of the Army. He made his reputation by modernizing Army logistics for the future. He was instrumental in reducing our logistic footprint by pursuing the use of a new logistics IT system called Battle Command Sustainment Supply System (BCS3) and pushing for more reliable equipment. More reliability meant fewer people required to maintain it and less hardware to fix it. Tom completed our team.

As I mentioned, I'm a huge fan of *The Wizard of Oz*. In many ways it's an example of Diversity 101 for the military and corporate America. Dorothy was short on self-confidence, but she had the unique ability to unite and inspire others through her kindness. She also had the basic common sense that many leaders lack as they overlook important details. The Scarecrow was in search of a brain, but he provided emotional support and served as a calming influence for Dorothy. As her first partner along the Yellow Brick Road, he became a trusted lieutenant. The Tin Man lacked a heart but was always quick to stand up for Dorothy whenever she was threatened in the Land of Oz. Good leaders, particularly in the Army, always value the people willing to take a bullet for them without hesitation. As for the Cowardly Lion, he appeared to be a hopeless case. We all are familiar with people who are all bark and no bite, but Dorothy had the compassion to bring him into the fold. Like the Tin Man, the Lion became a loyal friend whose courage grew because Dorothy believed in him. Although created on the silver screen, this type of diversity and understanding can be invaluable in a corporate setting.

Diversity can mean different things to different people. For me it really is about diversity of thought, and I was always looking for diverse personalities as well. I have always been a big fan of the Myers-Briggs Type Indicator Test. For those who have not taken the test before, it's a leadership tool that portrays individual personality preferences and styles. Not only does it reveal how you prefer to think, lead, and interact, but it also measures the degree or intensity of your preferences.

I'm an ENFP (Extroverted, Intuitive, Feeling, and Perceiving). When I first took the test the administrator told me that less than 1 percent of the Army officers were ENFPs, with the vast majority being ISTJs (Introvert, Sensing, Thinking, Judging), just the opposite of me. Your typical ENFP tends to be an idea person, enthusiastic, adaptable, and creative—a real people person. If you ask people who know me, they would tell you that pretty much hits the mark.

My husband is an ISTJ, so opposites do attract. His profile traits lean toward being organized and decisive, and he maintains an "if it ain't broke, don't fix it" approach. There are no good or bad personality types, and there are only sixteen different combinations. They are just a reflection of how you prefer to process and react. So as well as finding a good balance of talented people of different races, religions, backgrounds, and genders, I liked to get a good balance of leadership preferences as well.

When the Army decided to disband the WAC and integrate women into the regular Army, I was as excited as I was determined to help lead the effort. From that time forward, even as a 2nd lieutenant, I pushed back on any efforts that would clump women together, whether it was an all-female squad or an all-female PT formation. I didn't want to be the female platoon leader of all the women in the company, and I didn't want to be the platoon leader responsible for inspecting women's uniforms in the company; I wanted to be responsible for leading and supervising an integrated platoon of soldiers.

When I returned to Fort Bragg in 2000 as the first female general officer ever assigned, it was a big deal in the local media. At the change of command ceremony where I took command of the 1st COSCOM I saw row upon row, column after column of soldiers. Black, white, brown, and red men and women—all standing tall at attention. They were proud, they were a team, and diversity was obvious and thriving.

Soon after my return several women who I had served with before approached me, and they had a plan. To honor my return to Fort Bragg as a general and put the spotlight on the accomplishments of women, they wanted to do an all-women parachute jump, complete with an all-women flight crew from our neighbor installation at Pope Air Force Base. They were far along in their planning and were so excited.

Ma'am, I'm Major Cindy Pollock, XO for the 530th. Congratulations on coming back to Fort Bragg and commanding the 1st Corps Support Command. We are so excited. If I may be so bold to suggest to you . . . but we thought in honor of your return and your assignment . . . perhaps we should organize an all-female jump . . . you know, women pilots, women paratroopers, women jump masters, and women safeties. What do you think?

I was taken aback. All of my career I had fought for the integration of women, and now someone was proposing a segregated event. I was honored she felt so proud, but I couldn't see the value of this event. I saw no upside to drawing this attention to ourselves. I told her, "I've spent my whole career trying to support the integration of women into the Army, and this kind of activity seems to counter that. Don't get me wrong—I'm so proud that we could even have the opportunity to conduct an all-women event like this." When I told her I was very appreciative but didn't think it was appropriate to celebrate my return to Fort Bragg with an all-female airborne operation, she was very disappointed.

I hope, like me, that she is proud that in 2011 a male battalion commander at Fort Benning, Georgia, home of the Army Airborne School, determined it was time to celebrate the four decades of women in the airborne community. This officer had witnessed the contributions of female paratroopers and respected the fact that they all trained together to the same standard. He had seen the emergence of female "Black Hat" instructors at the school and felt that the time was right for an all-female jump to commemorate the anniversary.

When I saw the video tape of the 2011 all-female jump I couldn't help but think we had come full circle. I thought back to the poster from when I was a student at Fort Benning, "Paratrooper: last step to becoming a man." I thought about my 82nd Airborne Division commander who wouldn't even allow female paratroopers on his plane. The integration was now invisible, and the celebration by our male counterparts had more impact than any celebration we could have done for ourselves.

What I did learn over the years is that female-only sessions are important and necessary. Women talk about female issues a lot more freely when they are not surrounded by the guys they work with every day. Discussions about harassment, assault, respect, fitness, and pregnancy are discussions that will be much more open, honest, and candid without the presence of their male counterparts. Similarly, males will be more open to discuss their own issues, biases, and challenges with female soldiers in their ranks without women present. Since my retirement I have participated in women veteran forums, and it is clear that women-only forums like Veteran Women Igniting the Spirit of Entrepreneurship (V-WISE) provide a safe haven for honest and open discussions for women who have different issues from men.

Confusion over what diversity really means and why it is considered a strength will likely remain for the foreseeable future. I believe the strength in diversity comes from being able to leverage diversity of thought. It's about creating teams of people from various backgrounds to solve complex problems. They need to strategize and provide a full range of alternatives and ideas that allow leaders to make the best-informed decisions.

To maximize potential—be it in a war zone, Wall Street, or Main Street—leaders need to look in the mirror and at their immediate surroundings to figure out what's missing. Those courageous enough to embrace the power of diversity will thrive.

eight

✶ ✶ ✶ ✶

CALL ME COACH

"Form Your Winning Team"

AS A SIXTH GRADER, I couldn't wait for recess. Most of the boys pretended to be Johnny Unitas or Bart Starr. But those Hall of Famers had nothing on my all-time favorite quarterback: Mrs. Faulkner. She was tall and lean with dirty blonde hair. She wore the same uniform in the classroom and on the playground—a black, midcalf, A-line skirt and a white blouse. Her plain-Jane appearance belied her athleticism. She would rifle bullet spirals as the kids shouted, "Mrs. Faulkner! Mrs. Faulkner! Over here! Over here! Throw it to me, Mrs. Faulkner!"

I never wanted anyone to say I threw like a girl or a boy. I wanted to throw like Mrs. Faulkner. She motivated me to excel in academics and sports.

"Ladies, you can be smart and athletic," she would always tell the girls in the class.

Many of my earliest memories involved sports. I always played— kickball, tetherball, dodge ball . . . anything. I was a sports omnivore.

Back in those days we had the annual President's Fitness Awards program started by President Kennedy. Bar hang, fifty-yard dash, softball throw, pushups, and situps. It was a mini-Army PT test. If you excelled, you got a patch. I earned one every year. When I moved to middle school in seventh grade my physical education teacher and coach was Mrs. Snodgrass. She was about five-foot-five with short blonde hair and a head-turning laugh that would fill a gym or playground. She encouraged me to get into tumbling and, eventually, gymnastics. I was pretty good at tumbling and floor exercise. I also learned the basics of the balance beam, uneven bars, and vaulting. Prior to Mrs. Snodgrass and Mrs. Faulkner, most of my female PE teachers seemed better suited for home economics.

Through sports I traveled all over Europe in the late 1960s and early 1970s. My dad was stationed in Belgium, and I attended a Department of Defense (DOD)–sponsored high school all four years. We didn't have organized leagues the way kids do now. Our teachers did their best to moonlight as coaches. They would load us into vans and drive to competitions against the other DOD schools throughout Germany, England, and Belgium. It was great fun. Although they weren't highly trained coaches, our teachers made it fun. They also were my inspiration to pursue a career in coaching and physical education.

My graduating class had just fifty-five students. As a small high school, we were doing well just to field boys' football and basketball teams. Cheerleading was the most popular activity for girls. It was rewarding and gave us a taste of freedom. My cheerleading teammates, including my younger sister Jackie, were terrific friends. Girls' athletics in my high school equated to doing the splits, handsprings, and high jumps on the football field and the basketball court instead of on a gymnastics apparatus. The skills and team spirit I had learned in junior high had transferred well. I was on the cheerleading squad throughout high school.

My mom pushed all of her kids to be active in sports. She was a hell of a tennis player. Mom was about five-foot-two, 110 pounds, and her legs and arms were toned. Her ever-present suntan made her look even more athletic. Her mom had severe arthritis, and growing up I can't ever remember seeing Grandma without a cane or a walker. Mom was supersensitive to and even in fear of inheriting her mom's health issues, so she stayed on the go. My sisters and I could hardly keep up with Mom as she double-timed through the shopping malls.

. She played tennis at least three times a week right up to the day she suffered a stroke. She stretched every morning, even though it hurt to "get out all the kinks." She was such a competitor on the tennis court, competing and winning age-group tournaments with her dear friend Roberta in their late seventies. I rarely beat my mom. Her drop shots and precision volleys were the stuff of Billie Jean King. If you were her doubles partner and hit a ball long or into the net, she'd give you a look before saying, "That's all right—we'll get the next point." She would celebrate every winning point with a high-five, a fist pump, or comment like, "All right, let's go!" When she won she was ecstatic, and when she lost she was somber and almost pouty, but only for a minute or two. She fought being old, she fought being slow, and she fought inactivity. Even when Mom was in the hospital after her stroke, she kept that champion spirit. Roberta came to visit her in the hospital, and as she was leaving, Roberta told Mom she would be back to see her in a couple of days. "Bring your racquet!" Mom replied.

While living in Europe I traveled to Spain with my friend Donna to attend Lew Hoad's tennis camp. Hoad was star player from Australia who won four major championships and was once the top-ranked amateur in the world. As teenagers, we felt like grownups traveling by ourselves. The experience solidified my love for the game.

When it came time to attend college I selected the State University of New York at Cortland largely because it had one of the country's top physical education programs. It also was only a few hours from my mom's hometown of Randolph, New York.

That's where she was heading with my younger siblings, Bill and Jackie, while Dad prepared to deploy to Vietnam. I sensed that she wanted me closer to home while Dad was so far away, fighting another war.

I inherited Mom's passion for all sports. I continued to play at the highest levels available to women in college. I loved my four years at Cortland. I was challenged socially, intellectually, and, of course, athletically. Those were the days just before Title IX. Cortland was an athletics-minded university that had a robust offering of NCAA-sanctioned teams for men: basketball, football, baseball, and lacrosse. The sports opportunities for women were limited. But I wasn't resentful about the male sports and rooted the guys to victory, although I did wish we had more opportunities for women.

Today I have four nieces who all excelled at Division I sports. In the pre–Title IX days, however, that wasn't possible. My biggest frustration was that women couldn't letter in most sports or earn athletic scholarships; instead, we received certificates. They weren't even typed. I recently stumbled across one of the many I earned from gymnastics and tennis.

The magic marker used on the paper is fading. It reads,

Certificate of Athletic Award
    This Certifies that
    Ann Dunwoody
    of State University of New York College at Cortland
    has been awarded this certificate for
    Intercollegiate Gymnastics (Floor Exercise)
    May 17, 1972

My tennis and gymnastics coaches weren't deterred. They were always positive and upbeat. They focused on teaching us, training us, and having a winning spirit.

Sylvia Stokes was my tennis coach at Cortland State. She wasn't even on the Cortland faculty, but she volunteered to coach our fledgling tennis program. She taught me to never confuse enthusiasm with capability. That lesson has saved me time and time again. I was a sparkplug and loved being on the team. In addition to getting us prepared, Coach Stokes was adept at soothing the bruised egos of players who would have to sit out.

I played singles and, occasionally, doubles. Quite frankly, it meant more to me to be part of the team than to win my individual match, despite my ultracompetitive nature, which I credit to my mom. When Cortland honored me with an honorary doctorate degree in 2007, I was tickled to see Coach Stokes in attendance. I thanked her for teaching us to believe in ourselves. She reminded me of my mom. Spirited, full of life, with endless optimism, she seemed to have infinite tips and tricks to give us an edge on the court. "Charge the net, hit it hard and deep, or hit a high lob with spin to the baseline." In doubles it was "hit down the middle or hit sharp angles left or right, look one way and hit it another." In the fall of 1972 we had a 7–1 record—the best in years for the women's team.

Our gymnastics program at Cortland was first-rate but still a far cry from the quality of today's intercollegiate programs. Dr. Toni Tiburzi is a real Cortland legend. She was Pat Summitt–esque long before Summitt led the Tennessee Volunteers to the pinnacle of women's college basketball. She would have made Jim Valvano proud with her "never give up" approach to life, school, and sports. She desperately tried to teach me, the hyper tomboy, a little bit of style and grace during practice routines. I was more of a tumbler than a ballerina. I still have nightmares about falling off the balance beam, and this remains a great source of humor for my husband. He laughs at the fact that I'm afraid of static heights, particularly ledges of any kind, even though I never thought twice about jumping out of airplanes anywhere, anytime. I guess trying to perform four feet off the ground on a four-inch-wide beam can be more intimidating than jumping out of a plane from one thousand feet while strapped with military equipment. Our women's gymnastics team won New York state champions three years in a row, with Queens College and Ithaca College behind us in second and third. The last year, 1975, I placed second for Cortland on floor exercise behind my teammate Pat Evans, who placed first. Pat went on to place third overall in the state championships.

In 2011 I was presented with the NCAA's Theodore Roosevelt Award in San Antonio, Texas. The "Teddy" is awarded annually to a person of national reputation and accomplishment who participated in intercollegiate athletics. I was thrilled to meet Bo Jackson, pro golfer Scott Verplank, and my favorite baseball manager, Joe Girardi. They were honored by the NCAA with Silver Anniversary awards. But the highlight of the evening was the surprise attendance of Dr. Tiburzi, who I had not seen since leaving Cortland in 1975. The following year I was inducted into the Cortland State Athletic Hall of Fame, and I got to visit with Dr. Tiburzi once again. We proudly discussed how much had changed. Title IX leveled the playing for female scholar athletes. It dared girls to dream. Women's sports are now big draws, thanks to women such as Mia Hamm, Michelle Wie, Laila Ali, Lindsey Vonn, Ronda Rousey, Missy Franklin, Venus and Serena Williams, and many others.

Girls are now as likely to try out for softball, basketball, and volleyball as they are dance and cheerleading teams. The game has changed. But one thing will never change: athletes can always learn from winning and losing, regardless of the level of competition. Sports instill discipline, teach teamwork, and build character and confidence. The military is no different.

I'M STRUCK BY THE various meanings and the startling similarities between the words *coach* and *command*. Those in position of authority in the military are in command. They are in charge. If you are walking the sidelines of a football game, you are also in charge. But instead of being a commander, you are the coach. I find this to be very comforting because before I joined the Army all I ever wanted to do was be a physical education teacher and a coach. During my thirty-eight years in the Army many people thanked me for coaching them, but no one ever referred to me as "Coach." I must have said, "Thanks, Coach" thousands of times in high school and college. But in my military career, instead of coaching and building competitive, high-performing sports teams, I was coaching and building professional, high-performing units in the Army.

SET THE TONE

In the early 1990s, during my days in the 82nd Airborne Division, we were having a problem with soldiers driving under the influence of alcohol. As incentive to improve, the division commander proposed a training holiday or a day off if we could go eighty-two consecutive days without a DUI. At the entrance gate he posted a big neon sign to chart the progress. Early on, the tally rarely reached double figures. After most weekends the count would return to zero. I didn't think we were ever going to make it. Soldiers worked hard during the week and then partied harder on the weekends. Many weren't mature enough to have a designated driver or call a cab. Plus, the police were always on the lookout for unruly soldiers who frequented the many bars and strip clubs often located near military bases.

Eventually we started going longer without any DUIs—20 days, 36 days, 52 days. And the neon sign continued to keep count. Several of the higher-performing units were getting fed up. They were staying sober or at least not being stupid enough to get behind the wheel of a car after one too many, so they started putting pressure on the units that were responsible for the DUI offenses. Soldiers from all units started to feel peer pressure because when one person messed up, all fourteen thousand paratroopers suffered the consequences. In time we finally made it—82 days without a DUI. As I remember it took us about four months to reach our goal. A little more than two months later we reached 150 days.

Will you encourage your workers to be innovative, or will you promote an environment where the status quo is good enough? Do you have mechanisms to allow all employees to voice opinions and provide feedback without fear of retaliation? Are you accessible, or are you insulated from your people?

Good leaders motivate by being seen, by communicating, by engaging, and by taking care of their employees.

SET AND ENFORCE HIGH STANDARDS

In the Army soldiers generally know what they're supposed to do. I try not to walk by a mistake without responding. My husband still gets a little embarrassed when I stop a soldier in a store after work in his brown T-shirt without his Army combat uniform jacket or when I see a soldier whose haircut is not within regulation. Normally my husband drives our car when we're going on a military installation. The security force is always courteous and salutes, saying, "Have a nice day, Colonel." But recently I drove myself on post in civilian clothes, and the guard simply said to have a nice day. I asked him whether they didn't salute general officers anymore. He did a double-take at my ID—he was so embarrassed. He apologized and said he thought I was a dependent, a family member. If you don't correct it on the spot, you just set a lower standard.

The same is true in industry. One of my good friends, a fellow retired four-star general, happened to be driving behind a garbage truck on trash pickup day. The driver was causing a mess, as trash swirled out of the truck and onto the highway. The truck had one of those signs that read, "How's my driving? Call XXX-XXX-XXXX to report any problem." My friend called the number and asked a manager, "Are you in the trash collection or trash distribution business?" The manager thanked him. He later called my friend back to say he had talked to the driver and corrected the problem. Falling debris from a truck on a highway can lead to accidents and deaths, just as seemingly trivial human error can turn into environmental disasters. Great companies incentivize employees to correct the small things before catastrophe strikes.

REWARD GOOD PERFORMANCE AND CORRECT POOR PERFORMANCE

Taking care of outstanding performers and dealing with substandard performers may be two of the most important aspects of your day-to-day leadership. Some adhere to the 80 percent rule, meaning 20 percent of the workforce does 80 percent of the work. I wouldn't go that far.

But almost every organization has top-notch performers, say, 10 percent, who are self-starters and always exceed your expectations. They are your go-to men and women, and we usually overwork these folks because we know they will deliver.

There's also another 10 percent who are substandard performers. You wonder whether they are sick, lame, or just plain lazy. These might be the soldiers who were arrested and the judge gave them the option of going to jail or joining the Army. They are low performers, trying to get away with doing the least, to get around the system, and to get out of work.

The remainder, that 80 percent, are in the middle of the pack. They see it all. These soldiers come to work wanting to do their job and not wanting to get into trouble. They don't come to work trying to be the best; they just come to work to do their job. These are your average soldiers who try to meet the standard, not necessarily exceed it.

You build a high-performing organization one person at a time. Recognizing and rewarding good behavior is key along with taking noticeable corrective action. One of two things need to happen to the bottom 10 percent.

- They are reprimanded and eventually eliminated for lack of potential to be a good soldier/employee.
- They have a life-changing experience from a supervisor who cares and works hard to gain his supervisor's respect and admiration. Some people never had a parent or a supervisor who took them under their wing and made a real soldier/ employee out of them. The reverse is more often true: great supervisors try to make each and every person the best they can be and do so by training, spending time with them, and acknowledging their progress.

If the people in the middle of the pack don't see any consequences for poor performers or the recognition of outstanding performers, you will in essence affirm that mediocrity is okay. As leaders, our responsibility to reward the good, take corrective action on the bad, and try to incentivize the average to be better.

It's also important for coaches, bosses, and leaders to stand up for their people. I have learned so much from watching other leaders. Some techniques I liked; others I despised. One of my brigade commanders threw books at his subordinates when he got mad. He drove more good captains out of the Army than anyone. I tried talking one offended officer out of leaving the Army, telling this particularly bright young man that not all leaders hurled objects like a petulant child. This, unfortunately, was his second bad experience. "I've had it," he said, "and I'm not going to put up with this crap any longer." He quit. The brigade commander had no clue that his behavior was driving away the best and brightest, nor did he care. Fortunately he was never promoted again.

I watched an assistant division commander curse out two of my officers for not following his specific guidance during a convoy live-fire simulation. The exercise recreates an ambush, using live ammunition, while driving or riding in a vehicle. Training ammo is relatively safe and won't kill someone; live ammunition is deadly, so safety concerns are paramount. General David Petraeus, then a lieutenant colonel and battalion commander, was shot and wounded during one of his own live-fire exercises at Fort Campbell, Kentucky.

We had to train this infantry battalion because support personnel generally are more familiar with vehicle operations than are infantry soldiers. These particular soldiers were preparing for deployment to Bosnia. I was about thirty yards away and could not believe what I was hearing. The one-star general was letting f-bombs fly. *Are you f—ing kidding? This is f—ing ridiculous. You f—ing idiots call yourselves officers? Don't you know who the f— I am? Don't you see this f—ing star on my helmet?*

He stormed off as I walked over to check on my guys. After hearing the facts, I told my officers, "Guys, don't pay any attention to that guy." They had done an incredible job setting up the range. He was so busy unleashing his diatribe that my officers never had a chance to utter a word or plead their case. I'm glad I was never on the receiving end of one his rants. I'm not exactly sure what I would have done, but he wouldn't have turned and walked away without hearing from me. Funny—I knew that general for many years and had heard stories about his tirades but had never witnessed one. To me he was always courteous. Maybe he talked to women differently or considered me a peer.

As we watched the one star fly away, his boss, the division commander, was on approach in another helicopter to see the convoy setup. My officers were dreading another round of verbal shrapnel. Thankfully, I knew the general from the 82nd. He had been a wonderful coach and mentor for me over the years.

He was not only my division commander at Fort Drum but had also been an assistant division commander at Fort Bragg. He helped me get my job at the Pentagon working for the Chief of Staff of the Army by calling me up one day and asking whether I was interested in working for the Chief and then promptly made it happen. If we were about to screw up the live-fire exercise, I knew Major General Burnette (later, he became a Lieutenant General) would correct the situation in a professional manner—and not with a demoralizing profanity-laced outburst. He surveyed the setup and commended my officers for an exceptional job. "Guys, thanks for setting up the live-fire range on such short notice. It's very realistic. Glad you tied the medical evacuation drill into the range. This is exactly what I was looking for." He was so impressed that he gave each of them his commander's coin, a traditional token that recognizes outstanding performance on the spot. Burnette apologized for the ass-chewing my folks had just received. "I'll talk to him," he said. We exchanged salutes and off he went. After he left, I congratulated my officers.

BUILD A RECOGNIZABLE BRAND

People in uniform probably don't think of themselves as a walking, talking advertisement, but they are. Football players wear a uniform that promotes the team's brand. The logo is licensed and appears on Buccaneers T-shirts, Cowboys golf shirts, Saints hats, Giants purses, Broncos stadium cushions, and so on. People buy these items because they want to be identified with their team. When a technician comes to your house or office for a service call, chances are he'll arrive in a van or truck with the company logo and phone number on the side. Not only that, he will have a uniform or a shirt displaying the company logo that represents the corporate brand.

Military members are also branded by the uniforms and badges they wear. On my military work uniform was my name, DUN-WOODY, above one pocket and US ARMY over the other. On my left shoulder was a unit patch that told everyone that I was assigned to the Army Materiel Command. On my right shoulder was the distinctive Double-A of the 82nd Airborne Division. That patch told people I had been to a theater of war with the 82nd. Above my left pocket were two sets of wings, badges that denoted that I was a master parachutist and a parachute rigger. Our enlisted soldiers also wear distinctive unit crests on the front of the beret on top of the unit patch. The unit crests are also worn on the Army Service uniform to identify a soldier's unit. Every unit has their own unit crest and their own unit flag. Every soldier also has its current rank sewn on the front of its uniform right over their sternum. It's amazing how much a complete stranger could know about you before you ever say hello.

In 2008, I was proud to sew the AMC patch on my uniform for the first time. We were sixty-nine thousand strong, but only 3 percent were branded with military uniforms; the other 97 percent were civilians with no military identifiable brand. As I traveled around the organization I saw two corporate logos—one resembling the red, white, and blue AMC patch, and the other I thought was a relic, symbolizing our past: a yellow crest with "Arsenal of the Brave" stenciled on it. My first thought was that no Fortune 500 company would have two brands or logos, so why do we?

On my first trip to Rock Island, Illinois, to visit two of my subordinate commands, I received quite a surprise. As the first briefing started I noticed in the corner of each slide was a picture of a distinctive unit crest and no AMC logo. Not once during my visit did I even see a picture or sign of the AMC emblem. There was no evidence this command was even part of AMC. He was obviously very proud of his Army Sustainment Command. That afternoon I visited the Joint Munitions Command and saw the same thing. I quickly realized that these commanders and their employees had very little physical or personal connection to the AMC brand because they were not directly assigned to or collocated with my headquarters.

Imagine if every Nike store had their own logo, that the distinctive "swoosh" was nowhere to be found. I suspect their brand would be severely diluted. I started asking questions: "Why aren't you promoting yourselves as part of the AMC team?" No one had ever asked them that before. "Just doing what we've always done," they said. One slide that depicted all the partners they work with to get the mission done had fifteen different crests symbols, even though fourteen of the units depicted on the slide belonged to AMC. They were trying to show quantity, but I was more interested in unity.

Everyone is familiar with the AMC patch, but very few are familiar with the subordinate units' patch emblems or crests. "Guys, next time I come out here I want you to use the AMC patch with every AMC unit you have on this chart," I told them. "I want you to be proud to be part of the AMC team and help us promote the AMC brand."

"Yes ma'am."

Everyone wants to be on a winning team. Sometimes it takes the leader to show the workforce a little love and welcome them to the team. We launched a branding campaign by sending AMC branding "starter kits" to our sites around the world. The kits included flags, lapel pins, and signs. I rescinded all previous letters that allowed subordinate units to wear their own unit patch. Effective immediately, all military personnel were required to wear the AMC patch. Civilians, of course, weren't required to wear patches or emblems of any kind. But I made sure they would have access to an AMC lapel pin (a miniature red, white, and blue replica of our AMC patch).

Initially some wore the pins, but as others saw them, they wanted one too. Wherever I went I looked for the lapel pins. My admin folks got smart and started sending out boxes of lapel pins before every one of my visits so their work force would have access to them—they knew I'd be looking for them. When I saw someone wearing one, I'd stop and talk to them: "Hey, nice lapel pin. That pin looks real good on you. I'm proud to have you on the AMC team." I got smiles in return, some because they had just put it on and some because they probably would have never gotten one if I hadn't been on the lookout for one. People noticed. In short order it seemed that all of our senior executive civilians were wearing the AMC lapel pin instead of any other pin they previously wore.

People attending important client meetings could easily be identified with AMC. As our identity improved, our reputation skyrocketed. In Iraq AMC flags were flown and AMC emblems were painted on every facility we operated, even out in the most remote sites. When I held worldwide video conferences I could see the AMC emblem popping up in conference rooms and buildings. "Nice patch, but where is the AMC flag? I see your unit flag there," I'd ask.

"I'll take care of it, ma'am."

It was refreshing to see AMC branding become part of our karma. The Chief of Staff of the Army and the Secretary of the Army hold a holiday reception every year. They run shifts that last all day. I never said a word to anyone about wearing their lapel pin—they chose to. The vice chief in the receiving line said,

"Ann, I didn't know you had so many senior civilian executives until I saw so many AMC lapel pins coming through the line." I couldn't have been prouder.

Pride is not something you can order up; it's something the workforce has to feel. Wearing the AMC lapel pin was a signal to me that they were proud to be part of a global workforce. War fighters were no longer confused about who was providing the support on the battlefield. My four-star counterparts repeatedly complimented our work. "I never worried about logistics," they would say. That's the highest compliment a logistician can receive, especially during a period of constant war. Morale in our workforce soared. AMC had some swagger because people knew they were part of a winning team.

Brands also can be divisive. In the Army we used to have green tabs that denoted a select group of people. The highly coveted piece of green felt that was worn on both shoulders under the unit crest signified that you were a commander or a command sergeant major. In other words, you were a leader. The term was used frequently to announce various events like the "Green Tab run," the monthly four-mile, thirty-six-minute run for all the commanders and command sergeant majors in the division. Green Tab notes were sent out from division commanders to leaders throughout their divisions. When I was in the 82nd at Fort Bragg all commanders and command sergeant majors proudly wore the tabs. By 1990 I was the XO for the battalion when the new assistant division commander for operations (ADC-O) conducted a routine uniform inspection. "Major Dunwoody, why are your officers and NCOs wearing green tabs?"

"Sir, I received approval from Division Headquarters."

ASC-O: "Major Dunwoody, that is contrary to Army regulation. Green Tabs are only to be worn by combat arms leaders, not combat support or combat service support. Please inform your leaders they are not authorized to wear green tabs, and I will sort out guidance with Division Headquarters."

"Yes, sir."

Combat arms denotes the Infantry, Armor, Artillery, Air Defense, Aviation, and Special Forces of the Army. All others are considered support, and people in those career fields rarely rose to the top ranks of the Army. In some circles they were considered lesser roles or not as worthy as the combat arms. Even though, technically, it was policy that only combat leaders could wear the tabs, I never knew anyone who enforced it—letter of the law versus spirit of the law. It was an antiquated rule. I guess we were not worthy. I organized the ceremonial burning of all green tabs in our outfit. A bonfire was built, beer was poured, and the fire was lit.

One by one each person tossed their green tabs into the fire, saying, "Lord, I am not worthy." Other comments included, "I wonder if this means we don't have to participate in the green tab runs anymore," "Nothing quite like feeling like a second-class citizen," and "Yeah, this really makes you feel like part of the team."

Six years later I was commanding the Division Support Command at Fort Drum. Once again the division commander put out guidance that his commanders and command sergeant majors would wear the green tab—to hell with the policy. He believed leaders were leaders. During a visit to the Association of the United States Army (AUSA) annual conference, I wore my Class A uniform and green tabs. There is a wonderful opening reception in which everyone goes through a receiving line to shake the hands of the president of the association, the Chief of Staff of the Army, and the Sergeant Major of the Army. As I passed through the line, the Department of the Army Inspector General (DAIG), a three-star general, spotted me and questioned my audacity to wear the green tabs. He looked at me, then looked at my green tab–studded shoulders, and then looked back at me. "Colonel Dunwoody, why are you wearing green tabs?" *Here we go again*, I thought. At this point I didn't give a rat's behind if I ever wore or saw them again.

"Sir, I was told to wear green tabs by my division commander."

DAIG: "Well, you are not authorized to wear them—please remove them."

I responded with, "Yes, sir."

I called my division commander and told him what had happened. He was very apologetic and told me I needed to comply. "You don't have to worry about that, sir. They are already gone."

After a few beers at the next burning of the green tabs, pissed-off leaders commented, "This really sucks. I thought we were beyond this. Are we commanders and leaders, or not?"

I commented, "I'll never get suckered into putting these tabs on again, but we can't let this piece of green felt make us feel like second-class citizens."

Every service has certain symbols that can distinguish individuals or discriminate against them. These are not medals or badges that are earned but, rather, symbols. The green tab was the Army's way of recognizing the significance of the combat arms over combat support and combat service support. In the Air Force the highly sought-after brown leather jacket is a status symbol that only flyers can wear. In the Navy the aviators wear brown leather shoes instead of black. Although these are meant to be pride-instilling symbols, too often the pride turned to conceit or arrogance—a reason for the wearer to think less of others.

During his tenure as Army Chief of Staff, General Pete Schoomaker introduced the Army combat uniform in June 2004. It did away with branch insignia. He wanted the focus of the uniform to be on being a soldier, not whether he was a finance guy or an infantry guy. When the new Army service uniform, our service dress uniform, was introduced during this same period, it did away with green tabs altogether. The next edition of Army Regulation

670-1, Wear and Appearance of Army Uniforms and Insignia, which prescribes proper wear of uniforms, did not include wearing of the green tabs. Good riddance.

This new direction sent a powerful message to the entire Army: no matter what branch, no matter what your background, you are a soldier first. The uniform should always unite the force, not divide it.

As a high school and college athlete, I felt there was no greater feeling than putting on my uniform. Whether I was playing singles in tennis, competing at a gymnastics meet, cheering on the football and basketball teams, or encouraging my gymnastic and tennis teammates, being a part of a team was the ultimate adrenaline rush. We fought for each other. We pushed each other. We celebrated great victories and cried after heartbreaking losses. It taught me the power of team. It prepared me for life as a leader in the US Army.

I initially joined the Army as a timeout before I became a college coach and physical education professor. That transition never happened because the Army gave me the greatest coaching job. My mom, Mrs. Faulkner, Mrs. Snodgrass, Ms. Stokes, and Dr. Tiburzi prepared me well. I grew from a hyper tomboy, catching passes from Mrs. Faulkner and chasing down tennis lobs from Mom, to coaching a team of sixty-nine thousand. Hooah!

nine

* * * *

THE POWER OF
THE YELLOW BRICK ROAD
"Develop Your Strategic Vision"

MY MOST EXTENSIVE COACHING job came when I oversaw the Army Materiel Command. AMC has fifty-plus years of storied history, providing the logistics backbone for the US Army. Its baptism in conflict came during the Cuban Missile Crisis just two months after it was founded on August 1, 1962. This was a critical time in US history, and we truly were on the brink of nuclear war. The very first photos of the Soviet missiles in Cuba were developed in a building on Redstone Arsenal, right across the street from the new AMC headquarters we had just opened, before they were sent to President Kennedy at the White House. AMC was responsible for moving assets to Florida in response to the placement of Soviet missiles in Cuba. More than three hundred requisitions for HAWK missiles and repair parts were processed. Additionally, AMC's new subordinate command at Redstone Arsenal, the US Army Missile Command, conducted intelligence assessments on Soviet missile capabilities. So from its earliest days AMC has been there, shoulder to shoulder, with our nation's war fighters.

Over time much of its work has been focused on the nation's industrial base—the factories and depots that are vital for producing military hardware, vehicles, supplies, and ammunition. The command always has been facility and manpower intensive, with most of the workforce being civilian employees instead of members of the military. In days gone by, the initials "AMC" were said to stand for "a million civilians," with the implication that civilian employees were less dedicated and committed than their military counterparts.

After the Cold War ended, AMC began to evolve and streamline, a process that became more poignant after 9/11. Gone are the days when thousands of troops were stationed all over Europe, waiting on the inevitable attack by the Russians through the Fulda Gap. No longer did we have thousands of troops at the ready, keeping peace in Japan and South Korea. We are keeping tabs on the unpredictable North Korean army and a watchful eye on the always powerful Chinese military, now using technology instead of strength. Those drawdowns led to a consolidation of logistics. AMC took on research and development duties and became responsible for all Army contracting. Many of the functions AMC employees previously performed were outsourced to contractors. AMC oversaw the contractors and focused more of its resources on the operational side of logistics. Direct support to the war fighter became the top priority.

When I assumed command of the AMC in November 2008, we were beginning our eighth year of war, supporting operations in Iraq and Afghanistan along with responding to natural and manmade disasters in faraway places. From nuclear accidents, tsunamis, earthquakes, disease, and famine, AMC had a role. We were sixty-nine thousand people strong, with a presence or activity in all fifty United States and approximately 145 countries around the world. It was daunting to contemplate the responsibility associated with the operational demands and the sheer magnitude of a command that size. As if we weren't busy enough, we also had a congressional mandate to move major elements of the command to new locations in accordance with the 2005 Base Realignment and Closure Commission (BRAC) plan.

BRACs are designed to consolidate military functions at viable locations while closing excess facilities. The announcement of a new BRAC commission worries politicians in communities whose own jobs and local economies were tied to military installations around the country. A BRAC decision can turn a healthy community into a ghost town or spark a struggling community to experience unprecedented growth. Pine Bluff Arsenal was boarded up and Fort Story, Virginia, shut down, while Petersburg, Virginia, and Redstone Arsenal were big gainers. There were winners and there were losers as a result of BRAC. When Army groups were directed to move to new locations, that meant more people and more money infused into the economy for food, housing, entertainment, gas, and transportation. Operational Army depots, arsenals, and ammo plants often become the economic engine of town, city, or state. These decisions are emotional and almost always highly political. No small town, city, or state wants to be on the losing side of a BRAC decision. Politicians and federal, state, and local officials work closely with chambers of commerce to design plans to reap gains and prevent loses. These leaders' own careers are hanging in the balance, and there is plenty of wheeling and dealing. In the end no one seems to care much about the impact on the respective workforces.

The 2005 BRAC decision had a direct impact on eleven thousand AMC employees. The effects varied from city to city, base to base. Some workers simply would move from one old building to a newer one up the street. Others would have to change locations and move across town or across the state. My own three thousand employees faced a more daunting transition: their headquarters at Fort Belvoir, Virginia, was being shuttered. We were moving seven hundred miles away to Redstone Arsenal in Huntsville, Alabama. For some workers the seven hundred miles might as well have been seven thousand, and their options were limited. They could move to Alabama, seek a new job within the civil service system, or leave government service altogether. Many of the employees were Virginia natives and had never lived anywhere else. The prospect of leaving their families was unsettling and not good for morale. Other folks were excited at the prospect of moving out from the shadow of Washington, DC, and away from the daily traffic snafus.

The personnel folks immediately went to work trying to get a sense of the impact. The news wasn't good, especially if you were in charge. It appeared that less than 30 percent of the workforce was receptive to making the move. As AMC's new commanding general, I was hit with the statistic like a Nolan Ryan fastball in the gut.

The thought of losing 70 percent of my workforce was incomprehensible. AMC is one of the largest commands in the Army. Our three-thousand-person headquarters was filled with highly experienced and generally more senior civilian personnel. These people literally ran the logistics enterprise for the entire Army. Huntsville is a great city with a robust scientific community and a history of excellence supporting the aerospace industry. But even in "Rocket City," where were we going to find a couple thousand new people who had the skill sets and expertise needed to run logistics for the Army?

One of the special things about the Army is its family network. Even after you become a four-star general there are plenty of people who can coach and mentor you. Your fellow four-stars and your active-duty and retired brethren continue to reach out to help where they can. I was always pleased to receive an e-mail or phone call offering to meet for lunch or coffee, and I rarely turned them down if the schedule permitted. General Gordon Sullivan, a former

Chief of Staff of the Army, remained a good friend and mentor, so I enlisted his help as we prepared for the move to Alabama. Over lunch he gave me a piece of advice: "Ann, you need to think about your vision for the command, and you need to be able to put it on one chart in a way that everyone can understand. It has to show where you're heading and how you're going to get there."

I had used vision statements in the past, but they were probably more like bumper stickers. "Be the *go-to* Corps Support Command," or "Be the sustainer of choice." Our typical Army banner statements were more about what we do and not enough about the how, why, or where we do it. I had always used a stack of briefing charts to try to make the compelling case for change. It worked for me in the past, but right now I was tuned in to General Sullivan as if I were listening to my favorite country song (Lee Greenwood's "I'm Proud to Be an American"). He pulled out a napkin and drew up the chart he had used to explain and manage the drawdown of the Army while still maintaining readiness. It was very simple and very visually compelling. When I returned to my office I sat down with my strategic initiatives group. "Hey guys, I want to go over my discussion I had with General Sullivan today about creating a vision so you can start giving the idea some thought." We then launched a brainstorming session to spark ideas of how we would explain our vision.

I started thinking about what Sergeant Wendell Bowen had showed me thirty years prior when he taught me how to influence 220 people. Now I was trying to inspire and convince 3,000 people to move with me to Huntsville. How do I get every person excited about what he or she is doing? How do I get them excited about our future and make them understand how important their contributions are to our success? I also wanted our 69,000 AMC employees to know how important they were to our overall success. The vision was going to be the unifier, and it almost became an obsession of mine. Thanks to General Sullivan, I had a new tool on my belt to describe that vision. It became the most powerful tool I had ever used to lead and motivate my people.

As our migration to Huntsville started in earnest, we already had about fifty people based at Redstone Arsenal, and all new vacancies for the command would be filled with people in Alabama instead of Virginia. Over the next two years there would be a steady flow of new and existing employees to our new location. Fort Belvoir would remain open during the transition, and I knew it would be important to retain some of our most experienced people as we operated out of two locations. I realistically had one year to convince a larger percentage of our workforce to make the move to Alabama.

We set out to create a vision for the command that would show everyone where we were headed and what life could be like in Huntsville. We had big plans to transform how we did business. We were going to take operational systems like PBUSE and link them to the national level system we were fielding, called the Logistics Modernization Program (LMP)—the first successful enterprise resource planning system the Army had ever used. We were creating a truly state-of-the-art control center for Army logistics. It was a huge undertaking, and I wondered whether it would be possible with a depleted workforce.

As a selling point we wanted to make it clear that the new headquarters would be a sparkling, modern facility. There would be a place and role for everyone who made the journey, and that's what it was going to be—a journey into the future. We were about to transform ourselves into a twenty-first-century enterprise. I knew that if our new headquarters looked and ran just like it did at Belvoir, we would have failed. We wanted to update our networks with the latest technologies. We wanted to eliminate stovepipes and create a collaborative team that would provide America's war fighters with a decisive edge. Yes, information was power, but we needed to take it a step further: shared information could multiply that power exponentially. We needed to fundamentally change the way we were doing business. We had to become more efficient and more effective so we could free up resources to help the Chief of Staff and the Secretary of the Army achieve their goal of rebalancing the Army.

The vision slide affectionately became known as the "Yellow Brick Road." It was one page, and it was bright. It explained what we did and for whom. It displayed our priorities, opportunities, and partners. The only elements missing were my beloved Dorothy, Toto, the Scarecrow, Tin Man, and the Cowardly Lion. When I was a wet-behind-the-ears 2nd lieutenant, I didn't know about

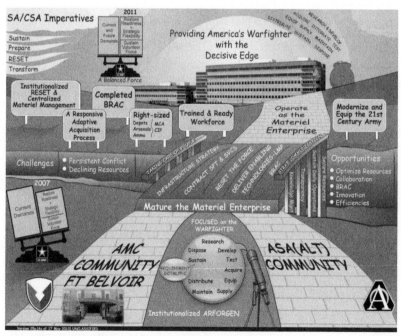

The "Yellow Brick Road" vision slide that we used to explain to the work force what the future in AMC would be like when we moved to Redstone Arsenal in Huntsville, Alabama.

strategic visioning—I just wanted to be the best 2nd lieutenant in the Army and with the best platoon. But as a general officer, I learned why strategic visioning was a cornerstone to our successes.

With things changing rapidly in today's environment, you always have to be thinking about the future. You have to be innovative, creative, and visionary. Those who lack those characteristics risk becoming less relevant or less competitive. A former Chief of Staff of the Army, General Eric Shinseki, once said, "If you don't like change, you'll like irrelevance even less."

When this one-page vision was complete, I took it to the rest of AMC staff for their review. Any vision that doesn't have support from the people who have to make it a reality is merely a pipe dream—visions have to be inclusive. Your people need to see it, believe in it, and bring it to life. The staff had a few tweaks and suggested additions, but most thought we had a compelling vision. The next step was to share our vision with everyone in the command. Those unsure about making the move had to see what they were going to miss. The stakes were high. We conducted in-house meetings to explain the vision, and we also took our show on the road. In addition to trying to convince the people at our headquarters to make the move, we wanted to show the entire command what the future of AMC held for everyone.

My operations officer was Major General Larry Wyche, who I have known and served with for many years. He has the brightest smile I have ever seen and is a real "can do" kind of guy. A former enlisted man, he still wears his sergeant's rank under the collar of his battle dress uniform as a constant reminder of where he came from and who his real customers are. He had plenty to do running AMC operations in support of the two wars. I sent him to visit commercial and government operations centers such as FedEx, NASA, CIA, and Joint Staff in hopes of incorporating the best business practices in our new command center. He saw state-of-the-art operation centers where information was analyzed in real time, allowing leaders to make informed decisions quickly. If FedEx had a plane down or a weather challenge, its leaders knew immediately and had multiple solutions at the ready.

Construction was already underway at our new headquarters, and we ran into some challenges trying to modify the plans on the fly to accommodate our vision. General George Casey did not ask me to move to Huntsville for the final sixteen months of my command, but I knew I could not lead the charge from Fort Belvoir. In April 2011 my husband, Craig, and I packed up the cars and our dog, Barney, and started our drive to Huntsville, Alabama. I drove our 1999 Volvo and Craig drove his Tahoe Z-71, towing my little convertible Thunderbird on a U-Haul auto trailer. It was a two-day trip, stopping overnight in Knoxville, Tennessee. We arrived on Easter Sunday and checked into guest quarters for three days while waiting for our furniture to arrive. The moving vans got there early the next week, and we officially began unpacking and moving into our home on Redstone Arsenal one day before devastating and deadly tornados hit Alabama, killing 238 people and leaving thousands more across the state without electricity and basic necessities.

The state's response to the natural disaster was inspiring. Citizens from all backgrounds didn't wring their hands; they rolled up their sleeves and got to work. First, they accounted for families, and then they comforted those who had lost loved ones and cared for those in need.

As Alabama rebuilt its communities I got to work building momentum for our new headquarters at Redstone. Over the next year we started to see changes in attitudes and in the number of people who were now interested in moving to Huntsville. We punched the accelerator on our drive to Huntsville. I learned who would be staying and who would be moving, allowing me to start interviewing and filling key positions. Prior to moving into our new headquarters our command was dispersed in decades-old and sometimes dilapidated buildings across the installation at Redstone. Staff meetings were an adventure because you couldn't hold one without teleconference connectivity between Huntsville and Northern Virginia. Every staff section was now represented in Huntsville, and we were developing timelines for the rest of the senior leaders to move. By the completion of the move more than 60 percent of the Fort Belvoir workforce had relocated to Alabama. When I asked people why they changed their minds, they said they were excited about the future and wanted to part of it. People bought into our vision.

When the CSA, General Ray Odierno, came down to visit our new headquarters in Huntsville and walked into our global operations center, he was so impressed that he said, "Can you put that capability [click-on icon] on my computer in the Pentagon so I could access the readiness of every unit in real time?" It was awesome.

People wanted to be part of a team that was making a difference. I've always posed this question to everyone on my team: "Who wants to be part of a high-performing organization?" Everyone always raised his or her hands. No one wants to be part of a mediocre company.

For me high performance means doing routine things in an outstanding manner routinely. For that to be a reality, the work force has to believe in the vision and the purpose of the outfit. They have to be able to visualize how they fit into the overall picture. When you take command in the Army your most important job is to coach. You want to coach your soldiers or your workforce to be their best. You want to form a winning team to be its very best. This sounds easy, but how do you accomplish it?

My husband and I both enjoy watching professional football, and it's always been interesting to see how the various teams are built. I remember back in the 1970s when George Allen was the Super Bowl–winning coach of the Washington Redskins. He built his teams based on experience and routinely traded away his draft picks in favor of proven and experienced veteran players. It was as though he had a disdain for young hotshots coming out of college. He viewed rookies as potential liabilities; win now and worry about next year next year. Today most coaches and general managers build a team through the draft while also adding talent through trades or free agency. The ability to build a strong team separates the winners from the losers.

GOOD LEADERS PROVIDE A STRATEGIC VISION

I have shamelessly and repeatedly paraphrased the conversation between Alice and the Cheshire Cat from Lewis Carroll's masterpiece, *Alice in Wonderland*. The exact passage:

> "Would you tell me, please, which way I ought to go from here?" asks Alice.
>
> "That depends a good deal on where you want to get to," replies the Cat.
>
> "I don't much care where."
>
> "Then it doesn't matter which way you go."
>
> "So long as I get somewhere."
>
> "Oh, you're sure to do that," said the Cat, "if you only walk long enough."

In my own version I like to say, "If you don't know where you're going, any road will take you there."

On June 15, 2011, we had a touchdown ceremony to officially commemorate the arrival of AMC to Redstone Arsenal, Alabama. The mayors of Huntsville and nearby Madison were both in attendance, continuing their duel claims as the hosts of the installation. The new building was christened, the ribbons were cut, and the cake was consumed. It was now time to get back to work. The "yellow brick road" was history, and we had a new vision to articulate as we sped toward AMC 2020 and our strategic plan.

How do you create a vision that inspires and motivates individuals to perform at a high level and to put their trust in you and believe in your vision? The starting point for me was having a clear understanding of what my boss was trying to do, to understand his vision. Everyone has a boss, whether it's many shareholders or just one person. For me, I knew what the Secretary of the Army and the Chief of Staff of the Army were thinking, so my starting point was to acknowledge that.

The next step was to develop the foundation. As a military professional, I knew that the most important element is trust—the vision had to be built on trust. The very basis for why soldiers fight the way they do is the trust they have in their teammates, their fellow soldiers. It's usually less dramatic off the battlefield but still equally important. Without trust in each other and trust in the institution, you will not be able to realize your vision.

Once you set parameters for your vision try to capture the essence of your organization. For AMC our strategic plan was called AMC 2020, and our vision was to become the globally networked logistics command for the Army. We were going to establish AMC as the four-star headquarters responsible for optimizing logistics capability and leveraging the latest real-time technologies to become more efficient and effective while enhancing Army readiness. For the vision to be taken seriously, the destination—or the goal—has to be attainable. Visions can be a matter of days, weeks, months, or years. It's *your* vision, so *you* need to determine the timing. With your destination now in focus, you need to describe who you are, what you do, and how you are going to get there.

We developed the "Bullet Train" as our next phase of the Yellow Brick Road. We had now reached our bright and shiny new

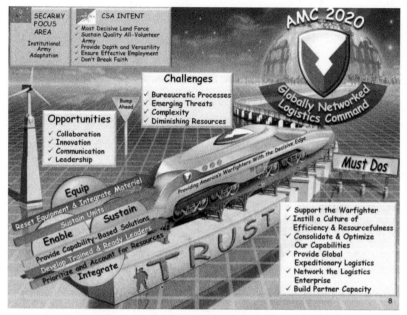

The "Bullet Train" vision slide we developed to articulate what we needed to accomplish by 2020 to truly be a globally networked logistics command.

home at Redstone Arsenal; it was time to speed into the future. The graphics or cartoons—whatever medium you choose for your vision—should make it clear to your workforce what you have in mind. I wanted to show that we were modern, fast, and zooming into the future.

We rounded out our Bullet Train vision with our must-dos—those things that are non-negotiable if we're going to be successful—and identified the opportunities and challenges that lie ahead. When you finish a vision slide, it should tell a story. It might take a half-hour to explain it, but once you have explained it, people should be able to just look at the slide to remember where their high-performing organization is going. Every person should be able to see himself riding that train into the future, with the secure knowledge that they're part of a winning team.

Properly done, the vision becomes the heartbeat of the organization and drives the prioritization of resources, people, time, money, and training. Leadership makes all the difference. People in high-performing teams look for opportunities to excel, and people feel empowered to make a difference. These things don't happen by accident; they happen because of good leadership—no matter the group, no matter the mission, whether you are running a war or running a business.

When I left the military I was ready. I was content with the progress and road map we established for AMC. I felt like a championship coach or a conductor of a fine symphony. We had built a high-performing organization by any metric. My nearly four decades as a coach in the US Army was about to end. I was proud of my run and all of the triumphs over adversity during an incredible military career that initially started as a two-year timeout from becoming a college coach and professor. But mostly I was content. It was time for the next chapter and challenge in my soon-to-be civilian life.

ten

★ ★ ★ ★

THE NEEDS OF THE
ARMY NOTWITHSTANDING

"Know When to Fold 'Em"

MY HEART WAS POUNDING and my hands were sweating as I walked to the mound in the brand-new Yankee Stadium, wearing my camouflage uniform and black beret. Forty-seven thousand fans were yelling, cheering, and jeering as the Mets were about to take on the Yankees for New York City bragging rights. It was Military Appreciation Day, June 14, 2009. The Army's prestigious Golden Knights parachute team had just jumped into the stadium with the American flag as part of the pregame ceremonies, raising the level of excitement and noise. Several of our wounded warriors were recognized, as were several surviving children of our fallen, prompting a standing ovation.

I was there to throw the ceremonial first pitch. A. J. Burnett, the Yankees' starting pitcher, was standing on the backside of the mound, looking impatient and deep in thought, clearly anxious for me to get on with it and out of the way so he could do his work. I walked up to A. J. and reached out to shake his hand and wish him good luck. He was not exactly Mr. Personality, but he shook

193

my hand and said, "Thanks." The noise in the stadium was deaf-ening, and seeing myself on the larger-than-life video scoreboard was unnerving. The comments of my fellow four-stars echoed in my head: "You're not going to throw like a girl, are you? You're going to throw from the mound, aren't you? You're not going to bounce it into the dirt, are you?"

Thankfully my husband Craig bought a baseball, measured sixty feet, six inches in our backyard (the distance from the pitching rub-ber to the plate), and made me practice every night after I got home from work. Even my command counsel and dear friend, Vince Fagg-ioli, another diehard Yankee fan, kept a ball and glove in the trunk of his car in case we had a chance to go out and throw a few at lunch time. By now my heart felt like it was in my throat, and the pounding was noisier than the crowd. *Okay, Ann calm down.* Craig had coached me well. He told me to take my time and motion to the catcher with my glove hand to give me a signal for the pitch.

I shook off Francisco Cervelli's first offering, and he cracked up and gave me the signal for a curve ball. I bent over at the waist, like pitchers do before they throw the ball, and shook my head signaling *no* again. Francisco chuckled, but it was time to get on with it. He flashed another sign, I nodded my head, and let it fly. The ball sailed straight and true and would surely have been a low strike, but Francisco made me look even better by coming out of his stance, snagging the ball over the plate, and stepping forward to shake my hand and present the ball all in one perfectly exe-cuted motion. The crowd cheered! Thank heavens it was over and now I could relax and enjoy the game. The Yankees won 15–0 that day.

When I was asked who I wanted to sign the baseball, I said Derek Jeter. He was my favorite Yankee. In the baseball world I always thought he was a great role model. Though most of my observations are from watching him on TV, the traits that jumped out at me were his passion for the game, his dedication to the team, his upbeat attitude and smile no matter if they were winning or losing, his commitment to fitness, and his willingness to give back to his community. He was, in my mind, a true example of someone, albeit in a different profession, who lived a higher standard. Today on my desk in my office sits my autographed baseball: "To Gen. Ann Dunwoody, Best Wishes," with his scribbly signature, "Derek Jeter."

As with every team, some days it's hard to be a Yankees fan, but it was never hard to be a Jeter fan. As I watched Derek announce his retirement, my first thought was, "Oh no, my hero is leaving the Yankees." But after I had time to let it sink in, my thoughts transformed into "Good for him!" He's retiring on his own terms. He's still fit, healthy, and able to play. He's had a wonderful career, and he made a difference. He was now hanging up his baseball cleats and starting a new phase of his adult life. As I reflected on his decision, it reminded me that I'd hung up my dog tags for many of the same reasons.

Not everyone has the resources to retire when they want to, but it's important and often difficult to recognize when it *is* time to step aside.

HAROLD HALSEY DUNWOODY is remarkable. Not only is he a war hero and a man of integrity, but my father is also a Renaissance man who could play most musical instruments by ear, had a photographic memory, and was fluent in French. At the end of my senior year of high school Dad was reassigned to the US Army Republic of Vietnam. I was furious. *Hadn't he already sacrificed enough for his country?* I didn't want my dad to earn a *third* Purple Heart— or worse. The distance and separation were also getting harder for my mom. But Dad was born to fight wars, not sit behind a desk. So off to Vietnam he went.

Dad returned from the war physically unscathed. He was hopeful he would receive a second star, but hope faded. The promotion never came. Had it happened, he would have willingly stayed in the Army. But on January 8, 1973, at age fifty-four and after thirty-one years of service, he retired.

My father left the Army when his service to his country was no longer needed. It was difficult for me to comprehend. Over the years he shared some of his jaded feelings about why some were selected for promotion while others, equally deserving soldiers, were snubbed. I remember him telling me that he wasn't one of "Westy's" boys. He thought General William Westmoreland might have kept him from advancing. His perception was that General Westmoreland had his "in crowd" of favorites who followed him around, and that certainly was not my dad. It made me realize at an early age that I wanted to call my own shots. It's one of the greatest life lessons I've ever learned.

Dad isn't one to harp or look back. But the Army was still on his mind, even if he wouldn't admit it. He continued to subscribe to *Army Times*, a weekly publication that focuses on all things military. As he got older he grew cynical about the service, the country, and the future. He would watch the evening news and bark at the reporters when he disagreed. "That damn Cronkite doesn't know what he's talking about." Mom would just look at him and say, "Oh, Bo"—Mom's way of scolding Dad in front of us.

Eventually he canceled his *Army Times* subscription. He still receives *West Point* magazine, an alumni quarterly. The magazine has a section called "Taps" that honors graduates who have died. A few years ago I asked Dad whether he was interested in going back for a class reunion. He joked that he wasn't ready yet because he was waiting for his class to "thin out a bit"—a typical comment from my proud father who undoubtedly is one of the last living members of the West Point class of 1943. The subject has never come up again, as it was clear that he has no interest in returning.

When he retired, Dad said his goal was to live as many years in retirement as he had served in the military. He and Mom planned on spending time together doing all the things that military life had forced them to postpone. Dad loved anything on water— fishing, sailing, and waterskiing. He grew up on a lake in Sheldrake, New York. He actually wanted to attend the Naval Academy in Annapolis, but my grandfather wanted him to continue the family Army tradition, and young men in 1938 didn't defy their fathers. Dad was admitted to the Naval Academy but forfeited his appointment in favor of West Point. Because he hadn't even applied to West Point, he attended West Point Prep, a one-year school designed to prepare officers to officially join the Long Gray Line.

After three decades of service, Dad set sail for retirement. He bought a twenty-nine-foot cabin cruiser. He captained his boat through the Finger Lakes and cruised through the Erie Canal. Mom and Dad also bought a camper. They parked it on the banks of Allegheny Lake, about thirty minutes from our house in Randolph. We'd go fishing and have cookouts. Dad also resumed his lost passions: playing the piano and doing woodwork. He even started painting.

Today, at age ninety-six, my father has surpassed his goal of years in retirement versus military career by twelve years. I can only pray that I've inherited his remarkable genes; after all, I definitely didn't get his photographic memory or musical gifts. He did, however, pass down his sense of humor, sense of timing, and the infamous "character-building" Dunwoody nose.

Although Dad prefers not to talk about his West Point days or his decorated career, I organized a surprise event for our family to celebrate his years of distinguished service. We held the ceremony on November 30, 2003, to roughly coincide with the thirtieth anniversary of his retirement. Dad was being recognized by the chief of the Armor School with the Order of St. Georges—a Bronze Medallion. This was the equivalent of induction in the Armor Hall of Fame. We hosted a Sunday brunch in a private room at the Ritz Carlton Hotel in Arlington, Virginia. Former Chief of Staff of the Army and current president of the Association of the US Army, General (Ret) Gordon Sullivan presided.

It's rare for a former Chief of Staff of the Army to present an award at a family function. General Sullivan spoke almost in deference to my dad. "It's so wonderful that so many of your family members could be here today," he said before introducing and welcoming each member of my family. He then asked Mom and Dad to come forward to the head of the table. General Sullivan told Dad, "This award is long overdue" and that he was "grateful to be the one to present it." General Sullivan spoke very slowly and deliberately, as he shared highlights of Dad's valiant career. He talked about Dad serving in World War II, Korea, and Vietnam and his two Purple Hearts. He also praised Dad for receiving the Distinguished Service Cross, the second-highest award next to the Medal of Honor. During a four-day siege on a Korean mountaintop in 1951 Dad was cited for extraordinary heroism when his battalion defeated a large enemy force. General Sullivan then presented my dad with a framed certificate and placed the Order of St. Georges medallion around his neck as we all applauded.

He then turned to our family's secret weapon: Mom. "Betty, we all know and understand the sacrifices you endured while your husband was serving," General Sullivan said. "Multiple moves, missed anniversaries and birthdays, all while raising this remarkable family, often on your own." At this point my normally stoic mom started tearing up. She looked out at all of us and said, "It was hard." General Sullivan continued, "We thank you for all your love and support that allowed Hal to carry out his missions." He then hugged her and presented her with a dozen beautiful red roses.

Mom and Dad were deeply touched. Dad never received his second star, but General Sullivan gave him something equally important that day: closure. It's common for soldiers to leave the military with mixed emotions. Our ceremony helped heal decades' worth of old wounds.

On July 28, 1997, the Chief of Staff of the Air Force, General Ronald Fogleman, asked the Secretary of the Air Force to relieve him of his duties a year before the end of his four-year term. In an interview with historian Richard H. Kohn the Chief of Staff said, "My values and sense of loyalty to our soldiers, sailors, Marines, and especially our airmen led me to the conclusion that I may be out of step with the times and some of the thinking of the establishment. You really do have to get up and look at yourself in the mirror every day and ask, 'Do I feel honorable and clean?'"

It marked the first time in history that a serving Chief of Staff voluntarily stepped down early. He clearly felt that the leadership under which he served no longer valued his opinion. General Fogleman said he had "become ineffective as a spokesman." He hadn't done anything illegal or immoral; he just "did not want the Air Force to suffer for my judgment and convictions."

As a young colonel, I remember thinking how difficult this decision must have been. "When you sense that you have lost the confidence of the folks you're dealing with—almost to the extent where the service will be punished—that's one reason to leave," he said. General Fogleman also said he had "simply lost respect and confidence in the leadership that I was supposed to be following." My husband had known General Fogleman and had admired him greatly. Craig thought he was tough, smart, and a no-nonsense leader, a leader for whom it was easy to follow. He felt it was a great loss for the Air Force.

From the very start I never knew how long I'd stay in the military. I figured if the Army didn't work out, I would find something equally challenging and fun. Having been retired from the military for more than two years now, I have learned that it's not that easy. I loved the Army, and I loved being a soldier. It was my essence.

Finding comrades like those I served with in the military or finding meaningful work that I was passionate about in the civilian sector requires patience, research, and luck. I took my time and didn't rush into anything until I was certain it was something I wanted to commit to doing. I have to laugh when people ask, "How's retired life?" I'm as busy as I've ever been, except now I make my own schedule. I see my husband every day. I finally get to spend regular quality time with family and friends. I no longer miss milestone events such as baby showers, birthdays, graduations, and weddings. I wrote this book. I started a consulting company, First 2 Four, LLC. I serve on multiple boards. I even continue to give speeches at universities and corporate gatherings, despite my continued fear of public speaking. But nothing—absolutely nothing—can replace the pride and purpose of being a soldier.

Not everyone is cut out for the military, but I do believe everyone can and should have the opportunity to participate in a national service endeavor of their choice. Serving in the military can make you a better citizen, employee, and leader. The military provides hands-on experience. It provides leadership training and builds a foundation for a strong work ethic. Corporate America has taken notice and regularly recruits soldiers just as it does Ivy League students. I feel so passionate about public service that I joined the Leadership Council for the Franklin Project, chaired by my friend and colleague General (Ret) Stan McChrystal. Walter Isaacson and the Aspen Institute sponsor the council.

The project's goal is to unite people eighteen to twenty-eight years of age from different backgrounds through a year of full-time paid national service aimed at ending the high-school dropout epidemic, conserving our national parks, transitioning military veterans back to civilian life, and many other noble endeavors. The Franklin Project is creating a new generation of leaders.

I always encourage young Americans to find something they love, something they are passionate about, and pursue it with conviction, regardless of what detractors might say. It worked for me. And it worked for Alicia Keys.

I met Alicia in March of 2009 at a Women's History Month event hosted by First Lady Michelle Obama at the White House. Alicia was wearing classy jeans and a cute, bling-studded top. She was clearly a lot more comfortable in her jeans than I was in my military blue jacket, skirt, and high heels. I introduced myself, "Hi, I'm Ann Dunwoody." She immediately gave me a hug while saying, "I'm Alicia." She seemed so young to already be so famous. She then introduced me to her equally stunning mother, Teresa.

We jumped into the back of a Secret Service–looking SUV and headed to Dunbar High School. We sat in the backseat together and started off with the usual get-to-know-each-other conversation.

"Where are you from?" I asked.

"Manhattan," she said. "How about you?"

"I'm an Army brat . . . kind of like a mutt," I replied. "I've lived all over."

She laughed. I asked her how she got into entertainment. She said singing and dancing had been her passion since she was a little girl. Then she talked about growing up in New York City. "Dad and Mom were separated when I was two, and my mom pretty much raised me." Her mom, a paralegal and part-time actress sent her to music lessons at an early age and taught her how to be a strong and independent young woman.

Alicia said the most important things to her were being respected for who she was and being successful based on her abilities and passion. She said there were a lot of bad people along the way who tried to tempt her to do otherwise. I was surprised that we had so much in common despite the age difference, career paths, and looks.

We went to Dunbar High School, currently ranked twenty-fifth out of the thirty-five high schools in DC. I can honestly say I have never been to a school like this one. It was an old, three-story brick building. Instead of hall patrols with safety belts, they had police standing around with guns in their holsters. When they led us into the school, they had to unlock the door, and it was an eerie feeling when they locked it behind us once we were in. We made our way up the back stairway to get to the library where we met with the students.

We took our seats in the library with a group of twenty African American students. Alicia and I had very different stories, but our messages were similar. Taking turns, we fielded questions—no PowerPoints, pie charts, or videos. Just a real conversation.

"How did you decide to join the Army?"

"How can I make it in music?"

"How do you find your passion?"

"What do you do when someone tells you that you can't do something you want to do?"

"What if you don't want to do what your parents have planned for you?"

Our answers echoed each other's:

"Stay in school and get an education."

"Immerse yourself in extracurricular activities."

"Don't be afraid to try new things, because you might discover your passion."

"Do what you like, and like what you do."

"Dream big."

"Don't let anyone tell you no."

"Believe in yourself."

When the session was over, the students looked like someone had just set them free. Most of the kids came from impoverished backgrounds. Their questions and promise, however, inspired us and enriched our lives. The students came up to us to say thank you for caring enough to take the time to visit.

On the way back to the White House I commented to Alicia, "What a great experience that was for me. I feel like I have just been touched by an incredible group of human beings."

Alicia smiled and said, "It was emotional for me as well."

We both agreed it shouldn't take Women's History Month to prompt another visit like this.

For Alicia and me our chosen professions were more than a job—they were a calling. Music can heal and unite. At its best, the Armed Forces can help rebuild countries and communities torn apart by hatred, ignorance, and war. It's the ultimate challenge. This sense of duty makes the choice between staying and leaving the military a difficult one for many soldiers.

I was saddened as I watched successful soldiers like my dad leave the service disappointed after not receiving that next promotion or assignment. The Army is a competitive business, especially when it comes to advancement through the senior ranks of colonel, brigadier general, and major general. Some of the very best are often bypassed. Appointments to the grade of lieutenant general and general are made by the president and confirmed by the Senate. The higher the rank, the fewer the promotions available. Although I was always competitive and wanted the next mission, I also knew that one day my name or Craig's might not be called. I always believed in the promotion-selection process.

I suspected my time was coming, and my name wasn't going to be called while I was assigned to Combined Arms Support Command at Fort Lee as a two-star. It was 2005, and I had been a two-star for three years. Based on the rumors about who was going where and when, it appeared that all of the potential three-star positions already had general officers projected to fill them, and mine wasn't in the mix. So I figured I would retire as a two-star. Although I knew I was capable of filling many of the three-star jobs, others had apparently been chosen. I'd be lying if I said I wasn't upset, but I also knew that there are always more qualified people than there are positions. I just thought it must be my time to retire.

Craig and I actually started getting excited about the prospect of retiring in Hawaii. Then, out of nowhere, I received an e-mail from the General Officer Management Office (GOMO). I was shocked. I was working at home in the evening and called Craig in to come look at the e-mail. General Schoomaker, the Chief of Staff of the Army, wanted to nominate me for a three-star position on the Joint Staff, a prestigious group representing all the military services that supports the chairman of the Joint Chiefs of Staff. There were already several nominees, and chances were slim I'd get the appointment, but General Schoomaker wanted to start floating my name around and put me in the mix. I didn't get that job, but several weeks after that I was nominated to become the Army G4, the three-star director of logistics for the entire US Army. Within the month I'd been confirmed. Retirement and beaches were put on hold.

Watching my husband get passed over twice for brigadier general at the end of his career tested my faith in meritocracy. Craig excelled in almost everything his entire life, from Boy Scouts to the California Boys State Delegate to the Air Force. He starred in sports, playing football and golf in high school. He was his high school's nominee for the Inland Empire Scholar Athlete Award. He went to Southern Utah University on a football scholarship, and there he discovered Air Force ROTC.

Craig's entry into the Air Force coincided with the oil embargo crisis of 1973. The oil cartels of the Middle East decided to reduce the amount of oil they would export. It was a pure power play, but it had the desired result, as the price of oil on the world market skyrocketed. In the United States it meant long lines at the gas stations, rationing, and severe cutbacks. Instead of going to pilot

training as he was slated, Craig entered the Air Force as a personnel officer. With the mandated cutbacks, only Air Force Academy
graduates would be going to pilot training for the next few years.
At the five-year mark he applied for and was accepted into the
Combat Control career field. Combat Control is crucial to many
air missions. Imagine Air Traffic Control in remote, often unim-
proved runways and calling in air strikes on enemy positions—
that's what he was training to do.

His entry into Combat Control coincided with the resurgence
of Special Operations Forces after the fatal attempt to rescue hostages in Operation Eagle Claw in 1980. In 1979 the American
Embassy in Tehran, Iran, was overrun by Iranian militants. The
Americans present that day were held hostage for 444 days. In
April 1980 a group of Army and Air Force special operations forces
along with Marine aviators using Navy helicopters was assembled
and trained to attempt a rescue of the hostages. The mission was
aborted when one of the helicopters crashed into a C-130 aircraft
that was parked on the Iranian desert waiting to ground refuel the
helicopters. As a result of the mission failure, congressional action soon followed with the mandate to revitalize and resource
a growth in our nation's special operations capability. Craig rode
the wave of that resurgence like a Waikiki beach boy.

He was immersed in the joint special operations world—he
was not only Airborne qualified but was also trained in high-
altitude, low-opening (HALO) parachuting and was trained to
be a combat diver—think skydiving and scuba diving at night
while carrying required military equipment like radios, navigation
aids, spare batteries, and ammunition. He spent so much of his
time training and associating with Army and Navy special warfare operatives that he was barely recognizable as an Air Force
officer. When he was selected for an advanced command and staff
service school, the Air Force, with some logic and common sense,

sent him to Fort Leavenworth, Kansas, to the Command and General Staff College to learn side by side with the Army. That's where we met.

When I arrived at Fort Leavenworth, Kansas, in August 1986 to attend the Command and General Staff Officer course, I was excited but anxious. Excited because I had been selected to attend the resident-in-house course instead of having to take it by correspondence, referred to as the nonresident course. The selection for the resident was very competitive. I was anxious because I had not served in a division and thought that might put me at a disadvantage with the other students, particularly combat arms officers, who had divisional experience—operational experience with our war-fighting divisions. Physically I was ready. I had run the Marine Corps Marathon the previous year. I was also comforted by the fact that two of my best running buddies, Jan Edmunds and Barb Doornink, were also attending the course. The Command and General Staff Officer course is a nine-month session of instruction designed to prepare midcareer Army officers, normally majors, for command and staff jobs at the battalion level or higher. There were a few Air Force, Marine, Navy, and Coast Guard officers attending as well as allies from foreign countries.

The instruction is delivered in three distinct forums. One is lectures by guest speakers, or subject-matter experts were delivered in Bell Hall, a seven-hundred-seat auditorium where nearly every seat was taken. Everything from national security, leadership, strategic Army operations, and joint operations from key leaders in the Army and the Office of the Secretary of Defense and industry. Bell Hall had baby-blue seats and baby-blue walls. Some of the lectures were terrible, and Bell Hall had the well-earned nickname "the blue bedroom." When not in Bell Hall, we were in sixty-person classrooms with four sections and moveable partitions. Some of the instruction was delivered to all sixty officers, but for more intimate discussions the classroom was divided into groups of fifteen officers. I was in section 10B, and although I didn't know him at the time, Craig was in 10A.

As with every school or course I ever attended, one of the first events on the agenda was a weigh-in and the Army physical training (PT) test. It consisted of maximum pushups for two minutes, followed by maximum situps for two minutes, followed by a two-mile run. As a thirty-year-old female, I had to do forty-five pushups and seventy-two situps to max the test. I'd never had any problem getting the maximum score. It was surprising to me that people would show up for this prestigious school out of shape or overweight, but it happened.

It was kind of funny, but my next-door neighbor was an Air Force guy who had never heard of the Army PT test when he arrived. "Hey Ann, can you come take a look at my push-up and see if I'm doing it correctly?" I couldn't believe my ears. A C-5 aircraft navigator by trade, he struggled to do five by-the-book pushups. His arms did not bend enough to make a forty-five degree angle as he was lowering his chest to the ground. As I got down on the ground to demonstrate an "Army pushup" I said, "Here, Charlie, this is what they will be grading you on." The correct pushup is feet together, on the toes, arms straight with hands on the ground at shoulder width apart, and back straight. One repetition is lowering the chest to the ground, arms at a forty-five-degree angle, and then returning to the straight-arm position while maintaining the rigid back position, then repeat. No head bobbing, no wavy back. To his credit, I saw him at the gym working out and practicing every day. He had no trouble passing the Army fitness test.

When the instructors posted the announcement that our group, Section 10, would take the Army PT test, I was looking forward to it. The morning of the test all sixty of us loaded onto two buses and headed down toward the airfield where they conducted the test. First came the pushups. Everyone was paired with another student so that while one did the exercise, the other would count the repetitions and ensure that the drills were done properly. People who struggled were not happy when a classmate disallowed a repetition for not adhering to the standard. Pushups were followed by situps, flat on your back, knees raised to a ninety-degree angle with hands behind the head and the fingers of each hand interlaced. A successful repetition was to sit up with elbows striking the knees and then returning to the flat-on-your-back position. It was September by now, but it was still midsummer hot. After the two exercises some were out of breath, with sweat-soaked T-shirts. It was then time to line up for the two-mile run. The course at Fort Leavenworth was unique. Normally you'd go to a standard running track that had a football or soccer field in the middle, but here they had a long, straight road. Run out a mile until you get to the orange cone, then circle the cone and run back. You couldn't see the cone from the start line. What happened over the next few minutes startled my classmates and me: a Hulk-looking dude was dusting us.

It was a two-lane road, so sixty people couldn't all be at the front of the group. Most didn't care, as they weren't trying to be the next Louis Zamperini; they would just wait for the start gun and complete the run at a moderate pace, much as they had during their careers to date. Others were elbowing their way to the front. I wanted to be close to the lead, but I wasn't going to be pushing and shoving anyone.

Bang! The starting gun sounded. One guy took off like it was the start of the hundred-yard dash. *Wow, look at that dude,* I thought. *He'll never last at that pace.* First off, it didn't appear as though he had a runner's frame—this guy was big. Six-foot-two, 210 pounds, with a buzz cut. He looked more like an NFL linebacker than a gazelle. Secondly, I didn't think anyone in our age group could sprint for two miles. By the half-mile point he was at least 100, maybe 150 yards ahead of the pack. Several runners picked up the chase, but they weren't making up any ground. Someone in our pack asked, "Who is that guy?"

Another said, "That's that big Air Force guy."

"An Air Force guy? No way," said another.

No way he can keep that pace up, I thought again.

As the orange cone came into our view, the front-runner was almost there. He rounded the cone and started heading toward us. As he closed in, I couldn't help but stare at him to see how he was doing. Surely he'd be huffing and puffing any second before dropping to the end of the pack. As he went by, I remember thinking, *He is not going to stop. Wow, he looks intense. Hmmmm, he's not bad looking.*

I crossed the finish line in just under twelve minutes, one of my best times. I was third overall out of the fifty-seven men and three women, but we were all well behind the big Air Force guy. When I asked an instructor what his time was, he said 10:45. That run and that guy made a lasting impression on me.

That weekend I talked to my sister Sue, just to check in. We caught up on family stuff. Her big sister senses kicked, and she asked whether I'd met anyone interesting. I told her about the Air Force guy, and we had a laugh. My sister had met her husband, Jim, an Air Force officer, while they both were attending Army helicopter training. They now have three kids. When we were saying good-bye she said, "Be careful."

Craig and I were married three years and three months later, just after he was assigned to Fort Bragg. This was Craig's second assignment to Fort Bragg, this time as a lieutenant colonel commanding forces in the joint special operations business. His airmen played a significant part in Operation Just Cause in Panama and in Desert Storm, the first Gulf War, and others that fall into the "If I tell you, I have to kill you" category. After three years zipped by, Craig was sent to senior service school at the Army War College at Carlisle, Pennsylvania. With his 1993 graduation he became the first Air Force officer to complete both Army service schools— Command and General Staff College and Army War College.

As I was heading off to command at Fort Drum in 1996 Craig was selected to command the only Air Force colonel-level Special Tactics Group—720th Special Tactics Group at Hurlburt Field, Florida. Even though we were at opposite ends of the East Coast, we made it work. We both knew in our hearts that I loved the Army, he loved the Air Force, and we loved each other. After two years in command he was selected by General Hugh Shelton, then the commander of the US Special Operations Command, to be the deputy Chief of Staff for the command in Tampa because, as one Army general explained, "We want to make you the first Red Beret general officer."

Although Air Force special operators like Craig did not wear the highly coveted brown leather jacket, they were the Army's equivalent of Special Forces and rangers. Senior leaders in the Army Special Operations business understood and valued the contribution of Air Force combat controllers. General Shelton and General Schoomaker were not only my advocates; they were Craig's as well.

For the next three years Craig's Army bosses were committed to getting him promoted to one-star. Unfortunately—and understandably so—the Air Force is responsible for selecting its generals. The Air Force hierarchy just didn't see the need for a ground combatant general officer to rise through its most senior ranks.

When I was selected for brigadier general (one star) in the spring of 2000, Craig wasn't selected. At that time, he didn't see the need to continue to fight a futile fight. He could have hung on, taken another assignment, and filled a space. He wasn't bitter. I was frustrated, however, that the Air Force was shortsighted and couldn't appreciate what his unique background, experience, and skill set could bring to the fight. But he retired happily and looked forward. The only time I think he missed serving was when the drumbeats of war sounded the following year, immediately after 9/11.

I was relieved that he left the Air Force healthy and smiling. We'd been married for eleven years, and half of those were spent apart. General Schoomaker was Craig's boss when he retired. They had known each other for twenty years, and it was only natural that the general would oversee the retirement ceremony. General Schoomaker, a private, reserved, and decorated patriot, was brief but gracious in his comments. He focused on the years of their association in joint special operations, the wars they had fought together, and the training they had completed together.

He recounted one story Craig and I had shared several times. General Schoomaker and Craig had desks next to each other when they both worked in Current Operations at the Joint Special Operations Command in late 1983 and early 1984. They were a major and captain, respectively. In those days one officer was assigned to stay overnight in the communications center in the basement of the headquarters in case there was an emergency call or a high-level inquiry from Washington. Late one afternoon, when General Schoomaker was slated for the duty that night, he received a call from his wife, telling him that her water had broken and he needed to come home. Craig had overheard the gist of the call and just told him to go take care of his wife: "Sir, get out of here, I'll take care of the night duty."

"Are you sure?"

"No sweat. Good luck."

Schoomaker's daughter Laura was born later that night. Years later he did everything he could to get Craig promoted to brigadier general, but it just didn't happen. His belief in Craig as a soldier meant so much to us, more than any star.

AFTER I COMPLETED MY battalion command tour in 1994 with the 82nd Airborne Division I was faced with one of the toughest decisions of my career. The Chief of Staff of the division asked me whether I would stay another year to be the division chief of logistics (G4). It was one of the best jobs for a former battalion commander. The division G4, a lieutenant colonel position, was the primary logistics adviser and policy maker for the division. It would have been another "first" for the division—this time the first female G4. But there were other factors to consider. I was on orders to attend Senior Service College at the Industrial College of the Armed Forces at Fort McNair in Washington, DC. There I would be reunited with Craig, who was working at the Pentagon as deputy director of the Special Operations Division on the Air Force staff.

I'd been with the 82nd for six years and had spent the past two of those geographically separated from my husband. We didn't want to concede that separation had become our new normal just because we were both pursuing military careers. We decided that being together was more important than my chance to be the division chief of logistics. I nervously called the Chief of Staff of the division to thank him for his faith in me. Then I respectfully declined. He said he understood. I'm not convinced that he really did, because the Army culture of the time reinforced placing the needs of the Army over family considerations. Without hesitation most soldiers immediately say, "Yes sir" to such an offer. I'm grateful he didn't pressure me to take the new position.

I was fortunate that I was never passed over for a big promotion. My only deflating moment came in 1999. Several senior logisticians said that I was going to be promoted to brigadier general a year early. It was common for senior general officers to want to make you feel like they were in the "know" and could share these predictions. Unfortunately what I learned after sitting on boards was that no one really knows who will be selected until the list is published. I didn't expect to be on the list because you truly never know, but I allowed myself to believe that this was my time. However, my name wasn't on the list. The selection system is fair, and only once the list is released do you know for sure whether you made it. But when leaders say you're going to be promoted and you aren't, it's disappointing. The following year I was elated when I received the promotion.

MOST OF MY DAYS IN the Army started just about the same way: alarm buzzing at 0500 hours, put on PT clothes, cup of coffee, and out the door. Maybe there would be a few exercises or stretches, but the cornerstone of the training was a four-mile run. A formation run with NCOs keeping cadence and running in perfect unison is a real morale builder. Sometimes it was just a small squad of eight or ten, sometimes a full platoon of seventy or eighty or a company of two hundred. On special occasions, like a Friday morning prior to a holiday weekend, it might even be a battalion of six hundred or so soldiers.

Once a year it would be an entire division. What a sight. In the 82nd Airborne Division we had such a run every May during All-American Week. Fourteen thousand paratroopers in formation, starting on Ardennes Street, then a right turn on Longstreet Road, all the way to the end at Reilly Road and back. Family, friends, and nearby residents lined the streets as units sang songs, hooted, and hollered. *Here We Go, On the Run, Gotta Be, AIRBORNE!* It was quite a celebration.

I've always loved running. Running for me meant fitness, clearing the cobwebs from a night's sleep, stress mitigation, and a chance to think about the day ahead. What I hated was the dark. I hated getting up well before sunrise. But most of all I hated running in the dark. For me it was just unnatural. I love being in the sun, I love sunrises, and I like to see where I'm going. Much later in my career I tripped on a curb and fell flat on my face. I shattered my wrist trying to break my fall. A metal plate and eight screws later, my wrist was fixed. During rehab I remember thinking, *I'm getting too old for this crap.*

Craig says he has never seen anyone who was more at peace when I announced, "I'm done, babe." Retirement wasn't unexpected. We had been talking about timing and circumstances for months. On this day, though, a cold winter day at Redstone Arsenal, I'd finally said no to one last feeler for another job. The Chief of Staff of the Army said he wanted to nominate me to be the next commander of the United States Transportation Command (USTRANSCOM) at Scott Air Force Base, Illinois. I would become the first Army general to command USTRANSCOM and the first female to command a combatant command. I was honored, but I didn't have the energy for it. We talked about the physical pain and the wear and tear. My back ached most days, and spinal epidurals had become my only relief.

For nearly four decades I had parachuted from planes, climbed mountains, marched hundreds of miles, and led thousands of men and women—far too often in times of war. I had few real vacations, rarely slept in, and participated in countless predawn training exercises. But I never second-guessed a second of it because I was given a chance to make a difference in the greatest military in the world. I had accomplished more than what was imaginable or possible when I signed up for the Women's Officer Orientation course in 1974. I had already stayed a year longer than my final appointment required. I was staring at sixty in the mirror. Although I probably wasn't going to live as long in retirement as my father has, I was ready to give it a try.

I had a three-year-old granddaughter whom I'd only seen twice. In a life of few regrets, my biggest disappointment was never having children of my own. A failed first marriage and meeting Craig much later in life derailed those plans. But Craig, ever Mr. Wonderful, has given me the most precious gift: his family. Although his boys are technically my stepsons, there's no technicality about our grandkids, DNA be damned. I'm their GiGi, short for Gorgeous Grandma. I stole that name from another Grandma I know—the wife of one of my high school classmates from Supreme Headquarters Allied Powers Europe (SHAPE) Belgium, Sharon Foster.

I wanted to enjoy life with family and friends and be healthy doing so once retirement rolled around. At sixty, I started to wonder whether that would be possible. A life of competitive sports, parachuting from planes, running in military boots, and being a thrill seeker were finally catching up with me. In addition to the spinal epidurals and the shattered wrist, I broke my ankle while Craig and I were on leave in Hawaii with his older son, Bryan. I told the CSA that I was ready to hang up my dog tags. Like my father and husband before me, I knew when it was time. I wasn't quitting; I just didn't want to take on another four-star assignment at that stage of my life. I'd done it my way. Like Fogleman, I felt honorable and clean.

Over the years I've come to realize that some people don't know how or when to retire. We do what we've been doing all of our lives until someone tells us it's time to go. In the military we are so busy that we don't even have time to think about retirement until it is upon us—myself included. Most continue to serve because they love it as I did. Some can't retire because of their belief in selfless service and loyalty: "They asked me to stay." What do you say? These are the values of our Army. These are all wonderful reasons to continue to serve. At the same time, however, these patriotic reasons for staying can lead to stagnation in promotion and or assignments of those we have been grooming to replace us. When you are promoted to three stars you receive a letter from the Chief of Staff of the Army saying congratulations on your promotion, but if in three years you are not promoted to four stars or asked to stay for another three-star assignment, you must submit your retirement papers. The Army also has mandatory retirement dates based on rank. Craig's mandatory retirement as a colonel was thirty years. He chose to retire after twenty-six. These arbitrary mandatory timelines assume everyone needs to go based on time rather than talent or lack of it. Boardrooms wrestle with the same issue, using tenure or age as the termination of one's board duty versus succession planning based on talent diversity.

Several months before retiring I attended the General Officer Transition course, a one-week program designed to prepare senior officers for retirement. The instructor compared retiring to the five stages of grieving: (1) denial, (2) anger, (3) bargaining, (4) depression, and (5) acceptance.

I had read ahead and knew what was coming. I lost it when he started in on anger. I raised my hand and said, "Excuse me, but retirement isn't a time to grieve. It's a time of celebration and reflection." My point was that everyone in that room, whether a one-star or a four-star, had a hugely successful career. No one should compare it to grieving.

For me a new life begins after retirement—especially in the military, where most of us retire long before average citizens. It might be scary for some. Soldiering is the only thing most of us have ever known. Leaving the Army is uncertain and exciting. Rarely does one get a chance to get this all figured out before they actually retire. So there is a period of unknown, and there was for me as well. But I certainly can't accept the notion that we should compare our departure from military service to grief or death. It took me a while to figure out what I wanted to do when I retired, but I never regretted retiring when I did. Nor did I compare it to grieving.

In October 2011 the Chief of Staff held his four-star conference at West Point, followed by a bus ride to New York City, where we visited Ground Zero, the 9/11 Memorial Monument, and the New York Police Department. I had not been to this part of the city in many years and certainly not since that fateful September morning. The visit caught me off guard, stirring up some strong emotions.

The monument is a remarkable tribute to the thousands who lost their lives on 9/11, a day that stands as a constant reminder of the evils of terrorism and the importance of service. As I stood there I tried to visualize what the towers had looked like. In 1993 I had accompanied Craig's Army War College class on a trip to this very spot. We had eaten dinner at the top of the North Tower in a restaurant called Windows on the World. Now I stood looking up as I'd done then, and of course it was all gone.

I walked along the monument and ran my fingers over two familiar names engraved in the granite. Lieutenant General Timothy Maude and Major Stephen Long, both killed as American Airlines Flight 77 crashed into the Pentagon. I knew Maude from my time in the Pentagon. Craig knew him from Saturday morning golf outings at Fort Belvoir. He was passionate and professional. He made the personnel system more responsive for the solider. Not unlike the Veterans Affairs system, personnel actions in the Army can take months to resolve. Tim Maude worked to expedite the process, getting orders for moving families or filling soldier vacancies with a sense of urgency. He made things better for soldiers.

Major Long was a Georgia boy who served with me as a lieutenant in the 82nd Airborne. He enlisted in the Army when he was twenty, served with the 2nd Ranger Battalion Airborne at Fort Lewis, and was awarded the Purple Heart in Grenada during Operation Urgent Fury. After earning his officer commission, Steve was assigned to the 82nd when we deployed to Saudi Arabia in support of operation Desert Storm/Desert Shield. He was thirty-nine years old when he died on 9/11 in the Pentagon. He is survived by his wife, Tina, and two stepsons.

On the day of his funeral we left the Post Chapel on Fort Myer, Virginia, after the memorial service and marched behind the flag-covered casket down to the gravesite. There was very little noise, most people deep in thought about the loss of this young officer. Family and friends walked side by side down to his final resting place on the hallowed grounds of Arlington Cemetery, passing by headstone after headstone of fallen comrades. I just walked in silence until we arrived. The chaplain gave his blessings, and the honor guard proceeded to move the casket in place and folded the American flag into a perfect triangular shape. I, in my service dress uniform, was handed the flag with the traditional slow, reverent exchange of salutes with the NCOIC of the burial detail. I then turned and presented the American flag to Steve's wife, Tina. I knelt down on one knee and presented the perfectly folded American Flag to her, saying, "On behalf of the president of the United States, the United States Army, and a grateful nation, please accept this flag as a symbol of our appreciation for your loved one's honorable and faithful service to his country."

With tissue in hand and tears in her eyes, she bowed her head and said, "Thank you." The three-volley gun salute was followed by the mournful playing of Taps. That solemn tribute gets to Craig and me every time we hear it.

Seeing the names of Maude and Long among many more was so somber, so stark, so surreal. The police commissioner, Ray Kelly, was our host, and he was accompanied by first responders who had been there that day. The opportunity to talk to the first responders brought a sense of pride, and I listened as they recounted their stories of courage—firefighters who headed into the burning towers, trying rescue whoever could be rescued, many who never came back out, and police officers trying to maintain order amid chaos no one had ever imagined. Many of the survivors remain devastated by the loss of their friends and coworkers. As we talked, we gained new appreciation for what they had done, and we discovered that we shared a common bond of service.

I stood with the senior leadership of the Army, who, like me, were one-star generals serving around the Army when 9/11 occurred. Over the past decade this collective group of four-star generals had deployed many times and taken the fight to the enemy. I was in awe, surrounded by these great Americans, knowing I had the privilege to serve with many of them. So much has changed during this pivotal period in US history. Saddam Hussein and Osama bin Laden were killed during US-led military operations. The first female four-star general in the US military was appointed. US citizens voted into the White House the first African American commander-in-chief.

During the visit to the monument I knew that my "brief two-year detour in the Army before becoming a coach and PE teacher" was finally over. In my heart I was as proud as I could be to be part of this great Army and this great nation. I was humbled that I was able to serve during critical times.

It's been two years since I retired, and what a joy it's been regularly visiting and tending to my ninety-six-year-old father. Although I still like to think of my dad as invincible, I know it won't be much longer until he'll reunite with Mom in heaven. I relish every moment with him. I cherish every e-mail that my tough-as-nails, artistic-soul father still sends, even as he approaches one hundred years on earth. I have found so many new joys since saying good-bye to my Army life, like flying to visit Craig's ninety-three-year-old mother, Helen, who lives in San Bernardino, California, or seeing the grandkids and visiting friends on my own timeline and in person, not via Skype or FaceTime with spotty Internet connection from a war-torn country at random hours.

Oh, and another thing—I love doing physical training in the daylight.

eleven

★ ★ ★ ★

LEADER OF LEADERS
"Build Your Bench"

EVERYBODY IS REPLACEABLE—kings and queens, generals, CEOs, Hall of Fame athletes. Great leaders should be prepared to fire themselves and help find their heir apparent. The military changed my life. It gave me a husband. It gave me self-esteem and confidence. It gave me the opportunity to see the world and make a small difference in the well-being of people in war-torn countries. What's most rewarding, however, is knowing that today's Army is infinitely better than the great one I joined forty years ago. It's also getting better without me. We are stronger and we are more diverse, though there is still work to do in getting more minorities in positions of leadership. We aren't perfect, but there isn't a better war-fighting machine and defender of liberties in the world. That's in large part because of the military's deep bench and people like "Bonecrusher."

A few months after I retired I received an e-mail from a young female Air Force fighter pilot looking for advice on her promising career. I was flattered that she reached out. She probably didn't need my insights. She already had the pedigree. She was born on an Air Force base in Germany. Her mother was one of the Army's first female helicopter pilots. Her father was an A-10 pilot and a fellow Air Force Academy alum. This young soldier in many ways is the new face of the military: a compassionate warrior.

She earned the nickname Bonecrusher because of her relentless style of play on the soccer field during a standout college career. During e-mail exchanges she always had several queries.

Bonecrusher: "If you aren't too busy, I was wondering if you wouldn't mind answering a few questions I had or providing me a little mentorship. I feel really blessed to be here in the chairman's CAG [special think tank for the chairman of the Joint Chiefs of Staff] and to have the opportunity to be surrounded by things I would never get to see or hear anywhere else. Almost every day I'm reminded how outside my comfort zone I really am."

Dunwoody: "Trust me, when I worked in the CSA's initiatives group I had to pinch myself everyday. . . . When I got e-mails from GEN Reimer asking for my thoughts and opinions I couldn't get used to the fact that the CSA was e-mailing me (a lieutenant colonel) for my opinion. What I realized is that it was his way of staying connected to folks who had just come out of the field, and we could lend a little reality to the discussion. I also realized after I left that it was more of a professional development assignment for me than anything I had ever had. I got to see the things you are seeing. How the Pentagon works, all the challenges and pressures. And when I went out to command my brigade I was now a disciple for the CSA because I understood the rationale behind some of the tough decisions. One of the most rewarding assignments I ever had."

Bonecrusher: "What was your approach to situations you didn't feel particularly comfortable in?"

Dunwoody: "I always tried to be like a fly on the wall. I wanted to learn and observe as much as I could from the discussion or the event, realizing I really was a 'student.' When asked my opinion I would always answer as honestly as I could while being respectful. I never was a good 'yes person.' I think that's the true value you can bring to the assignment. Sharing your perspectives from your experiences. Trust me, just being a female, you will bring new and refreshing perspectives to the problems. Sometimes I thought the guys would look at me like I was from Mars, but I do believe diversity of thought is a strength and that you can make a difference.

"That said, sometimes it's harder to be heard because you have a different view. But that doesn't make it any less important if you really believe in what you have to offer. I recommend you be very persistent if it is important and could make a difference in the long run. I've been in environments where guys yell louder to make their point. But it didn't make the point any better. I had guys try to patronize me, but not do anything. I've had guys try to minimize my inputs. But I would not let them get away with any of it. You have to fight for what you believe in on the battlefield and in the Pentagon."

One of most important jobs a senior leader has is to develop leaders or to "build the bench." This is common in sports, where a versatile bench is often the determining factor in whether a team survives the rigors of a demanding season while building a team for the future. Players get injured, go into a slump, or get traded. Employees get promoted, quit, or retire. Do you have players ready to step in when inevitable changes occur?

Throughout the military ranks, soldiers are being developed or are developing others. The Army has a very deliberate and specified professional education program. Creating leaders is what we do. The Army has an evaluation process that recommends good leaders for further schooling and advancement while nonselecting or weeding out others not deemed ready for advancement. Are parts of it subjective? Sure, but what isn't?

Beyond the structured leadership program there's an informal mentoring process that truly makes the Army special. The most important leadership lessons I learned throughout my career came directly from someone who took the time to teach, coach, and share ideas with me. Sometimes it happened in a classroom or a war zone, but just as often it happened during a run, over a beer, or at dinner.

Lieutenant General Tom Glisson is the only man I've ever met who could scold someone while laughing. A man of great character and a great sense of humor, he is the only logistics officer I ever worked for, and I worked for him twice. The first time we worked together I was a captain and he was a lieutenant colonel and the quartermaster branch chief at the Army Personnel Center. We worked hard, made time for a five-mile run every day, and laughed constantly. He is a great communicator and jokester. You always knew what he wanted or where you stood. He remembered everyone's birthday and always made a big deal about birthday cake surprises, from the clerk secretary to senior leaders. To this day he still sends cards to everyone.

As the three-star director of the Defense Logistics Agency, he hired me as his XO in 1998. This job technically made me joint qualified, which means that I understood multiservice operations—you need to be joint qualified to be eligible for selection to brigadier general. Surprisingly, General Glisson sat on the promotion board that selected me for promotion to brigadier. Because I was his XO and responsible for his calendar, I knew he was on the board. But true to his oath of secrecy, he never let on that I would be on the list.

When I first reported as his XO, I wasn't sure I'd last the day. I was now working in a very different capacity than the last time I had worked for him as a twenty-nine-year-old captain. Now, as a colonel, I was responsible for every piece of paper and every person who went in and out of his office. He lived and died by his calendar, and he told me that I would live and die by it too. The calendar could pinpoint his every move for six months. When I first took over as the XO, Glisson summoned me to his office every Monday to review the schedule. He often looked at me like I was the dumbest XO in the world, chuckling as he did so. He then proceeded to pick apart the calendar:

"You couldn't have informed me sooner? Why did I drive to Arlington for a lunch meeting only to find it's next week? How can we get from Fort Belvoir to the Pentagon in fifteen minutes? That's crazy! Where's my white space?" (White space is that precious time without an appointment—free time to make calls, work on a speech, or just breathe.)

At the end of these sessions, his secretary, Wanda; aide-de-camp, Harney; and I would retreat and fix the calendar. Attention to the most minuscule detail didn't come naturally to me, but I soon became adept at managing time to the second.

Franklin Covey would have been impressed. LTG Glisson's techniques worked. He helped me prioritize my time, become more detailed oriented, and put order into an otherwise chaotic schedule.

When I became a general officer I found myself parroting Lieutenant General Glisson as I lectured my staff about living and dying by the calendar: "You couldn't have informed me sooner? Why did I drive to Arlington for a lunch meeting only to find out it's next week? How can we get from Fort Belvoir to the Pentagon in fifteen minutes? That's crazy! Where's my white space?"

I had many great role models at crucial stages of my career. They helped develop me—and countless other soldiers—without bullying tactics. They didn't care about my gender; they cared about me. They pushed me physically and challenged me mentally. In the military you can't achieve your best without sound mind and body. Most important, they put their faith in me and put me on the bench.

In 1981 Lieutenant Colonel Henry Fitzpatrick selected me to command the Airborne Rigger detachment as a captain in Kaiserslautern Germany. He was tough and stern but fair. He had a very rigid and thorough inspection program. He had checklists for everything. There were no surprises. During my first inspection I thought most members of his inspection team were being too nitpicky, looking only for faults instead of the good.

Once, when I thought my command was doing exceptionally well, Lieutenant Colonel Fitzpatrick pulled a surprise inspection while I was on leave. They found faults and errors galore. When I returned I had a sealed brown envelope with the worst report and detailed listing of write-ups I'd ever seen, let alone received as my own. It was embarrassing. I tried to refute some of the findings, but he wouldn't hear any of that. Besides, he was right. Attention to detail is crucial in the military. He gave me thirty days to fix the problems. We passed the next inspection, and he commended us on a job well done. In private he reminded me, "Don't ever get too comfortable. There's always room for improvement."

Lieutenant Colonel Fitzpatrick was a motivator. During one of my first visits to his office I noticed a photo of him finishing the Marine Corps Marathon in Washington, DC. I thought, "Wow, that's neat. How impressive. I want to do that." I told him of my ambition to try it, and he told me he was sure I could do it if I set my mind to it. Four years later I finished the Marine Corps Marathon in three hours and thirty-three minutes. I checked that box, and that was my last marathon. Standing at the finish line in the mass of people was Henry Fitzpatrick.

Lieutenant Colonel Fitzpatrick never compromised. He demanded more from me than anyone I ever worked for. Those early days of surprise inspection tests annoyed me, but ultimately they made me better. About a year after plopping that brown sealed envelope on my desk, he gave me the greatest compliment. He was the first to comment in my evaluation report, "Captain Dunwoody will ascend to the highest levels in the Army."

While I was elated that he believed in me, I was also saddened because I had no one to share that special moment with. My family was thousands of miles away, back in the States. I hadn't yet met Craig. My mother used to ask me after my divorce, "Don't you ever get lonely?"

"Mom, I don't have time to get lonely. I work hard, I have a lot of friends in the Army who work with me, and they aren't married either. So we get together all the time for a run or dinner or a beer or a show."

Three of my best friends and my boss trained for the Marine Corps Marathon together—Jan, Barb, Andy, Tom, and myself. Three long months of six days a week training. I was never bored. But this was one of the few times that I did get lonely. I realized that having good friends was important, but not having a "significant other" to share the real hard times or, in this case, the real good times made me feel lonely.

AS A FOUR-STAR GENERAL and the senior logistician in the Army, I was responsible for helping the Chief of Staff of the Army build and manage the bench for logistical colonels and general officers. I used what we call "horse blankets" in the Army—large spreadsheets to list all the logistics general officers (about thirty-five total) by the year they were commissioned, the date they were last promoted, current assignment, past experiences (joint, strategic, institutional, operational, and any specialties), and mandatory retirement date. Then I listed all the logistics general officer assignments and who was scheduled to rotate out or move on. Finally I provided the top three names for each position as potential candidates to fill the position when vacated. We worked this strategy six months out so officers had sufficient planning time once approved by the Chief at the four-star conference. I would coordinate each recommendation I made with the officers involved and with the gaining and losing four-star general officer to get their support and buy-in before the four-star conference. This made for a smooth process. The four-stars were always supportive of the nominations and appreciated my coordination efforts. It was a lot of work, but it was very effective.

As one progresses in the Army she will develop her own reputation based on performance and, just as important, potential. In one of my officer evaluation reports as a captain my PERSCOM boss wrote, "She is a possible future General officer and must be developed accordingly." I was surprised. At that point I didn't even think I was going to stay in the Army. He was identifying my potential early on so I could be monitored—or until I proved him wrong. Evaluating me as a lieutenant colonel, my division commander wrote, "She is destined to wear many stars—the sooner the better."

Once I learned to identify the standouts it became my responsibility to become their champion. Although it is fairly easy to identify the standouts, it is also important to look for talent and potential that might not be so apparent. You can't do effective succession planning without first growing and filling the bench. Despite being terminally ill with cancer, Steve Jobs made sure he had his successor in place long before his death because he wanted Apple to succeed for generations. Walt Disney Corporation recently extended the contract of uber-successful CEO Bob Iger for two more years, in part so he can help the company find his successor.

In August 2003 General Pete Schoomaker was named the thirty-fifth Chief of Staff of the US Army. His selection was surprising, but not because he wasn't superbly qualified. He is one of the strongest leaders I've ever known. He's a visionary with a keen intellect and common sense. He's as determined as Jobs and rivals all great CEOs with his vision, acumen, and intellect. He's also a very private person who doesn't seek the spotlight. He appointed me as his three-star director of logistics for the Army in 2005. He also planted the seed with the other four-stars that I had the potential to be the next head of the Army Materiel Command.

What made Schoomaker's appointment a head-scratcher was that he had been enjoying a happy retirement when he was called on to serve his country again, stepping down as the fifth commanding general of the US Special Operations Command in the fall of 2000. Before he retired the first time he knew me more as Craig's wife than as an Army colonel. They had served together in joint special operations units dating back to 1981.

When Secretary of Defense Donald Rumsfeld convinced General Schoomaker to come out of retirement, there was disbelief and disappointment. No one questioned General Schoomaker's qualifications, but he was retired. Did the Secretary not trust us? Did Secretary Rumsfeld not think the Army's bench of four-stars was deep enough? What type of message was he sending to active and decorated leaders who had served their country proudly and successfully for three or four decades? Did the soured relationship with the previous Chief of Staff so poison the well as to make it improbable for a trusting relationship between the Army and the Department of Defense?

Few understood Rumsfeld's exact reasoning. A two-star at the time, I knew there were people ready to step in and lead the US Army. Although I think General Schoomaker's tenure as Chief of Staff was one of the most successful in history and was an important period for my professional development, his appointment made me wonder whether civilian leadership simply didn't know or appreciate the talented leaders ready to step in and serve.

A good way to evaluate how well you've done at growing the bench is to ask yourself: Who will replace you, and who could eventually replace your successor? Succession planning involves more than just identifying replacements; it requires putting rising stars in the tough jobs and helping them succeed. Sometimes it requires sending folks from cushy offices to the field or back to school. Sometimes it requires investing in professional development and life-coaching courses. Few leaders were born with "it"; most are molded and developed deliberately or indirectly.

Succession planning can be difficult because our culture drives us to focus on being number one. A lot of sports coaches fail at developing the bench because the pressures of winning are often overwhelming and their primary concern is survival. There are basically two types of coaches: those who have been fired and those who will be.

It's difficult for alpha leaders to admit their services won't be needed. Thinking about finding our replacement seems counterintuitive. We think we are in great shape physically and sharp mentally. We don't want our top employees to think we're going to abandon them. Instead, we're busy trying to show why we're the best person for the job. The same culture exists in many boardrooms today. There is a push by activist investors and governance agencies to refresh boards—in other words, reduce the number of graybeards. Although it's crucial that we continue to innovate and invigorate, age, just like gender or race, shouldn't be the deciding factor in succession planning. Finding and developing those with the most potential to lead the unit, corporation, board, or team to greater success will ultimately be a leader's greatest legacy.

Young CEOs in particular have difficulty planning to walk away. But I always ask leaders, "What happens if you get smacked by an Abrams tank tomorrow?"

I have taken over two commands where my predecessors kept their entire key leadership teams in place until the day they departed. Once they left, their entire teams departed as well. I was left to form a new team—recruit, select, and train. Inheriting organizations like that made me even more determined to formalize the process of succession and transition planning.

Successful transitions must be a collaborative effort. Let your team know your plans and that you have faith they will continue to build on your joint accomplishments. If your team is part of the process and the future, they will be much more energized to tackle the challenges. This isn't just for senior executives; entry-level employees, middle management, and C-suite leaders should pay it forward with the hungry, ambitious kid in the mailroom, the idealistic intern, and the single mom going to night school, trying to improve the opportunities for herself and her children.

Change is hard, and bureaucratic organizations tend to be resistant to it. This is true at the Pentagon, Capitol Hill, 1600 Pennsylvania Avenue, and on every street from Wall Street to Main Street. People are so afraid of messing up that they would rather not challenge long-entrenched institutional norms and, instead, play it safe. But great leaders don't show up at work just to rubber-stamp policy or simply cash a check. The people who suffer from bad succession planning are the employees and customers. War fighters were my customers. Making sure they had basic necessities from toilet paper and three squares to tanks and missiles was AMC's responsibility.

GENERAL GEORGE CASEY pushed my nomination for a fourth star up the chain of command and ultimately to the White House for the final approval. He was a wonderful and supportive boss. He would visit my headquarters once a quarter on a Saturday morning, in civilian clothes, to talk about the tough issues of the day, things like logistics support for the war fighters or whether it was smart to extend the contract or send the requirement back out to industry and let service providers compete for the work. It was informal and informative. By the time he left each session he had a greater grasp of the issues that my team faced. He did this with all of his major commands.

It was during one of our quarterly meetings in the fall of 2010 that General Casey and I first discussed the succession planning for AMC. I was two years into my expected three-year term. There was still much work ahead to complete our headquarters move from Fort Belvoir to Redstone Arsenal. Typically the Army would identify my replacement and there would be a change of command almost exactly one year later. In a closed-door session with the Chief, I laid out the transition plan. What became immediately obvious was that my retirement would be within just months of the retirement of my military deputy and the command sergeant major as well as the replacement of my civilian deputy, who was not moving to Redstone. Plus my operations officer and Chief of Staff were scheduled to be reassigned. Just two months after the closing date when AMC needed to be settled in Alabama, the entire leadership team would have just changed, be changing, or about to change.

For General Casey the answer was clear: he asked me to stay another year. In short order I laid out a new transition plan and took it to the four-star conference. Some of the hardest decisions we make involve people we know and trust. Often they have served well and faithfully. These decisions can become emotional and ruin lifelong relationships if they are not handled correctly. I asked for approval to retire my military three-star deputy early so we could get a new three-star on board who could spend some time transitioning with the outgoing deputy. His successor would then have a year in the saddle before my retirement.

My command sergeant major decided not to make the move but thought he might be able to stay in the job while flying back and forth from Washington, DC, to Huntsville. I needed a full-time go-getter to help the command settle in at Redstone, and I asked him to retire as well. I extended my operations officer and my Chief of Staff.

As I was thinking about AMC's succession plan I called Dennis and asked him whether he would be interested in the deputy job. The conversation went something like this:

"Hey, Dennis, how are you?"

"Ma'am, what a pleasure to hear your voice." I could practically see his smile through the phone.

"Dennis, we are doing great things and are busy with the move to Huntsville, but everything is going well. Don't fall out of your chair when I ask you this next question, but I was thinking about your situation there and was wondering whether you would be interested in being my deputy?"

There was a short pause. "Are you kidding?" he asked. "That would be fantastic. I would be honored." It reminded me of my phone call to Sergeant Bowen, asking him whether he would like to be my 1st sergeant.

"Great, Dennis, I was hoping you would say that." Then I told him I had not talked to anyone about it yet but wanted to make sure he was interested before I threw his name in the ring. He must have thanked me four or five times for even considering him for the job. "Keep fighting the good fight," I told him, knowing how hard it is to get anything done in the building. "I'll be in touch. "

"Take care, Airborne!"

After I received permission for my military deputy to retire early as a three-star, the next question from the four-star conference was: Who would replace him? This was a busy time for AMC. We were overseeing the retrograde of combat equipment out of Iraq, and my military deputy was on the scene, making sure this critical logistical chess game was being played to win. When it was clear to the four-stars that we didn't have a two-star logistician who was ready to move up on such short notice, the names came flying in from all over the room. This infantry guy could do it, that artillery guy could do it, or this engineer could do it. It's funny sometimes how combat arms guys think a combat arms guy can do anything, even logistics, whereas they think logicians can only do logistics. Actually, it's not so funny.

I threw out Lieutenant General Dennis Via's name, and it stuck. LTG Via was a major in the 82nd Airborne when we first crossed paths in 1990. He was a smart, likable guy. An African American Signal officer from Martinsville, Virginia, he was the Distinguished Military Graduate from Virginia State University in 1981. Dennis had commanded one of AMC's two-star-level commands for two years and knew our business and the command as well as anyone. When I promoted Dennis to four stars I said, "My great-grandfather Brigadier General H. H. C. Dunwoody was one of the Army's original Signal corps officers." He was Teddy Roosevelt's Signal officer when they took San Juan Hill in Cuba. Sadly he was the last Dunwoody I know of to have any "IT" skills.

Dennis received his third star in August 2009 and became the director of communications for the chairman of the Joint Chiefs of Staff. In a cruel twist of bureaucratic fate, his three-star position on the joint staff was downgraded to two-star a short time later. The military is constantly reviewing the number of general officers required as well as the level of seniority of the general officer needed for each assignment. Under the rules Via would need to be nominated for another three-star job, revert to a two-star position, or retire as a two-star. This doesn't happen often, but the law is clear. These promotions are appointments, and an officer is supposed to have three honorable years in grade (i.e., their rank) before they can retire at that rank. But there are always exceptions.

Everyone in the room liked Dennis and knew he was facing a raw deal with the recent downgrade. I recounted his previous experience with AMC. He had commanded AMC's Communications Electronics Command for two years. I shared with them what a great job he had done getting the politicians and his workforce on board with the BRAC decision to move his headquarters from Fort Monmouth, New Jersey, to Aberdeen Proving Grounds in Maryland. It was hard government work, but he was very successful. We soon had the nod of approval from around the table.

Of course Via's appointment didn't solve who would replace me as the commanding general. After his first six months in the job, Via had shown me, without a doubt, that he was the one to replace me. He understood the command and the transformational initiatives underway. We were realigning all of the strategic logistical capabilities under our command to have the premier logistics headquarters responsible for all Army logistics. Maintenance and supply activities were scattered around the Army under different headquarters, keeping us from being as efficient and effective as we could be without some consolidation and optimization.

We were transforming the way we did service contracts, and we were in the process of becoming the lead materiel integrator (LMI), a single point of contact, a single headquarters now responsible to the leadership of the Army to manage and advise on all logistical matters, our core competency. Via was a believer in the vision of command and the brand. He helped promote our AMC branding campaign—notably while he was deployed to Kuwait. When I made my visits to see our men and women in Kuwait, Afghanistan, and Iraq, everywhere I went I saw the red, white, and blue AMC patch proudly displayed, even in the remotest areas. It made me feel good, and it made me proud. I never passed up an opportunity to champion Via and trumpet his credentials. I went out of my way to make sure the Chief and the other four-stars knew why I believed he was the best person for the job.

With the sudden announcement of General Marty Dempsey as the new chairman of the Joint Chiefs of Staff, we now had a new Chief of Staff, General Ray Odierno. I knew he would make the best decision for the Army, and he would have my unwavering support. These years at war brought war fighters and logisticians together. I was delighted when Ray was named to be our Chief. I saw Ray more times in Iraq than I ever saw him in the United States. We would always have dinner. I learned so much from him, but I also appreciated the fact that at the four-star level you don't have a lot of folks you can talk to and just vent without fear of repercussions. Everyone has frustrations, from captains to four-stars, so you need trusted friends with whom you can share good things and bad.

"Chief, I know this is a big decision for you, and you're getting a lot of pressure from the other four-stars. Not only do I know that Dennis is the best candidate based on his performance and his potential, I also know why the other guys being considered are not the best candidates. We're in one the most complicated transformations, and Dennis understands it. To bring in a combat arms guy or someone who doesn't get it might slow or even defeat the transformation. But Dennis gets it. I think it's important that we have a talented black American on the bench, and we need to take advantage of adding him to the team, not only as a role model leader but also as a role model for black officers and Signal officers." (Dennis was the first Signal officer ever to be promoted to four stars.)

Ray told me he wanted to have an interview with him. I was glad about that. I called Dennis the morning of the interview. "Dennis, how are you? Listen, I just wanted to call you and say good luck. I know you will do well. Just be open and honest, and talk to him about all the initiatives you're involved with to make the Army more efficient and effective."

He said, "Thanks, ma'am, I'll keep you posted."

Ray selected him at the end of the interview. Dennis called me immediately and said, "Ma'am, I got the job."

"Yahoo!" I said. "Never a doubt! Now get back here and get to work."

"Yes, ma'am!"

Thank you, Lord, for giving me the strength to do the right thing for the right reason. The Army just had another first. A black American four-star was not a first, but being the first Signal officer four-star was. As general officers, we are just that— generalists. At the four-star level it's not the job skill that's most important; we need the best athletes and the best leaders to run our Army. Check parochialism at the door and recognize all the talent out there on the bench.

Our greatest accomplishment will not be how many parachute jumps we made, how many wars we fought in, or how many medals we've earned. Our legacy will be measured by the depth and quality of the leaders we develop. This is what we should do best. The temptation is to put building a bench on hold while focusing on imperative day-to-day duties. I have coached and mentored hundreds of soldiers from my early days as a 2nd lieutenant to my final years as the senior logistician in the Army. I was coached and mentored by many people, up to my very last second in the military. In fact, my mentors continue to nurture and guide me, even in my sixties. I still seek advice from Generals Schoomaker, Sullivan, McChrystal, Brown, Casey, Glisson, Cody, Shelton, Griffin, McNeill, McKiernan, and Ham. I talk to most of them regularly, and former bosses are still recommending me for panels, speaking engagements, and boards. I'm still on their bench.

Without consciously taking time to build your bench, you run the risk of hurting your organization for generations. If anyone is worried about the next generation of our military, worry no more. There are soldiers as committed to the fight as my great-grandfather Henry Harrison Chase Dunwoody was when he fought the Spanish-American War.

I'll never forget Sergeant Jack Shumocker, a twenty-four-year-old infantry soldier from Champaign, Illinois, and Sergeant Dennis Hollimon, a thirty-year-old quartermaster from Jacksonville, Florida. I met both noncommissioned officers at Landstuhl Medical Center in Germany one day after they had been evacuated from Afghanistan, one without a lower leg and one without an arm. I looked at their faces and their natural reaction to seeing a general officer, and they both instinctively wanted to jump to attention when I walked in. "Wow, I have never met a general in person," Sergeant Shumocker said, "not to mention a female general."

"What unit were you with?" I asked. "How did you get wounded?" Their stories were as incredible as any Medal of Honor recipients' I'd ever heard.

The two soldiers had been close friends for four years and were always competing with one another—a healthy competition. They told me that the latest competition was going to be a ten-kilometer race, in which the winner would get $100. I was standing by their hospital beds as they were telling me this.

When I asked them how they were wounded, they told me they were riding in a convoy in Afghanistan, close to the Pakistan border—very rough terrain, a real bad neighborhood. Sergeant Shumocker was in the gunner's turret of a vehicle, and Sergeant Hollimon was standing next to him. As their convoy made its way through a valley, the ridgeline on their flank lit up with crackling small-arms fire. All of a sudden their convoy was in the middle of an ambush. Sergeant Shumocker answered with his .50-caliber machine gun, while Sergeant Hollimon furiously fed him more ammunition. Finally they pushed through the ambush.

Suddenly they heard an explosion and were knocked down, and instantly their world filled with thick smoke. Sergeant Shumocker told me he felt something "weird." No pain, but something was wrong. Finally he realized his right leg was "disconnected" below the knee. He looked over at Sergeant Hollimon and saw that his buddy's left arm was missing. Sergeant Hollimon told me he felt only "numbness" and that he began to pray. Although missing his lower leg, Sergeant Shumocker somehow hoisted himself up and cleared the turret so a fellow soldier could take the gun and continue to return fire. But now the convoy was faced with a tough decision: continue the hour-long ride north to an outpost where medical evacuation was uncertain, or turn around and head south, back through enemy fire, so they could link up with a helicopter, ten minutes away. Well, you know what they did, don't you?

The convoy valiantly fought back through the ambush—a second time—and made it to their base camp. The two sergeants were quickly placed on stretchers and loaded onto a "bird." Inside the helicopter, side by side on stretchers, Sergeant Shumocker looked over at his silent, six-foot-three, 250-pound pal. He saw the extent of Sergeant Hollimon's injuries, and for the first time he feared that his friend was slipping away.

Sergeant Shumocker watched his motionless friend begin to stir. Then he saw Sergeant Hollimon open his eyes. Hollimon turned his head slightly and whispered, "I'll bet I could beat you in a foot race now."

When Sergeant Shumocker heard those words, he said he knew "they were both going to make it." These two wounded American soldiers never lost their sense of humor, never gave up on each other, and their story speaks volumes about our nation's unwavering spirit.

During my time with these two NCOs in Germany I was awestruck by their courage. Their only concern was contacting their small outpost back in a remote corner of Afghanistan. I was stunned that their bodies had endured such devastating wounds and yet their spirits were soaring.

I thought about my dad in World War II almost losing his leg, and then I marveled at the advances in modern medicine in combat. Had it not been for advanced medicine and talented doctors right there in the battlefield, these two NCOs might not have survived this kind of traumatic injury.

All they asked of me was to make a call to let their company XO and their buddies know they were okay. My command sergeant major, CSM Riling, said, "Ma'am, I'll take care of that." He told the soldiers that their team knew they were all right. The words back from the field were simple: "Thank you, CSM, for the call. We are so glad they are okay. Tell them we miss them and will see them as soon as possible."

I'm just as proud of the continuing legacy of selfless service in my own family. Bonecrusher is my niece, Major Jennie Schoeck Hall, the middle child of my sister Sue's three children. My big sister, retired Lieutenant Colonel Sue Schoeck, was the Army's third female helicopter pilot. My brother in-law, retired Colonel Jim Schoeck, was an Air Force A-10 pilot—like father, like daughter. They prepared the bench.

Watching Jennie's career evolve is like watching part of my life come full circle. Her mother inspired me to join the military forty years ago. When I entered college my dream was to play a sport, marry my West Point boyfriend, have a family, and coach. Jennie is living her dreams and that of so many female soldiers before her—and on her own terms. What she has accomplished in service and sports was unthinkable for women when her mother and I enlisted in the military. She is an A-10 (Warthog) fighter pilot with 158 combat flying hours and is now earning an advanced degree so she can teach, mentor, and build a bench of her own. She was a four-time All-Conference soccer player at the Air Force Academy—she still loves to play soccer when her knees say it's okay. She is a wife and mother of two. She is a war fighter, and she is already encouraging future leaders. Jennie says she just wants young girls to know that they can do anything they want to do if they work hard, are committed, and just put their minds to it.

Watching great patriots like Dennis Via advance to four-star general gives me faith that the Army will continue to break barriers and embrace diversity. Knowing that there are war fighters like Giunta, Shumocker, Hollimon, Hall, and hundreds of thousands of others who are willing to make the bravest sacrifices to protect the freedoms of people around the world makes me honored to be a soldier and an American. Watching my niece Jennie continue the family tradition makes me prouder than any mom. Jennie and her contemporaries are part of the newest Greatest Generation. They are what make this country and our military so special. They are our bench.

I loved being a soldier. I loved serving soldiers. My small kid dreams of being a coach unfolded in a way unimaginable when I was growing up. Although I didn't end up coaching tennis or gymnastics, I now know I had the greatest coaching job in the world—coaching men and women serving this great country. Unlike sports, there is no apparent track record, no win-loss score, no Super Bowl rings to label military leaders as winning or losing coaches. Our winning record comes in the form of thank you cards, letters, and phone calls from those whom we served with and from those we served for. I can think of no greater reward than to know you were able to make a positive difference in someone's life. If I had to do it all over again, I wouldn't change a thing.

For me it has been a wonderful journey. I tried my very best to live to a higher standard and left the military on my own terms, with no reservations or remorse. And one thing is for sure: I won't be coming out of retirement.

AFTERTHOUGHTS
"My Way to Continue the Conversation . . . "

THE US ARMY SHATTERED THE BRASS CEILING, NOT ANN DUNWOODY

During the ceremony marking my promotion to four-star general, the Secretary of Defense remarked that I had broken through this final brass ceiling. Although I admired and respected the Secretary and appreciated his remarks that day, I didn't quite see it that way. In my view this promotion was that final step, recognition that had been fought for and earned by the entire cohort of women who had joined the Women's Army Corps and then led the integration of women into the regular Army. It was a final validation that the work, the blood, the sweat, and the tears of so many who had preceded me was now valued and respected. The Navy, the Air Force, and the Army all had female lieutenant generals in their ranks. It was the Army that made the decision that the time had finally arrived. The real credit for breaking through whatever glass—or brass—ceiling belongs squarely on the shoulders of the US Army and its leadership.

LESS THAN 1 PERCENT OF THE AMERICAN POPULATION WILL SERVE IN THE MILITARY

While America's population continues to grow, the military continues to shrink, reaching its lowest force structure levels since the pre–World War II era. Simultaneously we are raising our first generation of children who are no longer required to learn the Pledge of Allegiance, say prayers in public forums, or even say "so help me God" when reciting the Oath of Enlistment. The traditions and rituals that I knew, that taught me to love my country, to be patriotic, and to value my citizenship are being swept aside.

Not everyone is cut out for the military, but I believe that everyone can and should have the opportunity to participate in a national service endeavor of their choosing. That is why I believe that our next best hope to create a positive environment for good citizenship is a national service program. For the sake of our future, we need to develop, fund, and support a program of national service in which every eighteen- to twenty-eight-year-old in the country would serve for one year doing something for the betterment of the country. I feel so passionately about public service that I joined the Leadership Council for the Franklin Project, chaired by General (Ret) Stan McChrystal and sponsored by Walter Isaacson and the Aspen Institute, who are going national to promote this BIG IDEA.

The Franklin Project is a policy program at the Aspen Institute working to create a twenty-first-century national service system that challenges all young people to give at least one year of full-time service to their country. The vision of the Franklin Project would create an America where people from different backgrounds come together through a year of full-time national service to get big things done, such as helping to end the high school dropout epidemic, conserving our national parks, or ensuring that veterans have a better transition back home. The opportunity for full-time national service will create a next generation of leaders who will think differently about their obligations to one another and to the country.

WOMEN ARE IN COMBAT—ALL SOLDIERS ARE RIFLEMEN FIRST

I have watched the doors of opportunity open for me, and I believe they will continue to open for women in the military. Regarding the current debate about expanding the opportunities for women in the Combat Arms arena, I believe the answer is simple: no job should be closed based on gender alone to any person who can meet or exceed the standards of training for that job. As for me, all I ever wanted to do was be able to do my job in peace and at war. Nothing sorts out the appropriate roles for soldiers faster and more honestly than sustained combat operations. Women have, for a generation, demonstrated the appropriateness of their role in such operations. Women have been fighting, dying, and distinguishing themselves on the current battlefield for more than a decade. More than 150 women have died in service to their country. With our current determined enemy, nothing is off limits, nothing is sacred, and no one is safe. The military's gender policy is finally catching up with reality.

SEXUAL ASSAULT WILL ONLY BE ERADICATED WITH CAPABLE LEADERSHIP AND ENFORCEMENT OF THE LAW

Sexual assault has become a national dilemma—in the military, on college campuses, in industry, in the sports world, white and blue collar America, and on our streets. In the military the problem is particularly egregious because it often involves soldier-on-soldier violence. In an institution that is built on trust, the thought of having soldier-on-soldier violence and then, worse yet, the perception that the chain of command is not adequately dealing with the issue by appropriate investigation and exercise of authority under the Uniform Code of Military Justice is unacceptable. One incident of sexual assault is too many. Good leaders do get it, and leaders who don't get it don't deserve the privilege of leading soldiers. This issue is about dignity and respect for one another. Congress very publicly chastised the military for not properly handling sexual assault cases and even proposed legislation to remove commander's authority to investigate and decide appropriate actions and punishments. The chain of command must be held accountable.

Only the chain of command can lead us out of this problem and restore the faith. The American public must know and believe that our military leaders will do the right thing for the right reasons and that those who do not will be dealt with appropriately. War is not an excuse for such behaviors. We are a profession, and those who wear the uniform must know that by wearing that uniform they represent a profession that is held to a higher standard. Until the National Football League scandals of 2014 came to light, most of America only heard about sexual assault and domestic violence as it pertained to the military. I hope that one day our society will shun committing sexual assault and domestic violence with the same energy and the same passion with which we denounce racism, discrimination, and bias.

THE MILITARY IS A DEMANDING AND DANGEROUS PROFESSION

I'm often asked what advice would I give a young eighteen-year-old female today about joining the Army.

Here's what I would tell her: 1. The Army/military is a noble profession. 2. It's also a dangerous and demanding profession. 3. I loved being in the Army and being a soldier. 4. With hard work and determination you can achieve anything. 5. I watched the doors open, giving me opportunities I could never have imagined. In your career, you will have opportunities that I could not imagine. 6. The Army is a learning and self-policing organization. Yes, a few bad apples make headlines, but there are far more heroes than zeros in the Army. Finally, I would tell her that it doesn't matter whether you stay for two years, five years, ten years, or thirty—you will be a better citizen because of the values, work ethic, and leadership skills you will learn. And yes, I would do it all over again.

WOMEN CAN HAVE WHAT THEY WANT!

There have been some pretty lofty debates as to whether a woman can have it all. Who says that to have it all you must have a happy marriage, your dream home, a highly successful career, and two perfect kids—a son who is the quarterback and captain of the football team and a daughter who is head cheerleader and homecoming queen? Stop it! No one gets to tell us what having it all is or should be. The more important question is: Can today's women have what they want out of life?

When I met Craig, he already had two sons from a previous marriage. At that stage of my life having children was not a priority, but finding my soul mate was. Life is full of choices, and we all make them. That does not necessarily mean that you have to compromise. For me I ended up with what I wanted! I enjoy a loving husband, a happy home, a wonderful career, two wonderful stepsons, and their families, and I get to be a Grandma! Did I get to have it all? By my definition, I most certainly did, and even more importantly, I have what I want.

OUR ELECTED OFFICIALS HAVE MADE THE BUDGETING PROCESS IMPOSSIBLE TO PREDICT AND MANAGE

Some politicians continue to think that they can cut and slash military budgets on a whim without acknowledging the unintended consequences of these reductions. The rhetoric coming out of Washington, DC, these days features an entirely new vocabulary. We face the threat of government shut down rather than governing. Instead of mindfully thought out budgets and appropriations, we have continuing resolutions and sequestration. The lack of predictability in defense spending by its very nature means inefficiency and waste in programs. When tough budgetary decisions are required, the tendency is to "salami slice," or spread the pain out equally rather than canceling lower priority programs. The military is not a "nice to have" organization that can make do with appropriators when it is convenient or affordable. It is a "must prevail" institution that must always have the resources to be trained and ready for the next potential conflict in order to protect and defend the nation.

THE UNITED STATES HAS NOT FORMALLY DECLARED WAR SINCE WORLD WAR II, AND THAT IS THE LAST WAR WE UNEQUIVOCALLY WON

President Truman described the Korean Conflict as a "police action" conducted under the authority of the United Nations—it was not a war. Vietnam was also a conflict—no declaration of war ever came about. The Cold War was a state of political tension between two competing super powers. The first Gulf War—not a war—was simply a coalition action, led by the United States, to expel the Iraqi invaders and restore the original border between Kuwait and Iraq.

When the Japanese Navy launched the surprise attack on Pearl Harbor on December 7, 1941, the United States entered World War II and the entire nation rallied in support of the war effort. The United States declared war on Japan and introduced combat forces into the Pacific as well as sending forces across the Atlantic to help our allies stop Hitler and the Nazis in their march across Europe. Pearl Harbor marked the first time that America had been struck on its own soil, even though Hawaii was still eighteen years from statehood. The nation was united and committed, and there were genuine feelings and concern that our national survival was at stake. Only victory would suffice.

Today we are in a new kind of war, and sadly, not only have we not declared war, but we are also reticent to even admit who the enemy is. The terrorist attacks on September 11, 2001, were perpetrated by radical Islamic extremists. They attacked the Twin Towers of the World Trade Center, a symbol of our economic strength and capitalism; the Pentagon, a symbol of our military strength, even though a vast majority of the employees are civilians; and they wanted to attack a symbol of our government—whether it was the White House or Capitol Hill we might never know.

This attack on our soil should have been another wake-up call for Americans. But somehow the motivating ideology of our enemy was then and remains difficult for Americans to comprehend. This new enemy is unlike any that America has ever confronted. The enemy is not another nation; there are no soldiers with recognizable uniforms, and they don't always use accepted weapons of modern warfare. A commercial airliner with passengers on board is no ordinary missile, and a suicide explosive vest worn by a woman or child is no ordinary bomb.

What we have to come to grips with is an enemy who hates Western culture, our values, and our freedoms. An enemy who is so intolerant and so hateful that they are willing to kill themselves to kill us, scare us, or denigrate our way of life. So what will we do now?

We have ended combat operations in Afghanistan and Iraq. We didn't declare war, we didn't identify the enemy per se, and we didn't win—we just stopped. We killed a lot of radical Islamic extremists in the process, but in the end we just stopped. They are still out there, and as Paris, January 2015, reminds us, they have declared war on us.

AMERICA OWES ITS MILITARY VETERANS A QUALITY OF LIFE EQUAL TO THEIR QUALITY OF SERVICE

We have been a nation at war for nearly fourteen years, and despite the political musings and desires to limit armed conflict, we still have determined and capable enemies whom we must continue to deal with for the foreseeable future. Thousands have been killed, and many more thousands have been wounded. All veterans will need our help, but the wounded and, particularly, the severely wounded will need America's support to level the playing field. Thanks to the genius of modern medicine, more and more of the wounded survive and, with unprecedented capabilities, to resume a normal life. But war is hard, and some of the wounds aren't so visible.

When soldiers come home today to get on with their lives, they deserve our gratitude and need our help. Some will return to start or resume college. These young people have had some unique experiences and will be mature beyond the years of their contemporaries. Others will have challenges, inner demons that came home from the war zone with them. They need our outreach, they need our understanding, and they need a helping hand.

Unemployment is high for our veterans, and our female veterans seem to be particularly hard hit. They need job placement help, and they have leadership skills and work ethics gained from their demanding military service. Our veterans, our returning service members understand what it means to work, to complete the mission, and now they are home to start anew. They want a hand-up and not a handout. We owe them that hand-up. We promised—let's keep that promise.

There are hundreds of charities that support our veterans and surviving family members of the fallen—providing service dogs, homes, education, support, confidence-building activities, and moral and physical support. There are men-specific as well as women-veteran-specific charities. There are multi-service charities and service- or career-specific charities—Navy, Army, Air Force, Marines, Coast Guard, Special Operators, and so on. On a personal level, my husband is on the board of directors for Special Operations Warrior Foundation, which is a non-profit organization that provides college education, counseling, and college preparatory support for every child whose special operator dad or moms killed in the line of duty. It also provides financial assistance to the immediate family when a special operator is seriously injured or wounded, so the family can travel to be at their loved one's bedside. My advice would be to get involved with something! Go to Charity Navigator, a renowned charity watchdog, and find a charity that deserves your support. I have my own special-interest charities, particularly women veterans. If you can find a charity to be passionate about, it can change your life and bring you closer to your destiny as an American citizen.

CHRONOLOGY

January 1953	Born at Fort Belvoir, Virginia
June 1971	Graduated high school
June 1974	Attended Army's Women College Junior Program
May 1974	Enlisted in the Army Reserve
June 1975	Graduated State University of New York, Cortland
August 1975	Commissioned as a 2nd lieutenant
June 1976	Reported to Fort Sill, Oklahoma
July 1976	Attended Army Airborne School
May 1981	Reported to Germany
April 1984	Reported to Personnel Command, Washington, DC
November 1985	Completed Marine Corps Marathon
August 1986	Reported to Fort Leavenworth, Kansas Command and General Staff College
October 1986	Met Craig Brotchie
November 1986	Promoted to major
May 1988	Reported to Fort Bragg and the 82nd Airborne Division

November 1989	Married Craig
September 1990–April 1991	Deployed to Saudi Arabia for Desert Shield/Desert Storm
February 1992	Promoted to lieutenant colonel
August 1994	Reported to the Industrial College of the Armed Forces
June 1995	Reported to the Pentagon to work for the Chief of Staff of the Army
June 1996	Reported to 10th Mountain Division, Fort Drum, New York
September 1996	Promoted to colonel
July 1998	Reported to the Defense Logistics Agency
June 2000	Report to 1st Corps Support Command Fort Bragg, North Carolina
January 2001	Promoted to brigadier general
Winter 2002	Deployed to Uzbekistan
September 2002	Reported to Military Traffic Management Command, Washington, DC
January 2004	Promoted to major general
September 2004	Reported to Combined Arms Support Command, Fort Lee, Virginia
October 2005	Reported to Logistics Directorate, Pentagon
October 2005	Promoted to lieutenant general
June 2008	Reported to Army Materiel Command, Fort Belvoir, Virginia
November 2008	Promoted to general
April 2011	Moved to Redstone Arsenal, Alabama
October 2012	Retired

Postscript

Leadership Strategies from an Army Life

- Meeting the standard will always suffice if you want to be average or just get by. Exceeding the standard and living to a higher standard can lead to success and the achievement of your dreams.
- Believe in something! Believe in yourself, believe in a creed, believe in your passion.
- A hero is an everyday, ordinary person who has done something extraordinary. Honor them, praise them, and hope you will stand for what you believe in during a time of need.
- Be disciplined. Know what right looks like.
- If you take nothing else from this book—never walk by a mistake, or you just set a new lower standard!
- Invincibility is a myth. Recognize your strengths and your weaknesses. Optimize your strengths, and deal with and minimize your weaknesses.
- Don't stop trying or fighting for what you believe in the first time someone tells you *no*.
- Don't compromise your principles.

- People are always watching you. What you do sets the tone for others.
- Have the guts—courage—to do the right thing for the right reason.
- The best way to have healthy debates and find the ultimate solutions to very complex problems is to have the best and brightest group of people who can offer diverse perspectives on the issues. Be inclusive, not exclusive; embrace diversity of thought in management and in key leadership teams.
- Build high-performing teams or organizations. Build a team that routinely does routine things in an outstanding manner.
- Provide a strategic vision. Visualize where you want your team to be in the future and then design a roadmap to get there. It is key that *every* individual in your organization understands how important he or she is to accomplishing the vision.
- Enjoy your job and make a difference. Some of the most difficult decisions we make in our lives center around deciding how long to stay, when to change, or when to leave. Don't leave these decisions to someone else or to chance—make them *your* decisions.
- No one is indispensable. Succession planning is one of the most important actions senior leaders do. Set your team or organization up for success with a methodical transition plan for key leaders.

ACKNOWLEDGMENTS

WITHOUT MY HUSBAND, Craig's, support throughout this effort, there would be no book. He coauthored this book with me and worked tirelessly and endlessly on every word, every chapter, and every version. During my promotion ceremony to four-star general I said, "I don't know if I would be where I am today without him, but I know I would not want to try." I do know this book would not have been possible without him. He knows me so well that he added words, phrases, and thoughts that sounded more like me than me. This has been a long two-year journey. The sacrifices he made to ensure we met deadlines and timelines, never settling for just okay—he was as passionate about the book and the leadership strategies as I was.

It's been fun, it's been hard, and at times it's been stressful. On November 19, 2014, nearly two years after starting the book, we celebrated our twenty-fifth wedding anniversary. Reliving the memories, recounting the stories, and talking through our leadership experiences brought us closer together. I am lucky to have Craig as my soul mate and my husband. I am proud of the book we produced together.

Mom and Dad, thank you for raising a loving family with values that endured a lifetime. Thank you for your tough yet compassionate love during the good times and the hard times. You believed in me, and because of that I never believed there was anything I couldn't do.

My brothers and sisters have been cheering this effort all along the way, just as they have done for everything else in my life. I am grateful to them.

To Sheryl Sandberg, a leadership champion of this decade. Not only has she reached out to millions of women around the globe with her book *Lean In*, encouraging women to aspire to get out front and be leaders in their communities as well as in the workforce, but she reached out to me. From our first engagement, Sheryl Sandberg, the Chief Operating Officer of Facebook, made me feel like I was having a conversation with my own sister—positive, engaging, energetic and supportive . . . leaders being there for other leaders.

After meeting Sheryl, I reflected on people in own my career, people and friends who provided a "safe zone" for an honest conversation. Having friends who serve as sounding boards or just someone to vent with, knowing you won't read about it the next day, is priceless. Thank you, Sheryl. Wife, mom, leader, and influencing voice.

After struggling for more than a year to make suitable progress on this book, a colleague I had met on a board of directors, Tomago Collins, offered to help. Tomago is a sports executive and editor based in Denver, Colorado. I didn't expect him to help write the book but perhaps help us edit it once we had a writer on board. I'm not sure why he did it, but he sent me an email and said, Ann, I want to help you do this, I think you have something special here, and unless you don't want me, you're stuck with me. There was no contract, just an understanding and trust-me kind of relationship that prevailed. In spite of his own demanding schedule, Tomago kept driving us to be better. Writing a book just might be the hardest thing I have ever done. Tomago helped turn our countless interviews into stories full of color and personality. He has a creative brilliance about him. He has a talented network of writers and editors who he enticed to lend their expertise to this book. Two of his former colleagues, journalists Aaron Lopez and Doug Tatum, helped throughout the process. Jon Werthiem and Larry Burke—two editors with best-sellers in their own portfolios—also jumped in with invaluable insight and constructive feedback. I've never met any of them in person; they did it because of their respect for Tomago. This book now has an entirely different aura about it. Tomago and his associates helped make it possible.

To my lifelong coaches, mentors, and friends, many mentioned in the book, and so many more—thank you. Thank you for believing in me. Thank you for taking a chance on me, for standing up for me, and for giving me opportunities I would have never had without your intervention. Thank you for training me and teaching me lessons in life that evolved into lifelong leadership lessons.

To men and women whom I was privileged to serve with and their families—thank you for your dedication to our country and for your personal sacrifices. You are the reason I loved being a soldier.

Thanks to those who lent their voice and support to the book: Sheryl Sandberg, General (Ret) Stan McChrystal, Walter Issacson, Frances Hesselbein, and Peter Economy. Our friends USAF Colonel (Ret) John Carney and his wife, Cindy; my friend, adviser, and AMC command counsel, Vince Faggioli; my friend and former Army Chief of Staff of the Army, General (Ret) Gordon Sullivan; and our Hawaii friends Bernie and Julie Coleman.

And finally, my thanks to the good Lord for showering my family and me with His many blessings every day.

NOTES

FOREWORD

xii   **"During World War I, thirty-five thousand women served . . . "**: Women in Military Service for America Foundation, *Highlights in the History of Military Women*, www.womensmemorial.org/Education /timeline.html.

xii   **"In 1942, President Roosevelt authorized the creation . . . "**: Women's History Month, U.S. Department of Defense, www.defense .gov/home/features/2012/0212_womenshistory; Women in WWII at a Glance, The National WWII Museum, www.nationalww2 museum.org/learn/education/for-students/ww2-history/at-a-glance /women-in-ww2.html.

xii   **"Still, at the war's conclusion, these trained and seasoned personnel . . . "**: Mary Wechsler Segal, "Gender and the Military," in *Handbook of the Sociology of Gender*, ed. Janet S. Chafetz (New York: Springer, 2006).

xii   **"In 1948 the Women's Armed Services Integration Act enabled women . . . "**: The US Marine Corps, History Division, Public Law 625: The Women's Armed Services Integration Act of 1948, www .mcu.usmc.mil/historydivision/Pages/Speeches/PublicLaw625.aspx.

xii   **"It also limited the number of women allowed in the military . . . "**: Jacqueline Escobar, "Breaking the Kevlar Ceiling," *Military Review*, XCIII (March–April 2013): 71.

xiii   **"In 1994, a new policy was implemented that allowed for a less restrictive . . . "**: Women's History Month, U.S. Department of Defense, www.defense.gov/home/features/2012/0212_womenshistory.

xiii   **"By 2012, when Ann retired from the military, women made up almost 15 percent . . . "**: 2012 Demographics: Profile of the Military Community 2013, 2013, iii, www.militaryonesource.mil/12038 /MOS/Reports/2012_Demographics_Report.pdf.

INTRODUCTION

2   **"The nomination made headlines around the world."**: "First Woman Ann Dunwoody Makes Four-Star US General," *The Australian*, June 25, 2008, www.theaustralian.com.au/archive/news/first-woman -makes-four-star-us-general/story-e6frg6tf-1111116725245?nk= b92cb89e221defafc57dfbb406dd04c5; "Army Gets First Female Four-Star General," *NBC News*, November 14, 2008, www.nbcnews .com/id/27718059/ns/us_news-military/t/army-gets-first-female -four-star-general/#.VKcQnivF9x0; "Ann Dunwoody Becomes First Female 4-star General," *Kansas City Star*, November 14, 2008; "Military Milestone," Scholastic, November 17, 2008, www.scholastic .com/browse/article.jsp?id=3750837; Major Sharon Tosi Moore, "Four Stars—Finally," *US Army Reserve Magazine*, August 2008; "An American Original," *SUNY Cortland Alumni News*, Spring 2009, www2.cortland.edu/dotAsset/306950.pdf; "Four-Star and First," *Fayetteville Observer*, November 16, 2008, www.fayobserver. com/news/local/four-star-and-first/article_0b39f68c-134b-5c42 -b1b5-785e7616e12a.html; "Dunwoody Becomes First Female Four Star General," *Seattle Times*, November 14, 2008, http://seattle times.com/html/politics/2008389813_apfemalegeneral.html.

2   **"US Senator Hillary Clinton, representative of my native New York . . . "**: Hillary Clinton, "Senator Hillary Rodham Clinton the Nomination of Lieutenant General Ann E. Dunwoody to the Rank of General," Press Release, June 23, 2008, http://votesmart. org/public-statement/352851/senator-hillary-rodham-clinton-the -nomination-of-lieutenant-general-ann-e-dunwoody-to-the-rank -of-general#.VKcS_yvF9x1.

6   **"Women were now being recruited, and the number of WACs . . . "**: "History of the Women's Army Corps," Women's

Army Corps Veterans' Association, www.armywomen.org/wac History.shtml.

13 **"My new job as leader of the Army Materiel . . . "**: Army Materiel: The spelling of materiel is often confusing. In this instance materiel refers to the equipment and supplies normally associated with a military organization.

CHAPTER 1

19 **"Months into my promotion Oprah's O magazine named me . . . "**: "O's First ever Power List, #11 of 20," *O Magazine*, October 2009.

27 **"Whether it's the military, a Fortune 500 company . . . "**: *Jim Collins, Good to Great: Why Some Companies Make the Leap—And Others Don't* (New York: HarperBusiness, 2001).

29 **"In spite of Specialist Giunta's courage, he sincerely downplayed his heroism . . . "**: Anna Mulrine, "Medal of Honor Recipient Salvatore Giunta Tells His Story," *Christian Science Monitor*, September 16, 2010, www.csmonitor.com/USA/Military/2010/0916/Medal-of-Honor-recipient-Salvatore-Giunta-tells-his-story.

30 **"Recently Sal told his own story in *Living with Honor: A Memoir* . . . "**: Sal Giunta, *Living With Honor: A Memoir* (New York: Threshold Editions, 2012).

31 **Quartermaster Creed, Airborne Creed, and Rigger Pledge:** **"Quartermaster Creed,"** Quartermaster Corps, www.quartermaster.army.mil/qm_creed.html; Airborne Creed, www.benning.army.mil/infantry/rtb/1-507th/airborne/content/pdf/Airborne%20Creed.pdf; History of the Parachute Rigger Badge, www.quartermaster.army.mil/adfsd/righist.html.

32 **The Soldier's Creed: The Soldier's Creed, Army Values**, www.army.mil/values/soldiers.html.

CHAPTER 2

38 **"There was a cover story in the *Atlantic* in 2014"**: Katty Kay and Claire Shipman (illustrations by Edmon de Haro), "The Confidence Gap," *Atlantic*, May 2014, www.theatlantic.com/features/archive/2014/04/the-confidence-gap/359815.

CHAPTER 3

55   "He replied that there is nowhere else he would rather be than
     with Soldiers . . . ": Heidi Shyu, e-mail with author.

70   "I recently read a book that's a darling on Wall Street, *The Out-
     siders* . . . ": William N. Thorndike, *The Outsiders: Eight Uncon-
     ventional CEOs and Their Radically Rational Blueprint for Success*
     (Watertown, MA: Harvard Business Review Press, 2012).

CHAPTER 4

74   "Major Mariam Al Mansouri is her country's first female fighter
     pilot. In an October 2014 interview with CNN . . . ": Dana Ford,
     "UAE's First Female Fighter Pilot Led Airstrike Against ISIS,"
     CNN, October 9, 2014, www.cnn.com/2014/09/25/world/meast
     /uae-female-fighter-pilot.

74   As Al Mansouri said . . . : Ibid.

75   "Deborah Sampson served for three years in the Revolutionary
     Army . . . ": Jane Ketter, National Women's History Museum.

75   "Sarah Edmonds, aka Franklin Flint Thompson, joined the
     Union Army . . . ": Donald E. Markle, *Spies and Spymasters of the
     Civil War* (New York: Hippocrene Books, 2004).

76   "Mary Hayes was a legendary soldier's wife from the American
     Revolution . . . ": Jone Johnson Lewis, womenshistory.about.com.

76   "Australia permits women to train and perform in combat jobs.":
     Agence France-Post, April 25, 2013, global post.com.

76   "Canada has no restrictions on females.": Ellen Symons, "Under
     Fire: Canadian Women in Combat," *Canadian Journal of Women
     and the Law*, 1990.

76   "In Israel 90 percent of the jobs are open to women": "Statistics:
     Women's Service in the IDF for 2010," Israel Defense Force, Au-
     gust 25, 2010.

76   "In New Zealand there are no restrictions, but it's also notewor-
     thy . . . ": "Maximizing Opportunities for Military Women in the
     New Zealand Defence Force," Evaluation Division, Ministry of De-
     fense, February 2014.

79   "By 2010 the number of women on active duty had grown from
     55,028 in 1973 to 202,070": Eileen Patten and Kim Parker,

"Women in the U.S. Military: Growing Share, Distinctive Profile," Pew Research, Social and Demographic Trends, December 22, 2011, www.pewsocialtrends.org/2011/12/22/women-in-the-u-s-military -growing-share-distinctive-profile.

CHAPTER 5

113 **"If it were publicly listed when I took over in 2008, with its $47 billion budget . . . ":** Fortune 500 2009, *Fortune*, http://fortune .com/fortune500/2009.

CHAPTER 7

144 **"The purpose of the task force is to increase awareness . . . ":** Army News Service, "Gen. Casey Announces Creation of Diversity Task Force," November 30, 2007, www.army.mil/article/6405.

145 **"The percentage of enlisted women has grown seven-fold . . . ":** Patten and Parker, "Women in the U.S. Military." Women in the U.S. Military: Growing Share, Distinctive Profile; Patten, Eileen; Parker, Kim; Pew Research Social & Demographic Trends, December 22, 2011. http://www.pewsocialtrends.org/2011/12/22/women -in-the-u-s-military-growing-share-distinctive-profile/ [accessed 2015 Jan 2].

145 **"Today the Army has a publicized diversity definition . . . ":** "The Army Posture Statement," U.S. Army, www.army.mil/info/institu-tion/posturestatement.

146 **"Coca-Cola Company ranked No. 33 on *DiversityInc*'s Top 50 Companies . . . ":** Journey Staff, "Coca-Cola Advances on Diversity Inc's Top 50 Companies for Diversity Ranking," Coca-Cola Jour-ney, April 23, 2014, www.coca-colacompany.com/stories/coca-cola -advances-on-diversityincs-top-50-companies-for-diversity-ranking.

CHAPTER 10

199 **"In an interview with historian Richard H. Kohn . . . ":** Richard H. Kohn, "The Early Retirement of Gen Ronald R. Fogleman, Chief of Staff, United States Air Force," *Aerospace Power Journal* 15, pt. 1 (Spring 2001): 6–23.

201 **"Then she talked about growing up in New York City . . . "**: "Keys, Alicia," Contemporary Black Biography, 2009, Encyclopedia .com, www.encyclopedia.com/doc/1G2-3233800039.html.

202 **"We went to Dunbar High School, currently ranked . . . "**: District of Columbia High School Rankings, SchoolDigger, www.school digger.com/go/DC/schoolrank.aspx?level=3.

CHAPTER 11

222 **"During e-mail exchanges she always had several queries . . . "**: Major Jennie Hall, e-mail with author.

228 **"Despite being terminally ill with cancer, Steve Jobs made sure . . . "**: Robin Ferracone, "An Outsider's View of Apple's Succession Plan," *Forbes*, September 13, 2011, www.forbes.com/sites /robinferracone/2011/09/13/an-outsiders-view-of-apples-succession -plan-3.

228 **"Walt Disney Corporation recently extended the contract . . . "**: Ryan Jones, "Iger Contract Extension Is Excellent News for Disney's Future," *Seeking Alpha*, October 6, 2014, http://seekingalpha.com /article/2541725-iger-contract-extension-is-excellent-news-for -disneys-future?page=2.

AFTERTHOUGHTS

246 **"The Franklin Project is a policy program at the Aspen Institute . . . "**: From a series produced by he *Huffington Post* and the Franklin Project at the Aspen Institute to recognize the power of national service, in conjunction with the latter's Summit at Gettysburg (June 4–6, 2014, Gettysburg, Pennsylvania). Mary E. Bruce and Ben Duda, "AmeriCorps Alums: Untapped Potential," *Huffington Post*, June 5, 2014, www.huffingtonpost.com/mary-e-bruce /this-is-why-national-serv_b_5453717.html.

INDEX